Evelyn Kelly

## By the same author

Nuremberg: the facts, the law and the consequences

Survey of International Affairs 1947–48

Survey of International Affairs 1949–50

Survey of International Affairs 1951

Survey of International Affairs 1952

Survey of International Affairs 1953

Middle East Crisis (with Guy Wint)

South Africa and World Opinion

World Order and New States

Suez: Ten years after (with Anthony Moncrieff)

Total War: Causes and courses of the Second World War (with Guy Wint)

The British Experience 1945–75

Freedom to Publish (with Ann Bristow)

Top Secret Ultra

Independent Africa and the World

From Byzantium to Eton: a memoir of a millennium

A Time for Peace

*Illustration opposite: Samuel and Eli by Sir Edward Burne-Jones; St. Martin's Church, Brampton, Cumbria.*

# WHO'S WHO
# IN THE BIBLE

## Peter Calvocoressi

VIKING

VIKING

Penguin Books, 27 Wrights Lane, London W8 5TZ
(Publishing and Editorial) *and* Harmondsworth,
Middlesex, England (Distribution and Warehouse)
Viking Penguin Inc., 40 West 23rd Street, New York, New
York 10010, U.S.A.
Penguin Books Australia Ltd, Ringwood, Victoria,
Australia
Penguin Books Canada Ltd, 2801 John Street, Markham,
Ontario, Canada L3R 1B4
Penguin Books (N.Z.) Ltd, 182 – 190 Wairau Road,
Auckland 10, New Zealand

First published in Great Britain by Viking 1987

Typeset in Sabon by Bookworm Typesetting, Manchester

Printed in Great Britain by Richard Clay Ltd, Bungay, Suffolk

*British Library Cataloguing in Publication Data*

Calvocoressi, Peter
  Who's who in the Bible.
  1. Bible —— Biography
  I. Title
  220.9′2      BS571

  ISBN 0-670-81188-2

 Library of Congress Catalog Card Number 87-50540

Published in association with Tigerlily Ltd

# CONTENTS

# INTRODUCTION

This book is about a special aspect of the Bible – the people in it. Some of these people are as famous as anybody has ever been. Others are less famous than that but still very famous indeed. Then there are just ordinarily famous men and women, whose names are familiar even when what they did is ill remembered. Finally, there is a large supporting cast of the unfamous. About all these people, except the last category, we feel from time to time the itch to know more – to learn, to recollect or to settle an argument.

A Who's Who is not an encyclopaedia. A Who's Who is a select directory, to which entry has to be gained by fame or favour. It is for those who delight in thumbing works of reference and the names in it are those which set the thumbs moving. The entries in this book range from the very short to the very long. Their main purpose is to record the facts stated in the Bible about each of the persons listed, but that is not their only purpose. Telling about people involves telling who they were, what they did – but also something more. This something more has two faces. First, comment: thinking and reading about such out-of-the-ordinary personages as Moses or David, Isaiah or Paul, shapes ideas about their attributes and personalities and so invites appraisal as well as narrative.

The second additional element is posthumous. The Bible's main characters have lived on, in the imagination of later generations and in their works of art. For 2000 years artists have retold the Bible's stories in stone and glass, in prose and verse, in paint and music. Generation by generation these works have shaped the Biblical figures who were first presented to us by the Bible itself. Some of these works of art are mentioned in this book – an inevitably small selection from the mass that could be cited. In some instances – most obviously, the main events in the life of Jesus from the Annunciation to the Crucifixion – the wealth of material is too enormous, but for the rest a selection, however abbreviated and arbitrary, helps to underline the perennial vitality of these people and shows at the same time how different ages have seen and displayed them: tradition interacting with the spirit of the times.

These artistic references are drawn largely from the later Middle Ages and the Renaissance, when the Bible was the unchallenged prime source for artists and for the patrons who commissioned them. It was not, even then, the only source, for there were other good stories around and also – for the graphic artist – the lures of natural beauty, including the beauties of the human body. But the Church was the fount of the most money, the most ostentation and so the most art. This ecclesiastical predominance was dented by the classical renaissance which diverted artists to the mythical and historical stories of Greece and Rome; and it was further dented by the self-esteem of patrons, aristocrats (including princes of the Church) and plutocrats who wanted pictures of themselves, their wives and their horses. But in spite of all this competition the Bible has held its place and has continued to fructify the artistic imagination. Within the last hundred years the Crucifixion has haunted poets as diverse as Housman and D.H. Lawrence, Edith Sitwell and Edwin Muir and Nikos Kazantzakis; Messiaen has devoted (the *mot juste*) his life to music in a spirit recognizably akin to that of the Middle Ages; OT and NT themes crop up constantly in the painting of Stanley Spencer; and the novels of Tolstoy, Thomas Mann, George Moore and Mikhail Bulgakov attest the vitality of these ancient tales.

To the artist an ancient story makes its appeal in two different ways. As a good story it demands to be retold: the artist as narrator does this. But the story needs also to be re-imagined, either in its original setting or displaced into the artist's own time. Thus when Raphael wished to paint Ezekiel's vision he had to form, in his own mind and then on canvas, his own idea of what Ezekiel saw and what he meant to convey. And when Kipling, in his poem called 'Uriah', tells the story of Jack Barrett, he is saying: 'It still happens.'

## WHAT THE BIBLE IS.

The word Bible means book in Greek but the Bible is not so much a book as a collection of books, a specialized library. The earliest Greek translation, the Septuagint, was not in fact called the Bible but the Old Testament, and the word Bible first appeared in Latin versions and in the plural: Biblia Sacra, Holy Books.

The division of the Bible into Old Testament, New Testament and Apocrypha goes back to earliest times: the Apocrypha antedates the NT. These three elements are very different from each other and add to the diversity of the entire corpus. The NT, considerably shorter than the OT, is also more homogeneous. Much the greater part of it is devoted to two topics: the ministry, passion and divinity of Jesus (the four Gospels), and the missions and teachings of Paul (Paul's own letters and the Acts of the Apostles). The whole of the NT was written in Greek and in the second half of C 1 AD or, in a few cases, a bit later. It deals with the events of no more than a single century.

The OT is not only much bulkier but much more diverse. It covers an immense stretch of time but a comparatively restricted area and number of people. Even excluding its initial legendary period it extends over the best part of two millennia. It tells the story of a select people which trekked in remote times from the lower Euphrates to lands bordering the Mediterranean; abandoned these lands, probably for economic reasons, and pushed on into Egypt, where it prospered and then suffered through several centuries; escaped *en masse* to regain lost, now Promised Land, and did so after a whole generation of privations and frustrations on the way; conquered but did not eliminate the peoples whom it found in the Promised Land; created for a brief period the healthy and wealthy kingdom of David and Solomon but fell victim to internal divisions and greater empires; was almost expunged from history but not quite, half of it extinguished by the Assyrians but the other half making a comeback from captivity in Babylon; fashioned a religion which, initially a complex of ritualistic observances and prohibitions, was infused by the Prophets with profound ethical and social values; and so preserved its religious and racial identity without (except in the hundred years of the Maccabee priest kings) political independence.

The material of the OT is not only a record of these ups and downs, it also contributed to the ups. Traditions keep a people going. In good times they fortify; in bad times they comfort and foster hope. In good times they are voiced in songs and yarns; in bad times they are nostalgically collected and written down. The OT was largely written down during the decline of the post-Solomonic kingdoms, in captivity in Babylon, or soon afterwards. The OT is these writings. But its sources include much older sacred and profane legends and annals, songs and tales; and its oldest surviving texts are much later.

The OT was never a unitary work. It was seen as a miscellany in three parts: the Law, and the Prophets, and the so-called Writings which could just as well be called 'the rest'. The Law – in Hebrew Torah – consisted of the first five Books or Pentateuch (Greek for five books). They were ascribed to Moses and put at the beginning of the Hebrew Bible; the guardians of the Law, the priests, had a vested interest in their primacy. But the Mosaic authorship was suspect as much as a thousand years ago and now nobody with an open mind believes in it. A French C 18 AD scholar pointed out that there must have been two authors, and C 19 AD scholarship has added to this number and has devoted much effort to disentangling them. The earliest known event in the emergence of the Law occurred in 621 BC when, in the reign of King Josiah of Judah, men engaged in repairing the Temple in Jerusalem discovered a MS which seems to have been Deuteronomy. Josiah was carried away by this discovery and inaugurated the trend, greatly boosted after the Captivity by Ezra and Nehemiah, of proclaiming the Law of (supposedly) Moses as a kind of constitution for a priest-kingdom. Deuteronomy is uncompromisingly monotheistic, more so than any known earlier document.

The Prophets were honoured almost equally with the Law. Many of them were also earlier. In this context the Prophets were, in the first place, Isaiah, Jeremiah and Ezekiel and, additionally, a group of twelve beginning with the earliest of them all, Amos. These so-called Minor Prophets constituted one Book of the OT before they were divided into their present separate Books. Their lives spanned C8-C6 BC: the Books which bear their names achieved their present shape by 200 BC. Besides their spiritual messages they are an important adjunct of the OT's historical section, which includes Joshua, Judges, 1 and 2 Samuel and 1 and 2 Kings – a record covering the period 1200-586 BC and committed to writing in its surviving form in C6 BC.

The third category of OT writing is a job lot. The Book of Psalms is a collection of poetry ascribed to David and, like any ancient anthology, derived in fact from widely different times (C8-C2 BC). There is a clutch of works (some of them in the Apocrypha) which, however disparate, may be subsumed under the heading of Wisdom Books, many of them attributed to Solomon and composed in C3 BC: Proverbs, Ecclesiasticus, the Wisdom of Solomon, Job. There are simple tales: Ruth, Esther, Tobit, Daniel; more purposeful pieces such as Ecclesiastes and Lamentations, and a lyrical interlude in the Song of Songs. Finally, a quartet of late works dedicated to the promotion of the priestly view of how things had been and should be: 1 and 2 Chronicles, Ezra, Nehemiah. (Chronicles, composed C 300 BC, is a tendentious version of the events related in Samuel and Kings. It is concerned only with the kingdom of Judah and leaves out anything discreditable to David or Solomon.) This third category of the OT is so various that it can be, and has been, broken down in more ways than one. It contains, however, a striking number of the Books which give the OT its special flavour.

The genesis and history of the Apocrypha are related in an entry in the main body of this book.

## THE LANGUAGE OF THE BIBLE

The original language of the OT was (with small exceptions) Hebrew; that of the NT Greek. The material on which they were written was at first papyrus and then, from C AD 400, vellum. Sections of papyrus were stitched together end to end, rolled in the form of scrolls and stored in cylinders. To keep the scroll from crumpling the end section was stitched on to the rest of the scroll across the grain (this was the 'protocol' – Greek for first leaf). Sheets of vellum were stitched or stuck together like a modern book instead of in rolls and the resulting object is called a codex. Among the surviving 2-3,000 Biblical MSS, which range from single Books or parts of Books to virtually complete Testaments and Bibles, those on papyrus are fewer and more fragmentary. Nothing like a first edition survives.

The text of the OT was fixed by AD 100. It was written in an early form of Hebrew (unvocalized – that is, in a script without vowels) and no version of it has survived complete. The earliest vocalized Hebrew text dates from C 10 AD and was first printed in Venice in AD 1524. In a discovery as astonishing as it was accidental hundreds of Hebrew scrolls were found in AD 1947 in eleven caves at Qumran by the Dead Sea after a young goatherd had stumbled on a cache which had been undisturbed for nearly 2000 years. The finds, which included at least fragments of every Book of the OT except one, were in some instances older than any previously known Biblical document, going back to C 3 BC.

The oldest surviving written OT is, however, not Hebrew but Greek. It is the Septuagint, a translation from Hebrew made in Alexandria in C 3 and C 2 BC for Greek-speaking Jews. Strictly speaking, the Septuagint was the Greek translation of the Pentateuch only, but the name was applied to the whole of the OT as the rest of it came to be added. For linguistic reasons the Septuagint acquired a wider currency than the Hebrew text among Christians and consequently many more Greek MSS have survived than Hebrew. The two versions have one major discrepancy: the Greek translators included in the Septuagint fourteen Books which were not and are not in any Hebrew text. These are the Apocrypha and they have continued to appear in Christian Bibles in spite of doubts about their spiritual value, doubts which have been expressed through the ages from St Jerome to our own time. St Jerome himself included the Apocrypha in his Latin Vulgate Bible only because these Books were already in the Septuagint.

Of surviving MSS of the whole Bible (or most of it) two were written in C 4 AD. These are the Codex Vaticanus, which is almost complete and has been in the Vatican for 500 years, and the Codex Sinaiticus, which is complete with a few uncanonical extras. The latter codex was discovered in AD 1859 in a monastery on Mount Sinai; it was presented to the Russian Tsar and is now in the British Museum. From C 5 AD two other substantial MSS survive: the Codex Alexandrinus, almost complete and with extras, also in the British Museum, and the Codex Bezae, with the text in Latin as well as Greek, now in Cambridge.

The Bible is the most widely disseminated book in the world. The root cause of this phenomenon is the demand for the Christian scriptures, reinforced by missionary zeal and a degree of *gratis* distribution unparallelled before the deluge of modern advertising. But this demand could hardly have been met without two major technical contributions: printing and translation. The printing of the Bible, which began in C 15 AD, made it possible to produce Bibles which were both identical and numerous; before printing, when Bibles were made by hand, they were relatively few and frequently discrepant. Translation has been an even more powerful aid to ubiquity. The number of translations into languages and dialects of languages is amazing. It is not a subject to be pursued in this book, but a brief note on translation into English will not be out of place.

The original language of the OT and NT ceased to meet the needs of readers as early as C 2 AD when knowledge of Greek was already on the decline in western Europe. Nor had Greek ever been current in those parts of north Africa where the Christian Church developed strongly in the first centuries AD. So Latin translations began to appear (and, for similar reasons, Syrian and Coptic translations). These early efforts were manifestly imperfect and in C 4 AD the Pope commissioned the immensely learned and immensely industrious St Jerome to produce a more reliable Latin Bible. The result was the Vulgate, completed in AD 405, translated mainly from Hebrew and Greek but with references to other intervening translations, a stupendous achievement although faulty in parts, the father of all medieval Western Bibles, still officially approved by the Roman Catholic Church although no longer the only officially approved version.

The Vulgate became the source for other European translators – for example, Bede who translated some of the Bible into Anglo-Saxon, King Alfred who translated the Psalms into English, and John Wycliffe who was the first to translate the whole Bible into English (1380-82). A century and a half later William Tyndale went one better than Wycliffe by translating from the original Hebrew and Greek, but he failed to complete his work because he was hounded, imprisoned and brutally executed before he could finish it. His work was completed by Miles Coverdale who used, chiefly, the Vulgate and a Swiss version of Luther's German Bible. Both Tyndale (1526) and Coverdale (1535) were printed in Germany. The first English Bible to be printed in England was Matthew's Bible (1537), a compendium of Tyndale and Coverdale by one Rogers, who used the pseudonym Matthew but did not thereby escape the stake in the Roman Catholic backlash of the Marian persecution. The Great Bible, published in 1539 and republished in 1568 as the Bishops' Bible, was the first official English Bible. It was a revision by Coverdale of Tyndale's published and unpublished work and was issued in France before it appeared in England.

Up to this point all important English Bibles since Wycliffe's stemmed from Tyndale and Coverdale, but the next two versions were fresh departures. Both were the work of exiles. The Geneva Bible (1560) was produced by Protestant exiles; it was translated from the original Hebrew and Greek, was printed about simultaneously in Geneva and London, was the standard English Bible until 1611 and retained its popularity for a hundred years after that date. Roman Catholic exiles were also at work: first in Rheims and then in Douai. Using the Vulgate they produced a NT in 1582 and their complete Douai Bible in 1610. The most famous year in the annals of English Bible Translation is 1611, when the Authorized Version, sometimes called the King James Bible, first appeared. Six committees worked on particular sections. At a second stage two members of each committee formed a reviewing committee, and finally the entire work was again reviewed by one bishop and one future bishop. All worked from the oldest known Hebrew and Greek versions and from later translations. This most famous English translation became and has remained, for the English themselves, the most authoritative and most loved version, even when imperfectly understood.

Two factors have contributed nevertheless to a stream of further versions. The first is Biblical scholarship, normally divided into Textual or Lower Criticism and the Higher Criticism – the former concerned with the establishment of an accurate text, the latter with everything else (sources, dating, history, meaning). New scholarship was the main spur to the revision of the Authorized Version of 1611 which was undertaken towards the end of C 19 AD and produced the Revised Version between 1881 and 1895. By contrast the main impulse behind the American Revised Standard Version (1952) and the New English Bible (1961 and 1970) was the desire to have a Bible more easily intelligible to people at large than was the language of 1611. In this endeavour the promoters of these versions were echoing the original NT which was written in current conversational Greek and not in the literary style of the receding classical age.

## DATES

Dates are a great help in giving context and reality to the doings of the characters whom this book enumerates. Dates, however, are elusive and so that useful adjunct 'c' appears with perhaps disconcerting frequency, e.g. in placing the reigns of kings of Israel and Judah. While the lengths of these reigns are correct, they may be displaced in time by a few years in one direction or the other. The alternative would be to enter into more detailed chronological debate than I have deemed appropriate for a book of this nature.

The problems of chronology may be broadly divided into two sections: the period before c. 1000 BC and the period after that date. No dates can be given for the legendary period from Adam to Noah: even if Noah's flood reflects a real event it is impossible to say which of many inundations over thousands of years was his. Biblical history begins with Abraham and the first half of it ends with the conquest of the Promised Land by Joshua. Abraham trekked to the land of Canaan. Moses and Joshua trekked back to it. In this period the outstanding events were Abraham's migration from Ur on the lower Euphrates, up that river and then westward into what was later called Syria; and the career in Egypt of Abraham's great-grandson Joseph, and the Exodus from Egypt under Moses which paved the way for the re-establishment of Abraham's seed in the land of Canaan, the Promised Land.

Abraham's dates have been shifted by historical research but remain uncertain. He used to be generally dated around 2050 BC, largely because of the belief that the king called in Genesis Amraphel was none other than the famous Babylonian monarch Hammurabi who flourished at that time. But it is now more widely, although not unanimously, believed that Abraham lived c. 1450 BC. At the nearer end of the period stretching from Abraham to Moses the Exodus is most commonly placed around 1200 BC. But this creates congestion. Between Abraham and Moses room has to be found for the generations between Abraham and Joseph (say, a little more than 100 years) and for the continued sojourn of the Israelites in Egypt after Joseph's death, which is traditionally fixed at 400 years. The simplest, and possibly the most accurate, way to dispose of this problem is to disbelieve the 400-year span, and there is some justification for doing so since the figure 400 is frequently used, in ancient and mediaeval parlance, to mean nothing more precise than 'a lot'. This computation gives 150 or so years as the space remaining between Joseph's pharaoh and Moses' pharoah (c. 1350-1200 BC). But it remains possible that Joseph did in fact reach Egypt much earlier, during the period when Egypt was being invaded by people (like himself) from the north: the Hyksos, northern invaders, ruled Egypt c. 1700-1570 BC. It is also possible that the Exodus took place c. 1500, which would return Abraham to his earlier era but creates problems yet unelucidated about what happened between 1500 BC and the deeds of King David c. 1000 BC. An interval of 500 years between Moses and David is uncomfortably long.

The high point in the history of the Jews as recorded in the OT is the kingdom of David and Solomon which flourished in C 10 BC. It was made possible by a time of troubles which occupied much of the preceding 500 years (1500-1000 BC) and covered the whole of a wide region, within which the Israelites inhabited a comparatively small part. In that time greater powers rose, clashed and dissolved. In Egypt the New Empire came into being shortly before 1500 BC. It did so by evicting the alien Hyksos and it re-established Egyptian power in western Asia as far as the Euphrates. But it came again under pressure from the north, this time from the Hittites who, from their base in what is now Asia Minor, inflcted a crippling defeat on the Egyptians in 1280 BC. The Hittites, however, did not long survive this victory. They were assailed in their turn by the Phrygians and towards the end of C 13 BC both Hittite and Egyptian empires disintegrated. In the general disorder of C 12 BC two events momentous for Bible history occurred: a new Assyrian empire began to arise in the east, while in the coastal lands of Canaan and Israel the Philistines established a domination which lasted until c. 1000 BC. These were to be the principal scourges of the children of Israel.

The chronology of the last millenium BC is easier to handle. The conquest of the Promised Land by Joshua and its settlement by the twelve tribes of Israel during C 12 BC were followed by the period of the Judges, who were *ad hoc* leaders of groupings of tribes against the peoples whom the Israelites had incompletely subjugated and who from time to time turned the tables on them. This inchoate phase ended with the creation of a unified state under, first, Saul and then David and his son Solomon. And from this point time-scales may be represented diagrammatically.

| | BC | |
|---|---|---|
| David<br>Solomon | 1000 | Recovery of Phoenicia under leadership of Tyre |
| Division of the kingdom into Israel and Judah | | |
| | 900 | |
| | | Assyrian revival |
| | 800 | |
| Amos, Hosea, Isaiah | | Tiglath-Pileser III of Assyria |
| Extinction of Israel | | |
| | 700 | |
| | | Sennacherib |
| Jeremiah | | Sack of the Assyrian capital Nineveh by the Medes<br>Defeat of Egypt by Nebuchadnezzar of Babylon at Carchemish |
| | 600 | |
| Babylonian Captivity of Judah | | |
| Returns to Jerusalem led by<br>—Zerubbabel<br>—Ezra<br>—Nehemiah | 500 | Cyrus the Persian conquers Babylon |
| | 400 | |
| | | Alexander the Great conquers Persia |
| | 300 | |
| | | Alexander's successors rule Seleucids in Syria, Ptolemies in Egypt |
| | 200 | |

| | | | |
|---|---|:---:|---|
| Maccabee revolt and rule in Jerusalem | | | |
| | | **100** | |
| | | | Pompey conquers Syria and Judaea |
| | Birth of Jesus | **BC** | Herod the Great, king of Judaea |
| | | **AD** | |
| | Paul | **1 AD** | Pontius Pilate, Roman governor of Judaea |
| Revolt of the Jews against Rome | | | Nero emperor |
| | | **100** | |

**Author's note**   An asterisk placed before a name indicates that that name has an entry of its own at the appropriate alphabetical spot. Although this is a register of persons I have included in it certain groups of persons – families, tribes, nations – for example, Israelites, Amalekites, Semites, Philistines. I have also included some individuals whose proper names are not given in the Bible: the witch of Endor, Longinus, the Prodigal Son, the Queen of Sheba, Salome, the Shulamite, the Shunammite. Lot's wife and Potiphar's wife are to be found in their husbands' entries. There are also a few general entries. These are: Apocrypha; Assyria and Babylon; Captivity and Return; Egypt; Judges; Pharisees, Sadducees, Zealots, Essenes; Prophets; Samaritans; Syria.

Dates BC are so marked, but I have used the prefix AD only where it might be confusing not to do so. The symbol C stands for century. Thus the tenth centuries BC and AD are abbreviated as C 10 BC and C 10 respectively.

In a few cases where the location of a work of art is not given the work is privately owned.

While working on this book I have laid family and friends under obligation for information and ideas, but my pre-eminent debts are to James Michie and John Whale, both of whom read my whole draft and gave me many comments on substance and style which have been a very great help.

Finally, I have made a large assumption: that the events narrated in the OT took place where everybody has for centuries supposed they took place, namely in or around Palestine. But not everybody supposes so now. Professor Kamal Salibi, for one, has argued that an area by the Red Sea in western Arabia fits the facts better, but since even he admits that his case, which rests on linguistic scholarship, needs to be reinforced by archaeology I have, in the absence of such reinforcement, followed the traditional geography.

# GLOSSARY

**Apostle:** A person who is sent out (Greek). Jesus picked twelve apostles whom he despatched to spread his teachings. See also Disciple.

**Ark:** A container or vessel. Two arks of very different dimensions figure prominently in the OT: Noah's ark, and the ark made to hold the Tables of the Law given by God to Moses and other sacred documents. For the adventures of the latter, see entry for Eli.

**Deuteronomy:** Second Law (Greek), i.e. the second Book of the Law, the first being Leviticus.

**Diaspora:** Dispersal or scattering of a people (Greek). Also used as a collective noun to denote the people dispersed as distinct from those who stayed put. The diaspora of the Jews was both violent and peaceful — violent from the destruction of the kingdoms of Israel by the Assyrians in C 8 BC and of Judah by the Babylonians in C 6 BC, but also more gradually fostered by improved communications and commercial opportunities, particularly by the spread of the Roman empire. See entry for Captivity and Return.

**Disciple:** A pupil (Latin). Besides his 12 apostles Jesus enlisted 70 further disciples to help with the work of spreading his teachings.

**Epistle:** A letter (Greek). The NT consists almost entirely of epistles and gospels. Most ot the former were written by Paul and these are the oldest surviving Christian documents. For details see under Paul.

**Evangelist:** One who brings or proclaims good news (from *evangel*, good news in Greek). See also Gospel.

**Exodus:** Going out (Greek), specifically the Exodus of the Israelites from Egypt under the leadership of Moses.

**Genesis:** Becoming or beginning (Greek), specifically the creation of the world by God.

**Gospel:** Good news, from Old English, particularly the good news of the coming of the kingdom of God. Many gospels were written in C 1 and C 2 AD, including the four which are in the NT. The author of a gospel is an evangelist.

**Messiah:** A person anointed (Hebrew). The messiah of the OT was a future deliverer of the Jews from alien rule and oppression in this world. In the NT the title is applied to Jesus and the role becomes other-worldly.

**Patriarch:** The ruler of a family (Greek). The Biblical patriarchs were the principal ancestors of the Jews: essentially Abraham, Isaac and Jacob; or these three and their remoter forebears; or, additionally, the twelve sons of Jacob. In later terminology a patriarch is the ruler of a church, notably the four senior eastern sees of Jerusalem, Antioch, Alexandria and Constantinople, but also Venice and a few others.

**Pentateuch:** The first five Books of the Bible (from the Greek for five vessels or books). They are Genesis, Exodus, Leviticus, Numbers and Deuteronomy. The Hexateuch (six books) is these five plus Joshua.

**Procurator:** A person deputed to act for another (Latin), as under a power of attorney; in the Roman empire, a governor of an imperial province – that is, a province with a large military establishment under the direct rule of the emperor as distinct from the less exposed 'senatorial' provinces. The procurator was the emperor's military and fiscal representative. The NT names three procurators of Judaea: Pontius Pilate, Antonius Felix and Porcius Festus.

**Sanhedrin:** A council (Hebrew, from the Greek for sitting together); more specifically the supreme council or tribunal of the Jews in Jerusalem. Its origins are obscure but it certainly existed in the Maccabee and NT periods, when its president was the High Priest. Its powers dwindled with the advent of the Romans, as the Gospel narratives show.

**Tabernacle:** A hut or other makeshift dwelling (Latin). In the OT, the tent reserved for the ark (*q.v.*) and other sacred objects from the Exodus from Egypt under Moses to the building of the Temple in Jerusalem by David and Solomon.

**Tetrarch:** The ruler of a quarter (Greek), originally a fourth part but also in the sense of any sub-division.

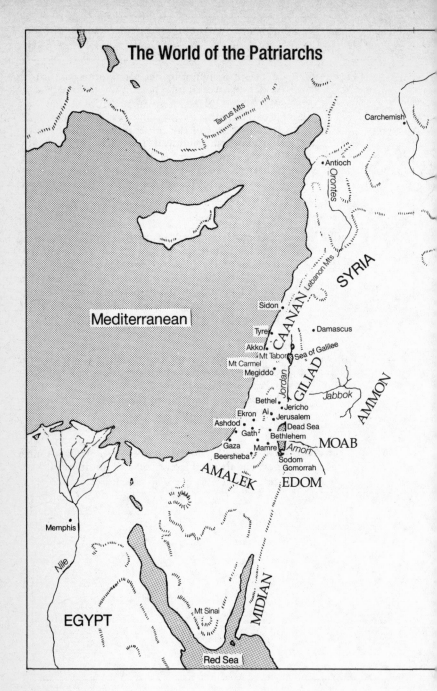

# The World of the Patriarchs

Carchemish

Taurus Mts

Antioch

Orontes

SYRIA

Lebanon Mts

Mediterranean

Sidon

Tyre

Damascus

Akko

CAANAN

Mt Tabor

Sea of Galilee

Mt Carmel

Megiddo

Jordan

GILIAD

Jabbok

AMMON

Bethel

Ai

Jericho

Ekron

Jerusalem

Ashdod

Dead Sea

Gath

Bethlehem

Gaza

Mamre

MOAB

Beersheba

Arnon

Sodom

Gomorrah

AMALEK

EDOM

Memphis

Nile

MIDIAN

EGYPT

Mt Sinai

Red Sea

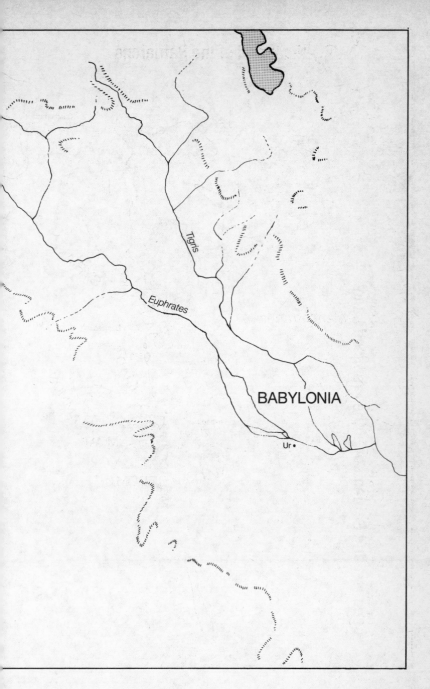

Tigris

Euphrates

BABYLONIA

Ur

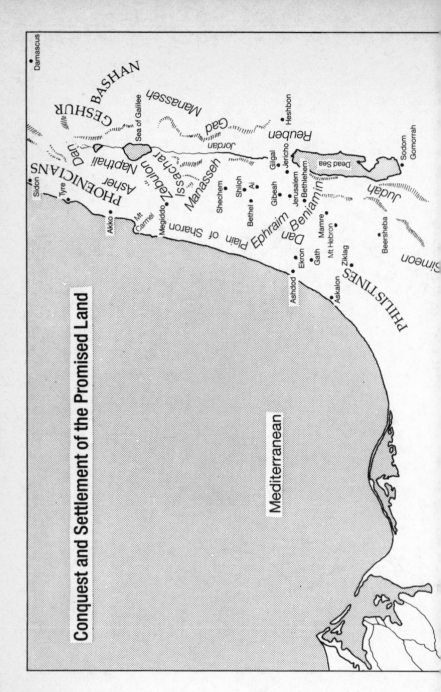

Conquest and Settlement of the Promised Land

Damascus

BASHAN

GESHUR

PHOENICIANS

Sidon

Tyre

Akko

Mt Carmel

Megiddo

Dan

Asher

Naphtali

Zebulun

Issachar

Sea of Galilee

Manasseh

Gad

Jordan

Manasseh

Shechem

Shiloh

Bethel

Ai

Plain of Sharon

Ephraim

Dan

Gibeah

Gilgal

Jericho

Jerusalem

Bethlehem

Benjamin

Heshbon

Reuben

Dead Sea

Sodom

Gomorrah

Judah

Ekron

Gath

Mamre

Mt Hebron

Ziklag

Ashdod

Askalon

PHILISTINES

Beersheba

Simeon

Mediterranean

xxiv

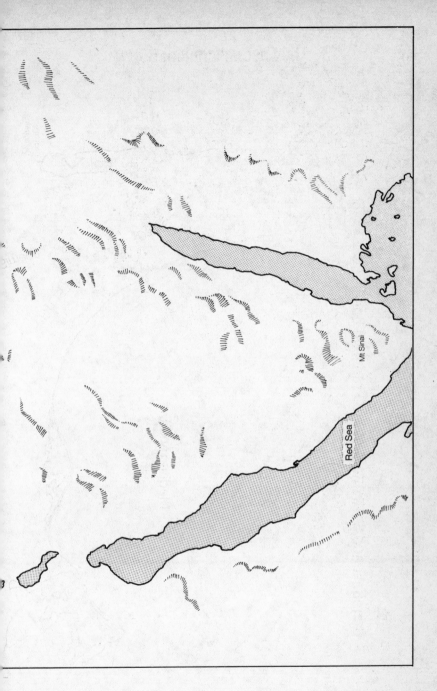

Red Sea

Mt Sinai

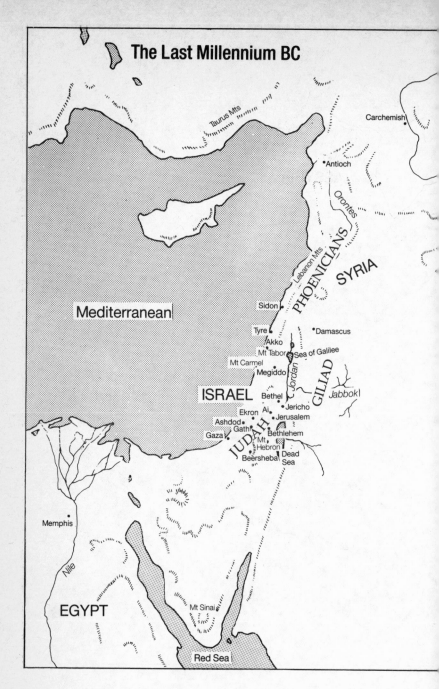

# The Last Millennium BC

Carchemish

Antioch

*Orontes*

Taurus Mts

SYRIA

PHOENICIANS

Lebanon Mts

Mediterranean

Sidon

Tyre

Akko

Mt Tabor

Sea of Galilee

Damascus

Mt Carmel

Megiddo

*Jordan*

GILIAD

*Jabbok*

ISRAEL

Bethel

Ekron

Ai

Jericho

Jerusalem

Ashdod

Gath

Bethlehem

Gaza

JUDAH

Mt Hebron

Beersheba

Dead Sea

Memphis

*Nile*

EGYPT

Mt Sinai

Red Sea

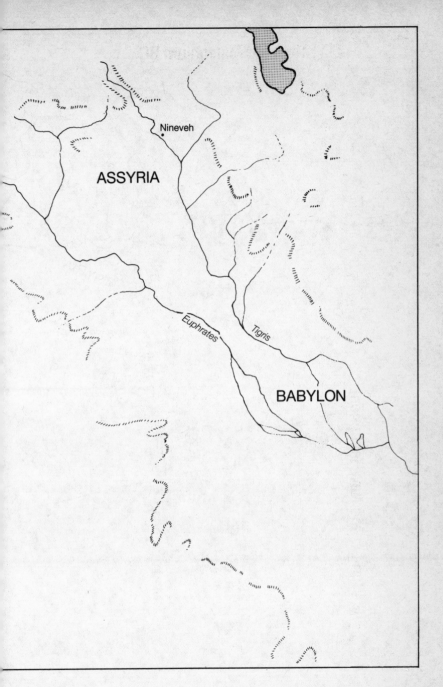

ASSYRIA

Nineveh

BABYLON

Euphrates

Tigris

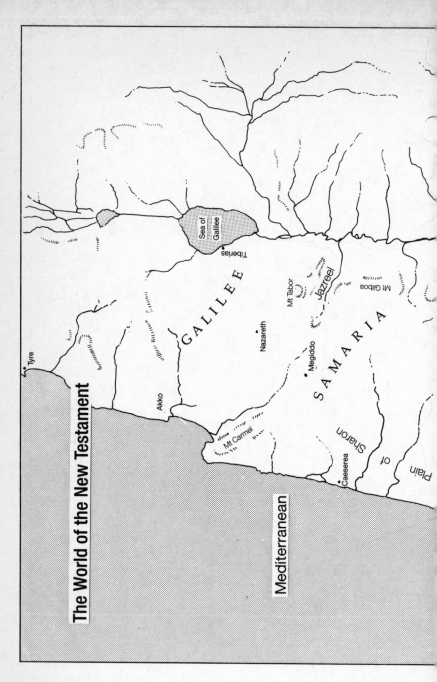

The World of the New Testament

Mediterranean

Tyre

Akko

GALILEE

Sea of Galilee

Tiberias

Nazareth

Mt Tabor

Jazreel

Mt Gilboa

Megiddo

SAMARIA

Mt Carmel

Caeserea

Plain of Sharon

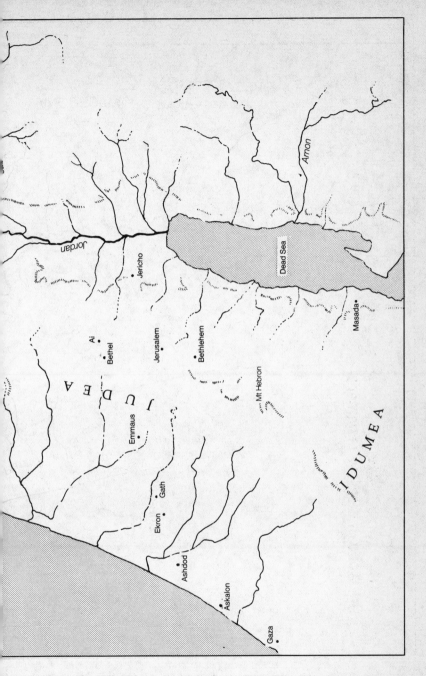

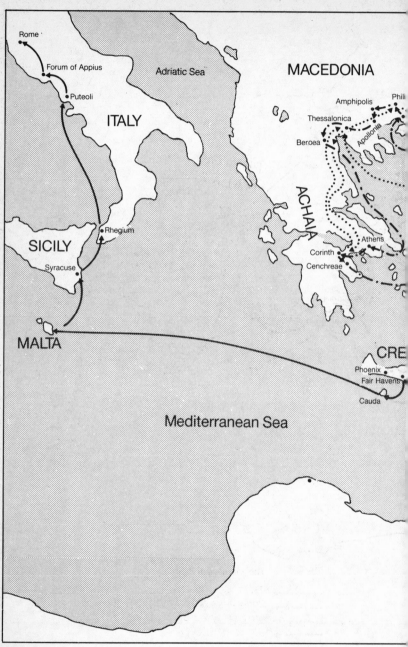

Rome

Forum of Appius

Puteoli

ITALY

Adriatic Sea

MACEDONIA

Amphipolis

Phili

Thessalonica

Apollonia

Beroea

ACHAIA

SICILY

Rhegium

Syracuse

Athens

Corinth

Cenchreae

MALTA

CRE

Phoenix

Fair Havens

Cauda

Mediterranean Sea

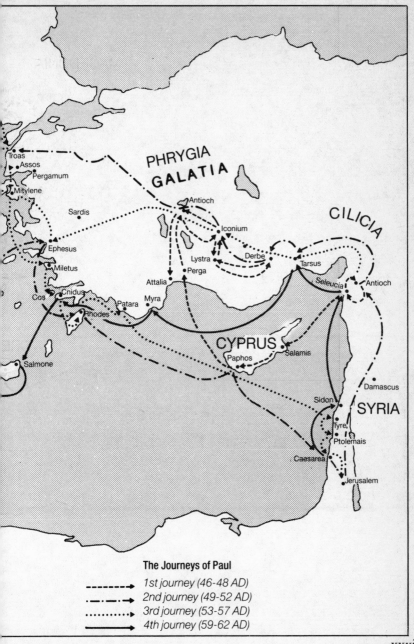

PHRYGIA
GALATIA
CILICIA

Troas
Assos
Pergamum
Mitylene
Sardis
Antioch
Iconium
Ephesus
Lystra
Derbe
Tarsus
Miletus
Perga
Attalia
Antioch
Cos
Cnidus
Patara
Myra
Seleucia
Rhodes
CYPRUS
Salmone
Paphos
Salamis
Damascus
Sidon
SYRIA
Tyre
Ptolemais
Caesarea
Jerusalem

### The Journeys of Paul

- - - - → 1st journey (46-48 AD)
–·–·–→ 2nd journey (49-52 AD)
········→ 3rd journey (53-57 AD)
━━━→ 4th journey (59-62 AD)

**Aaron** Older half-brother of *Moses and his closest companion and helper in Egypt before the Exodus and in the wilderness after it. He was more eloquent than Moses and played a crucial part in convincing the Israelites that Moses had a special charge from God and in the subsequent arguments with the pharaoh. His eloquence was reinforced by the miracles which his rod performed, changing at one time into a serpent and at another breaking into bud and fruit. In the wilderness Aaron was not totally loyal to Moses. On the personal level he and his sister *Miriam objected to Moses taking an Ethiopian wife. They also had some sympathy with those who complained that Moses' leadership was not getting them to the Promised Land fast enough. Far more seriously, during Moses' encounter with God on Mount Sinai (see Moses) Aaron acceded to popular clamour to make a god and, having collected a pile of gold earrings, turned them into a golden calf which he permitted the Israelites to worship naked. Nevertheless Aaron was invested with the insignia and functions of chief priest which, when he died, were transferred to his son *Eleazar. Aaron never saw the Promised Land. He died on Mount Hor in Edom when, at long last, the Israelites were leaving the desert behind them and trekking northward along the east shore of the Dead Sea to the point where, under *Joshua's leadership, they would cross the Jordan into the Promised Land.

In D.H. Lawrence's novel *Aaron's Rod* the hero, Aaron, is enabled by his flute (his rod) to challenge fate and to abandon colliery and family for a new world – London's Bohemia and travels through Italy – until flute and search are smashed by a bomb explosion in a café in Florence. The most celebrated depiction of the golden calf and its abandoned worshippers is by Poussin (London, National Gallery). A more decorous version by Cosimo Roselli is among the scenes from the life of Moses which cover one side of the Sistine Chapel in the Vatican. Botanically, Aaron's Rod is the name given to various flowering plants,

especially Golden Rod and Great Mullein.
(Exodus 4-7, 16, 17, 19, 24, 28, 30, 32, 40;
Leviticus 8-10, 16, 24; Numbers 1, 8, 16, 17, 20,
28, 33; Deuteronomy 9; Joshua 24; I Samuel 12; I
Chron. 6; Psalms 77, 99, 106, 115, 118, 133, 135)

**Abed-nego**     One of the three friends of *Daniel who were
thrown into a fiery furnace by command of
*Nebuchadnezzar. He was originally called Azar-
iah. The two others were **Shadrach and
Meshach. See Daniel.
(Daniel 2, 3)

**Abel**     Second son of **Adam and Eve. He was a
shepherd, his brother *Cain a tiller of the soil.
Both made gifts to God. Abel's was well received,
Cain's rejected. Cain killed Abel. Abel had no
progeny. He is a symbolic victim who exists to be
destroyed. In 'Abel's Blood' Henry Vaughan,
himself no stranger to family feuds and blood-
letting in C 17 AD England, took this first murder
to mean that blood must come before peace.
Titian depicts the very deed (Venice, Santa Maria
della Salute) and Thomas Arne wrote an oratorio
about it – one of his more successful works.
(Genesis 4)

**Abiathar**     Priest, son of *Ahimelech. He gave his powerful
support to *Adonijah's attempt to succeed *David
as king in opposition to *Solomon. When Solomon triumphed he had the chiefs of Adonijah's
party executed but spared Abiathar's life, merely
stripping him of his office and confining him to a
form of country house arrest. Abiathar was the
last representative of the line of *Eli which, as
foretold, lost the post of chief priest because of the
sins of Eli's family. Solomon gave the post to
*Zadok who had supported him against Adonijah

and whose line retained it until the days of the Maccabees in C 2 BC. Some thousand years later Abiathar's name was still popularly current: according to *Mark, *Jesus cited a story about Abiathar and David. In the OT (I Samuel 21) this story is told about Ahimelech, not Abiathar, but which is right we cannot now tell.
(I Kings 1, 2; I Chron. 15)

**Abigail** The beautiful wife of the churlish *Nabal whose rudeness to ten young men sent to him by *David brought upon himself an armed raid by David. Abigail did her duty by going out to meet David and diverting him from his murderous purpose, but God then killed Nabal and so Abigail was free to marry David. The use of her name to denote a servant or, more particularly, a lady's maid can be traced back to the C 17 play *The Scornful Lady* by Beaumont and Fletcher. This usage was probably popularized by the notoriety of Abigail Hill (Mrs Masham), waiting-woman to Queen Anne and royal favourite.
(I Samuel 25, 30; 2 Samuel 2, 3)

**Abimelech** King of Gerar in the time of *Abraham. When he arrived in Abimelech's lands Abraham pretended that his wife *Sarah was his sister. Without knowing the true state of affairs Abimelech took her but was warned by God in a dream that she was a married woman. God acknowledged that Abimelech had done no wrong and Abimelech chided Abraham for deceiving him and putting him in danger of mortal sin. Abraham's excuse was that he feared that Abimelech's kingdom was not a God-fearing land and that therefore Abimelech would kill him in order to get his wife; also that Sarah was in fact his sister, being his father's daughter although not his mother's. Abimelech gave Sarah back with sheep, oxen and servants and an invitation to Abraham to live

where he pleased in Abimelech's lands. In return Abraham prayed God to lift the infertility which God had put on Abimelech because of the episode with Sarah. Later, some of Abimelech's servants seized a well which Abraham had dug but Abraham swore to Abimelech that it was his well and the two made an amicable agreement; the place of the well was then called Beer-sheba. The story of Abraham and Abimelech is duplicated in the Bible by an almost identical story about *Isaac and Abimelech. Gerar is described in the Bible as a city of the *Philistines, although it is improbable that the Philistines got there until after Abraham's time. See also the next entry.
(Genesis 20, 21, 26)

**Abimelech**     Son of *Gideon by a concubine in Shechem. He persuaded the Shechemites to support a bid for kingship and got them to give him money with which he hired 'vain and light' persons with whose help he killed all but one of Gideon's seventy legitimate sons. After three years the Shechemites, instigated by an evil spirit sent by God, turned against Abimelech, but he triumphed over them, destroyed their city and sowed it with salt. He besieged and took the neighbouring city of Thebez, but a strong tower in the city held out and from it a woman threw a millstone which struck Abimelech and broke his skull. In order not to suffer the indignity of death by a woman's hand Abimelech ordered his armour-bearer to kill him, which he did. In this way God took vengeance on both Abimelech and his erstwhile supporters of Shechem. Abimelech tried prematurely to do what *Saul later achieved – create a united kingdom out of the several tribes of Israel. See also the foregoing entry.
(Judges 9)

**Abinadab**     The ark of the covenant (see glossary) was kept in

Abinadab's house in Gibeah for twenty years between its return to Israel by the Philistines (see *Eli) and its installation in Jerusalem by * David. (I Samuel 7; 2 Samuel 6; I Chron. 13)

**Abiram**  One of the leaders of the revolt, led by *Korah, against the authority of *Moses in the wilderness of Sinai. These dissidents complained that the Israelites were taking far too long to reach the Promised Land flowing with milk and honey. Their protest cost them their lives. The earth opened and swallowed them up alive with all their kin and cattle.
(Numbers 16)

**Abishag**  A Shunnamite girl who was bedded with *David in his old age to keep him warm. After David's death *Adonijah, one of his sons, asked for Abishag as wife. This request was a move in his bid for the throne against *Solomon, who had him killed in consequence. Rilke wrote two touching poems about the coldness of the king's body and the coldness of the girl's feelings. In similar vein Miguel de Unamuno meditates – in *Abishag the Shuamite,* a section of his *Agony of Christianity* – on the agony of the loving girl whom David was too old and cold to know sexually.
(I Kings 1, 2)

**Abishai**  Son of Zeruiah, was with his brothers **Joab and Asahel one of *David's staunchest supporters in his conflicts with *Saul. He was with David on the occasion when they surprised and could have killed Saul but David refused to take the life of the Lord's anointed. Abishai was an accomplice of Joab in the murder of *Abner in revenge for the death of their brother *Asahel.
(I Samuel 26, 2 Samuel 2, 21, 23; I Chron. 11, 18, 19)

**Abner**    Son of Ner, captain of *Saul's army. He remained faithful to Saul in his conflicts with *David and was the moving force in making Saul's son *Ish-bosheth king after Saul's death. In the seven-year war that followed, Abner's principal adversary on David's side was *Joab. Abner and Ish-bosheth fell out when Ish-bosheth accused Abner of taking one of his father's concubines, *Rizpah. Both made their peace with David. But Joab had a private feud with Abner who had killed his brother *Asahel. So Joab enticed Abner back to David's headquarters after peace had been concluded and, to David's distress, murdered him. (I Samuel 26; 2 Samuel 2-3)

**Abraham**    First of the patriarchs of Israel. He was born in Ur on the lower Euphrates. With his father *Terah and his nephew *Lot he left Ur during a time of troubles occasioned by the collapse of the current (semitic) empire of Babylon and travelled north-west to Haran, which lay between the Euphrates and the Tigris near the modern frontier between Syria and Turkey. There Terah and his followers settled and Terah died. After his father's death Abraham was directed by God to resume his travels. He trekked south, through the land of Shechem, between Bethel and Ai to Hebron, and into the Negeb (see map on p. xviii). Abraham and Lot possessed by this time large flocks and herds. They were comparatively wealthy men, but wealth of this kind is precarious. To keep their beasts in good condition the patriarchs needed wide tracts of land and were always at the mercy of the elements. A famine could wipe out their wealth with terrifying speed and a famine drove Abraham – as another, later, drove his grandson *Jacob – to Egypt, where he lived for some time. In Egypt he pretended that *Sarah, his wife, was his sister because he was afraid that the pharaoh would covet her for her beauty and kill Abraham in order to get her. The pharaoh was in fact enchanted by Sarah, took her into his household and loaded

Abraham with good things; but God inflicted diseases on the pharaoh and his court, the pharaoh discovered Abraham's trick, gave back Sarah and ordered Abraham to be off.

Back near Bethel Abraham told Lot that their combined wealth was such that the land could not support it without friction and feuding. He proposed that they separate and gave Lot the choice of which way to go. Lot chose the well-watered valley of the Jordan and settled in Sodom. Abraham, with God's promise to give him and his descendants all the lands that he could see in every direction, settled at Hebron. He became a power in a modest way, involved himself in the wars between the kings of the east and the kings of the west (the kings round the Euphrates against those round the Dead Sea) and laid the foundations of the military power of his race (see further under **Amraphel, Lot, Melchizedek).

He also founded a dynasty. He had at this point no legitimate heir, although he had a son Eliezer born of a slave, but God told him in a dream that after 400 years his descendants would have all the lands between Egypt and the Euphrates. Sarah, still childless, gave Abraham her Egyptian servant *Hagar as a concubine and she bore him *Ishmael. Another thirteen years passed and Abraham was in his hundredth year when God promised to fulfil the covenant he had made with him and give him fruitful legitimate issue, on condition that all his descendants should be circumcised as a sign of that covenant. Three men appeared to Abraham as he was sitting at midday in front of his tent 'at the terebinths (turpentine trees) of *Mamre' in Hebron and told him that Sarah would bear him a son. Sarah overheard them and laughed, for she was long past child-bearing. But she conceived and gave birth to *Isaac. By this time Abraham had moved from Hebron (presumably there was another famine) and back to the Negeb, where he lived as an alien in the land of *Abimelech, king of Gerar, once again going through the pretence that Sarah was his sister.

Abraham was commanded by God to sacrifice his beloved son Isaac. He prepared to obey
but was spared his odious duty when at the last
moment an angel told him to desist and sacrifice
instead a ram which was caught by the horns in a
nearby thicket. Abraham returned to Hebron
where Sarah died. He bought from *Ephron, a
Hittite, for 400 shekels the cave of Macpelah
where he buried Sarah and was himself later
buried by Isaac and Ishmael. After Sarah's death
Abraham married again – *Keturah, by whom he
had six more sons. His last recorded act was to
find a wife for Isaac from his native land (see
Isaac).

From Abraham and his brothers stemmed a
large part of the large cast of the OT, not only
Israelites but also **Ishmaelites, Midianites, Edomites, Amalekites, Moabites, Ammonites: see
family tree B. His dates are a matter of con-
troversy – C 15 or 21 BC, with modern scholarship
veering to C 15 BC: see the note on dates in the
Introduction to this book.

Abraham is the first of the patriarchs, the
historical first father of the Israelites, more real
than their legendary father *Adam. His essential
character is fatherhood and the essential Abraham
story is the testing of that fatherhood in the
sacrifice of Isaac. Unlike practically every other
major OT figure he failed no big test and died
untainted by deviation from duty or humanity. In
the north porch of Chartres he turns his head
aside as, enigmatic and benign, he cherished with
one hand his small son Isaac. Abraham's bosom
became in the Middle Ages the name for a section
of the afterworld. It was the place where the souls
of the dead who were not hopelessly damned
waited for the prayers of the living to secure their
passage into Paradise. This area has been called
the ante-chamber to Paradise. Powerfully promoted by St Augustine, this notion was an ingredient in the development, towards the end of the
Middle Ages, of the idea of Purgatory. When
Purgatory was fully approved by the Roman
Catholic church in C 16, Abraham's bosom

ceased to have function or location, but it has survived as a figure of speech denoting comfort or asylum, even sometimes Paradise: 'The sons of Edward sleep in Abraham's bosom' (Shakespeare, *Richard III*, iv, iii). Abraham has a prominent place in Muslim, as well as Jewish and Christian, legend.

(Genesis II-26, 28, 31, 50; Exodus 3, 32, 33; Matthew I, 3, 22; Mark 12; Luke 13, 16, 19; John 8)

**Absalom**  The third of *David's 17 sons. His mother was a daughter of the king of Geshur (north-east of the Sea of Galilee). Absalom made two big splashes in his life before his pitiable death entangled in the branches of an oak tree: he was involved as avenger in the case of the rape of his sister *Tamar, and he revolted against his father David in an attempt to seize the throne. (Tamar was Absalom's full sister. *Amnon, who raped her, was their half-brother.) For two years Absalom did nothing about the outrage but then invited all his brothers to a sheep-shearing party and there had Amnon murdered. In fear of his father he fled to his father-in-law in Geshur. David's general *Joab, seeing that David longed to have Absalom back, organised a charade by getting a woman of Tekoah to spin David a tale which was in all essential points Absalom's tale and pointed to the need for forgiveness. David got the point and told Joab to tell Absalom to return to his house in Jerusalem but stay away from David's presence. For two years after coming back Absalom tried in vain to see Joab and get him to intercede further with David, but Joab evaded him until Absalom forced an encounter by setting fire to Joab's field, which adjoined his own property. Joab agreed to speak to David, who sent for Absalom and kissed him.

Absalom was famous for his luxurious head of hair. When once a year he had it cut the tresses weighed 200 shekels of silver; but they were the death of him. Discontented and ambitious, he curried favour with the people, raised a rebellion against David and drove him out of Jerusalem. Against the advice of his chief counsellor *Ahithophel he allowed himself to be duped by *Hushai into taking personal command of his army and crossing the Jordan, where he was defeated by Joab in the wood of Ephraim. David had urgently enjoined Joab to see Absalom safe but Joab disobeyed. Absalom, riding a mule, was caught by the hair in the branches of an oak and left hanging when the mule moved on. Joab found him and stabbed him to death. On hearing that Absalom was dead David burst out: 'O my son Absalom, my son, my son Absalom, would God I had died for thee.'

Rilke's *Absalom's Abfall* relates the prince's progress from splendid confidence to the misery of his death, hanging defenceless in the tree. In Dryden's *Absalom and Achitophel* Absalom stands for Charles II's rebellious son Monmouth (the oldest of that king's 14 attested bastards) while Charles himself is portrayed as David and *Achitophel represents the Earl of Shaftesbury. William Faulkner gave Biblical titles to his two moving tragedies on the themes of guilt, shame and crime inherent in the inability of whites to accord an equal humanity to blacks in the American South: *Absalom, Absalom!* and *Go Down, Moses*. The pavemented floor of Siena cathedral shows Absalom caught in the tree and skewered by his enemies. Absalom's fate inspired an early C 18 jingle: 'O Absalom, Absalom my son, Had'st thou but worn a periwig Thou had'st not been undone' – which catches the bathos in which the advertising profession has continued to excel.

(2 Samuel 13-18)

**Achan**     The first of very many sinners whose sins were visited upon the *Israelites after their arrival in the Promised Land. Achan 'took of the accursed

thing' and so God caused an attempt by *Joshua to take the town of Ai to fail. An elaborate procedure detected, first, the culprit's tribe, and then his family, and finally himself. Achan confessed that he had stolen part of God's share (in Greek, the anathemata) of the war booty. He and his sons and daughters were all cursed (anathematized) and stoned to death and burned. The assault on Ai was renewed, and succeeded.
(Joshua 7)

**Achish**    King of Gath and so one of the chief princes of the *Philistines. He developed a friendship and alliance with *David when David was on the run from the jealousy of *Saul. David fled to Gath, where he pretended to be mad, and thence fled again to the cave of Adullam. After once failing to become reconciled with Saul he fled a second time to Achish, who gave him a place to live at Ziklag, near Gath. When the Philistines raised a confederate army against Saul, Achish wished David to have a place in it; but the other Philistines objected and David was sent back to Ziklag where he found that his home had meanwhile been wrecked by the *Amalekites, and his womenfolk, including his two wives **Abigail and Ahinoam, abducted. He chased the Amalekites and defeated them and got his wives back.
(I Samuel 21, 28-29; I Kings 2)

**Adam**    First man; uniquely made, not born. He engendered the entire human race but by succumbing to temptation he abased it. The Book of Genesis gives two accounts of his creation. In the one, man was created after everything else. In the other, he was created before God planted the garden of Eden and before He populated it with the animals and birds which Adam helped to name. God then made *Eve by putting Adam into a trance and taking from him a rib, from which he made Eve.

Adam and Eve were free to enjoy all that was in the garden of Eden except that they might not, on pain of death, taste the fruit of the Tree of Knowledge of Good and Evil. But the serpent – Satan in disguise – told Eve that if she tasted the fruit she would not die but would gain all knowledge. Eve succumbed and led Adam to succumb too. When in the evening God came to see Adam he hid, afraid because he was naked. God asked him how he knew that he was naked and charged him with having eaten the forbidden fruit. Adam blamed Eve and Eve blamed the serpent. In order to prevent Adam and Eve from eating also the fruit of the Tree of Life (and so becoming immortal as well as knowledgeable) God evicted them from Eden. He condemned Adam to hard labour all the days of his life, to gain his bread only by the sweat of his brow: 'Dust thou art, and unto dust shalt thou return.' After being driven out of Eden by the archangel Raphael, Adam and Eve had three sons, **Cain, Abel and Seth: see family tree A.

With this story the Book of Genesis offers an explanation of the puzzle of a human race which is at once the creation of an omnipotent and benevolent God and yet perennially subject to pain and grief. The answer is to be found in the sin of disobedience, originating in Adam and Eve and inherited by all their progeny.

The most splendid rendering of these events is Milton's *Paradise Lost*. The most original of the thousands of graphic representations of Adam is a sculpture at Bourges showing God in the act of thinking Adam into existence: Adam appears as an idea emerging from the side of God's head. Adam's creation and his death have been most famously depicted by, respectively, Michelangelo (Vatican, Sistine Chapel) and Piero della Francesca (Arezzo, S. Francesco). Jacopo della Quercia sculptured a creation-to-expulsion sequence on the west front of S. Petronio in Bologna and Raphael designed another which was executed by his pupils in the Vatican. Adam's first sight of Eve, by John Martin in an unusually restrained mood,

seems to be unique (Glasgow, City Art Gallery).
On the other hand Adam's eviction with Eve has
been painted and carved over and over again,
never more movingly than by Masaccio (Florence,
S. Maria del Carmine). Adam amd Eve together,
heads only, with the half-eaten apple were drawn
by Holbein (Basel, City Museum). Haydn's *Creation* ends with the couple still obedient to God and
blissfully happy in Eden. Purcell's *Sleep, Adam,
Sleep* is a most beautiful song. Rilke's pair of
sonnets, 'Adam' and 'Eve', reflect their gothic
figures on the outside of Notre-Dame in Paris.
(Genesis 1-5)

**Adoni-bezek**    A king who was served his own disgusting
medicine. In his heyday he cut off the thumbs and
big toes of 70 kings and made them scramble for
food under his table. When the tribes of **Judah
and Simeon made war on him and defeated him
they did the same to him.
(Judges 1)

**Adonijah**    Son of *David and contender for the throne when
David lay dying. His attempt to pre-empt his
younger brother *Solomon was a failure in spite
of the support of a number of the great men of
David's court – notably **Joab and Abiathar.
Against them were **Zadok the priest, Nathan
the prophet, Benaiah and others. Guided by
Nathan, Solomon's mother *Bathsheba prevailed
on the dying David to re-affirm Solomon's claim
and when Zadok and Nathan anointed Solomon
king Adonijah's support melted away. Adonijah
then put in a request to be given the girl *Abishag
as wife. Since she had shared David's bed this was
tantamount to a claim to stand in David's place
and Solomon had Adonijah killed.
(I Kings 1, 2)

**Adoni-zedek**   King of Jerusalem who assembled a coalition of five kings against *Joshua after his capture of Jericho and Ai. It was too little and too late. Joshua won his most memorable victory, aided by God, who rained hailstones on the enemy and stayed the sun in its course in order to give Joshua extra time for the slaughter. The five kings – the others were Hoham of Hebron, Piram of Jarmuth, Japhia of Lachish and Debir of Eglon – took refuge in a cave where they were walled up while the battle went on and then brought out and hanged.
(Joshua 10)

**Aeneas**   A man of Lydda sick of the palsy and cured by *Peter.
(Acts 9)

**Agabus**   He prophesied in Antioch the famine which was to befall in the days of the emperor Claudius. The Christians in Antioch made a collection and sent **Barnabas and Paul with it to Jerusalem. The same Agabus or another prophesied Paul's arrest by the Jews of Jerusalem.
(Acts 11, 21)

**Agag**   King of the *Amalekites. He was the occasion of God's change of heart about *Saul. When Saul defeated the Amalekites he spared Agag's life and, in deference to the wishes of the Israelites, also the best of the Amalekites' flocks and herds. But God had commanded that the Amalekites be destroyed utterly. Samuel was sent by God to do what Saul had failed to do. After reprimanding Saul, Samuel summoned Agag who, apprehensive, 'came unto him delicately'. And Samuel 'hewed Agag in pieces before the Lord in Gilgal'. To tread or walk like Agag means to proceed gingerly in a tricky situation.
(I Samuel 15)

**Agrippa I**   Also called Herod Agrippa, king of Judaea AD 37-44, grandson of *Herod the Great. He was crowned king by his friend Caligula – he continued the family tradition of making the right friends in Rome – upon the death in AD 37 of Tiberius, who had put him in prison. He was given the lands of his half-uncle *Philip the Tetrarch (see glossary) to which were soon added those of his other half-uncle the tetrarch *Antipas, whom he traduced to Caligula. When Caligula was assassinated in AD 41 Agrippa, who was living in Rome, transferred his attachment to the new emperor Claudius who gave him the Roman province of Judaea as well as the tetrarchies and so made him king over the reconstituted kingdom of Herod the Great. Agrippa I is the king called Herod in Acts 12 who had the apostle *James, son of Zebedee, killed and would have done the same to *Peter if he had not escaped with the help of an angel to the house of Mary, mother of *John Mark. Three years later Agrippa died, Judaea became once more a Roman province governed by a procurator, and his son, *Agrippa II, had to make do with a much limited inheritance. The name Agrippa came into the Herodian family through the friendship of Herod the Great with Marcus Vipsanius Agrippa, the general and counsellor and son-in-law of the emperor Augustus. See family tree F.
(Acts 12)

**Agrippa II**   King of Chalcis 48-100, son of *Agrippa I. His domain lay within the Roman province of Syria, beginning with the small region of Chalcis (now called Beqa'a) but extended until it embraced roughly the whole of his great-uncle *Philip's domains. His life covered the Jewish rising against Rome, which was begun AD 66 with the seizure of the armoury at Masada and the refusal of the priests in Jerusalem to continue the ritual sacrifice in honour of the emperor. After the capture of Jerusalem by the future emperor Titus in AD 70, and the destruction of the Temple and the final Jewish defeat in AD 73, Agrippa seems to have lived mostly in Rome, where his sister *Berenice was for a time the mistress of Titus.

(Acts 25, 26)

Ahab
King of Israel c. 869-850 BC. His father *Omri had seized the throne after the collapse of the kingdom's first two dynasties, had saved it from chaos, revised its foreign policies and built a new capital, Samaria. On this basis Ahab came nearer than any other king of Israel to recreating the great kingdom of *Solomon. He extended Israel's rule to Gilead and Bashan (east of the Jordan) and dominated for a while both Judah and Moab (east of the Dead Sea). But he warred too much, overstrained his resources and could not make up his mind whether to pursue Israel's traditional feud with *Syria (with which Israel had perennial frontier problems) or to make common cause with it against *Assyria. He also sowed discord within his own realm by marrying a foreign wife *Jezebel and allowing the worship of her gods, or *Baals, greatly to the scandal of strict conservatives whose champion was the prophet *Elijah. Their high-handed treatment of their subjects – for example *Naboth – exacerbated discontent. Ahab got Judah to join him in war against Syria but in spite of going into battle in diguise he was killed at Ramoth - Gilead by a man 'who drew a bow at a venture'. He was succeeded by two of his many sons, but his line was dethroned and exterminated by a coup led by his general *Jehu eight years after his death.

(I Kings 16-22; 2 Chron. 18, 22)

Ahasuerus
King over 127 provinces from India to Ethiopia who put away his wife *Vashti when she refused to obey his summons to come and display her beauty to the people. *Esther was promoted to her

place. Ahasuerus had a favourite, *Haman, and ordered all to bow to him. *Mordecai, a Jew and Esther's uncle, refused to do so. In revenge Haman planned to liquidate all the Jews in the king's realms. But the king discovered in time that Mordecai had previously uncovered a plot against his life and also that Haman's plans would involve Esther's death too. He had Haman hanged on the gallows which Haman had prepared for Mordecai, countermanded Haman's orders for the destruction of the Jews, empowered them to kill non-Jews instead, and made Mordecai the great man that Haman had been. Ahasuerus is commonly identified wth the Persian king Xerxes, famous for losing the battle of Salamis. Jan Steen shows him, very angry, starting up at Esther's banquet, scattering food and crockery, as Haman cowers in terror at his fate to come (Birmingham, Barber Institute). Ahasuerus is the traditional name of the wandering Jew who, in mediaeval legend, was cursed for scorning Jesus on his way to his crucifixion.
(Esther)

**Ahijah**   The *Shilonite, prophet. He intercepted *Jeroboam as he was fleeing into Egypt as a rebel against *Solomon. Ahijah caught hold of Jeroboam's new coat, tore it into twelve pieces and told him that he would be king over ten of the twelve tribes of *Israel. Ahijah's second encounter with Jeroboam took place when he had become king but had done things displeasing to God. One of Jeroboam's children was ill and Jeroboam sent his wife in disguise to ask about the child's fate. Ahijah recognized her in spite of her disguise and told her that the child would die, which it did.
(I Kings 11, 14)

**Ahimaaz**   Son of *Zadok the priest. Ahimaaz and *Jonathan (son of the priest *Abiathar) were chosen to take

intelligence about *Absalom's intentions from Jerusalem to *David, who had fled in the face of Absalom's rebellion. Before reaching David they had to hide in a well but they succeeded in delivering their vital information, which caused David to withdraw across the Jordan and so entice Absalom to his doom. After the battle Ahimaaz was one of the two runners sent to tell David of the victory of his armies but he was unable to answer David's first question: whether Absalom was safe. Only upon the arrival of the second runner, *Cushi, did David learn that Absalom was dead.
(2 Samuel 15, 18)

**Ahimelech**    Priest in Nob who paid with his life for befriending *David against *Saul. He succoured David in flight from Saul but his action was betrayed to Saul by the governor of Nob, *Doeg the Edomite. At Saul's command Doeg killed Ahimelech and 85 other priests, but Ahimelech's son *Abiathar escaped to David and became one of his main supporters for the kingship on the death of Saul.
(I Samuel 21, 22)

**Ahinoam**    A woman of Jezreel and one of *David's wives. Together with *Abigail she was taken to wife by David after his first wife *Michal was taken away from him by her father *Saul. Ahinoam was the mother of *Amnon who raped his half-sister *Tamar.
(I Samuel 25, 30; 2 Samuel 2, 3)

**Ahithophel**    Chief counsellor of *Absalom in his attempt to seize the kingdom from his father *David. At a crucial point in his rebellion Absalom preferred the advice of *Hushai, who was secretly acting in David's interests, to that of Ahithophel, who

thereupon hanged himself. In Dryden's political satire *Absalom and Achitophel* the latter represents Anthony Ashley Cooper, first Earl of Shaftesbury, the leader of those who wished to exclude Charles II's brother the Duke of York from the succession, campaigned for the legitimization of the king's bastard son Monmouth and incited his unsuccessful rebellion. Unlike the real Ahithophel Shaftesbury did not kill himself but fled to Holland, where he died.
(2 Samuel 16-17; I Chron. 27)

**Aholah and Aholibah**  Fictitious lewd women who whored in Egypt and with countless Assyrians and Babylonians. They stand in *Ezekiel's prophecy for the kingdoms of **Israel and Judah which whored after strange gods.
(Ezekiel 23)

**Amalek**  A grandson of *Esau and ancestor of the Amalekites. See family tree B.
(Genesis 36; Exodus 17)

**Amalekites**  Recurrent foes of the *Israelites. They were nomads in the zone between Egypt and Canaan. They obstructed the Israelites at the time of the Exodus from Egypt and in their progress from the wilderness of Sinai into the Promised Land. They were denounced by *Balaam, defeated by **Joshua and Saul, tried unsuccessfully to get their own back against *David in Ziklag. In the OT their most eminent figures are their king *Agag, who was hewn in pieces by *Samuel, and *Haman, whose anti-Israelite vendetta was defeated by Queen *Esther.

**Amasa**     A nephew of *David who joined *Absalom's revolt against his father. Absalom made Amasa commander-in-chief in place of *Joab (also David's nephew). After the revolt was defeated Joab came upon Amasa, gave him a friendly greeting and killed him.
(2 Samuel 17, 20; I Kings 2; I Chron. 2)

**Ammonites**     Descendants of *Ben-ammi – as, for example, the Israelites were the descendants of *Israel. The people or tribe most nearly related to the Ammonites were the *Moabites. They lived east of the Dead Sea. See also Nahash and family tree B.

**Amnon**     The eldest of all the sons of *David. His mother was *Ahinoam of Jezreel. He lusted after his half-sister *Tamar and listened in an evil hour to his friend and cousin *Jonadab who advised him to pretend to be ill and ask for Tamar to nurse him. She came and baked him some cakes but he refused to eat them until they were alone together. He then raped her but immediately came to hate her and had his servant throw her out. Tamar's full brother *Absalom bided his time for two years before inviting all his brothers to a sheep-shearing party where he had Amnon murdered.
(I Samuel 13)

**Amorites**     One of the people whom the *Israelites came up against in the Promised Land. The Amorites were Semites who had ruled in Babylon in the 2nd millennium BC. Defeated by northern invaders they moved west and created with the *Canaanites a new power (c. 1800-1600 BC) which extended at its peak over Asia Minor and perhaps into the Aegean. This power was overcome and reduced to dependence by the Egyptian New Empire, and by the time the Israelites arrived in the Promised Land the Amorites were a remnant who retained a certain identity in hilly areas. The Israelites lumped them together with the Canaanites and others with whom they disputed the Promised Land. See also Mamre.

**Amos**  A rough-hewn shepherd and forester from Tekoa who made a sharp and angry incursion into the public life of Israel and was quickly thrown out, c. 750 BC. It is not certain whether the Tekoa whence he came was the Tekoa near Bethlehem in Judah or another Tekoa inside Israel. Amos was a shrewd observer of man and nature, no mere roughneck but well informed as well as indignant, passionate and severe. He was among the sterner monotheists, insisting that Jehovah was not merely the only God for the children of Israel but the one and only God anywhere.

The voice of Amos is a voice of doom. He had five visions of the defeats and destruction to be visited on Israel because its people had revolted from their God. He stopped little short of foretelling destruction total and inevitable, but he conceded that God might save a remnant to perpetuate the house of *David. His denunciations were both religious and social. He deplored the abandonment of old rites and forms of worship and, no less, the destruction of Israel's small independent farming communities. Hating what he saw, he foresaw it all coming to a bad end – which it did when, not many years later, the *Assyrians destroyed Israel without trace. Amos set a pattern for all the major prophets who followed him, a pattern of cataclysm mitigated by the hope of salvation. If Amos himself gave only frail hopes of salvation, his close contemporary *Hosea was less pessimistic and in the long run more influential. See also Prophets.
(Amos)

**Amram**    Father of *Moses

**Amraphel**    King of Shinar (Sumeria). Together with three other kings from the east Amraphel made war on five kings in the general area of the Dead Sea, including the kings of Sodom and Gomorrah. The cause of this war was the attempt of the latter five kings to escape from the overlordship of the former. The confederacy of Dead Sea kings was put to flight. In the course of these commotions *Lot, who was living in Sodom, was captured, but *Abraham, his uncle, mounted a rescue operation and the kings of the east who had defeated the Dead Sea kings were in their turn defeated by Abraham. After his victory Abraham was blessed by the mysterious *Melchizedek, gave him a tithe of his battle spoils and restored everything else to the king of Sodom. The identification of Amraphel with the great Babylonian law-giver Hammurabi, once generally accepted, creates serious chronological difficulties since Hammurabi flourished around 2050 BC while Abraham can fairly confidently be assigned to 1500-1400 BC: see note on dates p. xiv. Amraphel's allies were called Arioch, Chedorlaomer and Tidal.
(Genesis 14)

**Anak**    A giant and father of giants. The spies sent by *Moses to gain intelligence about the Promised Land reported that there were giants – Anakim – to be contended with. When the Promised Land was conquered and *Caleb was given his share of it round Hebron he had to dispossess the sons of Anak.
(Numbers 13; Deuteronomy 9; Joshua 15)

**Ananias**    With his wife Sapphira sold his possessions but gave only part of the proceeds to the apostles and upon being rebuked by *Peter fell down dead. Ignorant of this fatality Sapphira came three hours later practising the same deception and, being discovered, also fell down dead. See also the next two entries.

(Acts 5)

**Ananias**  A disciple in Damascus sent to *Paul in the street called Straight to give him back the sight which he lost at the moment of his conversion. See also the preceding and following entries.

(Acts 9)

**Ananias**  High priest in Jerusalem who ordered bystanders to strike *Paul on the mouth but 'God shall smite thee, thou whited wall,' retorted Paul. See also the two preceding entries.

(Acts 23)

**Andrew**  A fisherman of Bethsaida and the first to be called of the twelve apostles. He was the brother of *Peter and that is almost all the NT has to say about him except for two anecdotes related in John's Gospel. When *John the Baptist acknowledged that *Jesus was the son of God he was overheard by Andrew who went to his brother and told him that they had found the Messiah (see glossary); and Andrew was the disciple who found the boy with the original loaves and fishes (see Jesus). Post-Biblical stories have taken him far afield – even to Scythia – and he was supposed to have been martyred on a saltire, or X-shaped, cross at Patras in Greece, whence his body was taken to Constantinople. He became the patron saint of that city and also of Scotland. Domenichino (early C 17) painted a sequence of pictures about his life in the church of S. Andrea della Valle in Rome.

(Matthew 10; Mark I, 3, 13; Luke 6; John I, 6, 12; Acts I)

**Anna**     A prophetess who spent her life serving God with fasting and prayer night and day. She happened to come into the Temple when *Simeon was praising and thanking God for the advent of *Jesus into the world. She too thanked God and began the task of spreading throughout Jerusalem the good news of the redemption of man. Other Annas are *Tobit's wife and the mother of the Virgin *Mary. (Luke 2)

**Annas**     High priest in Jerusalem and head of the family which virtually monopolized this office. He was deposed by the Roman procurator Valerius Gratus in AD 15, but was succeeded after a short interval by his son Eleazar, his son-in-law *Caiaphas and by three other sons. The office and the family were the focus of Jewish nationalism in the tradition of the *Maccabees. In *John's Gospel Annas has a behind-the-scenes role in the suppression of *Jesus, who is taken, after his arrest, to Annas before being passed on to the reigning high priest, Caiaphas. See also the next entry.
(Luke 3; John 18, 24; Acts 4)

**Annas**     Leader of the opposition to the apostles' preaching in Jerusalem after the Resurrection of Jesus and his Ascension. See also the foregoing entry.
(Acts 5)

**Antipas**     Also called Herod Antipas, tetrarch (see glossary) of Galilee 4 BC – AD 39, son of *Herod the Great. He received on his father's death his domains lying east and north of the Sea of Galilee. Antipas seduced and married *Herodias, his sister-in-law and cousin and mother of *Salome by her earlier marriage, for which misbehaviour he was condemned by *John the Baptist. Beguiled or inflamed by the dancing of his step-daughter, Antipas promised to give her anything she might ask up to half his kingdom. Prompted by her mother, Salome demanded the head of John the Baptist on a charger (dish) and Antipas, although disgusted, complied.

Antipas was in Jerusalem for the Feast of the Passover when *Jesus was brought before Pontius *Pilate at the behest of the high priest. Pilate sent Jesus to Antipas in an effort to sidestep his duty, but the tetrarch refused to accept any responsibility and passed it back to the procurator. Antipas was one of the ablest and least likeable of the Herods. His end was dramatic. Hailed as a god, he was smitten by the God of the Jews and eaten by worms before he died.

The Prado in Madrid has an unusual picture of the Feast of Herodias in C 17 costume. About 40 feet long, it shows Herodias, in a pool of light, peeling a pear at the banqueting table and surrounded by scores of hovering courtiers. At the other end Salome, her breast popping out of her dress, simpers towards them while servants in the background carry the head of the Baptist. The painting is now ascribed to Bartolemaus Strobl and some of the figures in it may protray the emperor Ferdinand II, King Henry IV of France, Wallenstein and other notabilities.
(Luke 3, 23)

**Apocrypha**  A Greek word meaning hidden things. It applied at first to any writing which was restricted to the private eye of members of a secret society or sect. Among Christians it was applied to Biblical literature which was never hidden in this or any other sense but was of dubious or secondary value. There are two categories of apocrypha. The first consists of those Books which, although they are not found in the Hebrew OT, were included in the Septuagint – the pre-Christian Greek translation of the Hebrew (see Introduction). Their presence in the Septuagint has ensured their continuing inclusion in Christians' Bibles in spite of the persistent doubts of divines and scholars. St Jerome, although himself one of the doubters, could not bring himself to leave out of his Latin Bible, the Vulgate (405 AD), anything that he found in the Septuagint. The Greek Orthodox Church has followed the Septuagint. For Roman Catholics uncertainties were removed by the Council of Trent which declared in C 16 AD that these Books were worthy of equal status and veneration with the rest of the scriptures, a ruling reaffirmed by the Vatican Council in 1870. Protestants, however, beginning with Luther, have felt freer with their doubts, have reduced the apocryphal Books to the category of the 'useful' and print them as an appendix to the OT instead of scattered in the body of the OT, as they were in the Septuagint.

The second and very much larger collection of apocrypha comprises some 40 books, or passages from books, relating to OT personages and an even more voluminous number of Gospels, Epistles and Acts analogous to those in the NT. Many of these works are known to have existed but now exist either as fragments or not at all. For various reasons and at various times they have been denied scriptural authority and they appear in no orthodox Christian Bible.

The Books of the Biblical Apocrypha are: I and II Esdras, Tobit, Judith, The Rest of Esther, The Wisdom of Solomon, Ecclesiasticus, Baruch with the Epistle of Jeremiah, The Song of the Three Holy Children, The History of Susanna, Bel and the Dragon, The Prayer of Manasses, I and II Maccabees.

**Apollos**  An eloquent and learned Jew from Alexandria who went to Ephesus where he imbibed *Paul's teaching from *Aquila and Priscilla. He proceeded to Corinth and became a pillar of the Church there.
(Acts 18, 19)

**Aquila and Priscilla**   Jewish Christians evicted from Rome and settled in Corinth, he a tentmaker. They were *Paul's hosts in Corinth and accompanied him when he left to go back to Syria. They settled in Ephesus. (Acts 18; 2 Timothy 4)

**Archelaus**   Ethnarch of Judaea, 4 BC – AD 6, son of King *Herod the Great, received on his father's death about half his kingdom with the diminished title of ethnarch, i.e. national leader. His portion included the Jewish heartlands of Judaea and Samaria and his family's ancestral Idumaea (formerly Edom) to the south. Young, weak and rapacious, he was removed by the emperor Augustus, who turned Judaea into a Roman province of a minor kind governed by a procurator (see Pontius Pilate, Antonius Felix, Publius Festus) with its capital moved from Jerusalem to the new coastal city of Caesarea built by Herod the Great and named after Augustus. (Matthew 2)

**Archippus**   Owner of the runaway slave *Onesimus who was converted by *Paul and whose forgiveness and freedom Paul seeks in the letter which he addessed to *Philemon. (Coloss. 4; Philemon)

**Aristarchus**   A Christian from the Greek city of Thessalonica who accompanied *Paul on his last visit to Jerusalem and also to Rome. At some point he was a fellow prisoner with Paul. (Acts 19, 20, 27; Coloss. 4; Philemon)

**Asahel**   Son of Zeruiah. With his brothers **Joab and Abishai, Asahel was a staunch supporter of

*David against *Saul and the Saulite party led,
after Saul's death, by *Abner. When Abner had
suffered a defeat Asahel, who was 'as light of foot
as a young roe', chased after him and forced him
to combat in which Abner killed him. Asahel was
later avenged by his brothers.
(2 Samuel 2; I Chron. 11, 27)

**Asenath**    An Egyptian, wife of *Joseph and mother of their
sons **Manasseh and Ephraim.
(Genesis 41)

**Asher**    One of the twelve sons of *Jacob and progenitor
of one of the twelve tribes of Israel. He and his
brother *Gad were the sons of *Zilpah, the
servant of *Leah. His tribal territory was along
the coast north of Carmel and so debatable land
with the *Phoenicians. See family tree C.
(Genesis 30, 35, 42-50; Joshua 17, 19))

**Assyria and**    The two principal empires in the Tigris and
**Babylon**    Euphrates valleys in Biblical times. Civilization in
these valleys began in small city states, some of
which grew into imperial centres. Such was Ur
where *Abraham came from. The first Babylonian
empire, whose most famous king was the law-
giver Hammurabi, flourished c. 2100-1600 BC. It
was destroyed by the *Hittites. For the next three
centuries the whole area of the Two Rivers was
dominated by a variety of invaders of Indo-
European stock. Then Assyria began its rise to
empire (c. 1300 BC). It was interrupted (c. 1150
BC) by a Babylonian renaissance but reached a
first peak with Tiglath-Pileser I (c. 1090-1060
BC). Its heyday began when Tiglath-Pileser III,
called in the Bible *Pul, seized the throne in 747
BC. He overran **Syria and Israel. Shalmaneser V
(727- 722 BC) took king Hoshea of Israel captive,

and Sargon (722 -705 BC) destroyed Israel's capital Samaria and carried off 30,000 of the children of Israel to Nineveh where they became the Lost Tribes of Israel. Israel was colonized and the sister kingdom of *Judah, although still nominally independent, became an Assyrian satellite. Assyria was temporarily weakened by the loss of Babylon to the usurper Merodach-Baladan in 721 BC and this weakness tempted king *Hezekiah of Judah into an anti-Assyrian alliance with Egypt; but the Assyrian king Sennacherib (705-681 BC) defeated all his enemies. He was the Assyrian who 'came down like a wolf on the fold' (Byron) to besiege Jerusalem but he failed to take it – probably bought off by Hezekiah. His successors Esarhaddon and Ashur-bani-pal (669-626 BC) conquered half Egypt but by mid-century Assyria was in decline, threatened not only by Babylon from the south but also by Medes and Scythians from east and north. These sacked Nineveh in 612 BC. The Assyrians disappeared almost as completely as the Lost Tribes. Their last great king became, under the name of Sardanapalus, a byword among Greeks and Romans for orgiastic self-indulgence, effeminacy and exuberantly dramatic suicide. Delacroix's vast picture of his last hour (inspired by Byron), although virtually unknown for half a century after it was first exhibited, is now an acknowledged masterpiece of early C 19 AD painting. Byron's tragedy, a very free versification of a section of the histories of Diodorus Siculus, and dedicated to Goethe, gives the king manly virtues as well as epicene vices.

The new Babylon which took Assyria's place lasted less than a hundred years. It was established in 625 BC by Nabopolassar whose armies, besides sharing in the sack of Nineveh, defeated the Egyptians at Carchemish in 605 BC. His son *Nebuchadnezzar put an end to the kingdom of Judah and deported many of its inhabitants to exile and forced labour 'by the waters of Babylon'. His main purpose in taking Jerusalem was to protect his western flank against Egypt while facing a threat from the Medes to the north. His feeble successors were supplanted by a new line; the threat from the Medes gave way to a greater Persian threat; the last king and his son *Belshazzar were overthrown in 538 BC by the Persian king *Cyrus the Great who initiated the return of the Jewish exiles to Jerusalem (see Zerubbabel, Ezra, Nehemiah). Babylon long remained a prosperous city but never again became an imperial capital.

**Athaliah**  Wife of Jehoram king of Judah (c. 849-842 BC) but herself a daughter of the heathen house of *Ahab king of Israel and a worshipper of *Baal. Her son Ahaziah was killed after a single year on the throne and Athaliah then seized the crown for herself. She slaughtered all the royal seed of Judah – with one exception. Ahaziah's infant son Joash was saved by an aunt, kept hidden for six years and then placed on the throne by a military-ecclesiastical coup led by the priest *Jehoiada. Athaliah was killed. Racine's *Athalie*, written inappropriately for a girl's school, relates with all the disciplined passion of his later years the heathen queen's fight with the God of Israel and her defeat. It was translated into English within a few years and used by Handel as the basis for an oratorio (first performed in the Sheldonian theatre at Oxford) in which he enters gleefully into the spirit of celebrating the deplorable and heightens the drama by inventing for Athaliah a scene in a dream with the equally deplorable *Jezebel.
(2 Kings II; 2 Chron. 22, 23)

**Baal**  The word Baal or Bel means god. It is used in the OT for gods other than the God of Israel. To the *Judges or *Prophets Baalim were either alien gods with whom the Israelites must have no truck or they were false gods, not gods at all. The worship of Baal tended to spread among the

Israelites for two main reasons. They lived close to and intermarried with peoples who worshiped one Baal or another and, until admonished to the contrary, saw little reason why they should not admit a local Baal to a share in their religious observances. Secondly, diplomatic moves or alliances might lead a king of Israel or Judah to take an accommodating view of a neighbour's god, as for example when king Ahaz of Judah was seeking alliance with Assyria. The principal gods of the *Philistines were Dagon, Ashtaroth (Astarte) and Beelzebub (Baalzebub); among the *Phoenicians the most potent local Baal was Melkarth of Tyre.

**Baanah**    A servant of king *Ish-bosheth whom he murdered in expectation of reward from *David, who ordered instead that he be executed along with his fellow ruffian *Rechab.
(2 Samuel 4)

**Babylon**    See Assyria and Babylon.

**Bagoas**    Chief eunuch of *Holofernes. See Judith.

**Balaam**    A man of standing to whom *Balak, king of the *Moabites, turned for help against the Israelites after they had defeated the kings **Sihon and Og and were threatening to 'cover the earth'. Balak sent for Balaam to curse the Israelites. God warned Balaam not to help Balak, but when Balak raised the inducements Balaam set off to parley with him. An angel barred his road, unseen to Balaam but seen by his ass, which shied off the road. Balaam belaboured it back again. The road was bounded on each side by a wall and Balaam's

foot was crushed. The ass fell down, Balaam cursed it, the ass spoke back and Balaam saw the angel. The angel instructed Balaam to go on to Balak but not to help him. On his arrival Balaam refused to curse Israel and maintained this refusal in spite of various manoeuvres by Balak. Much to Balak's vexation Balaam praised the Israelites and prophesied their coming victories over Moab and others. He went back home but later the Israelites killed him, a piece of monstrous ingratitude for which the Bible offers no explanation or excuse. Balaam's ass, one of the more engaging animals in the Bible, has made appearances in carving, stained glass and other memorials to animal sagacity. It was a favourite with Romanesque sculptures, e.g. at Autun. In the professional jargon of printers the word Balaam is used for the nonsensical matter kept in type to fill up odd spaces.
(Numbers 22-24, 31; Joshua 13, 24; Nehemiah 13)

**Balak**   King of Moab. He took fright when *Moses, having defeated *Sihon king of the *Amorites and *Og king of Bashan, threatened the land of Moab (east of the Jordan at the head of the Dead Sea). Balak tried to organize a coalition against the Israelites. He sent for *Balaam to curse the Israelites but Balaam praised them instead and foretold their victories.
(Numbers 22-24)

**Barabbas**   A man in custody on charges of insurrection and murder at the time of the indictment of *Jesus before Pontius *Pilate. Pilate, vaguely aware that the priests' indictment of Jesus was malicious, tried to get out of his dilemma by offering to release Jesus to the crowd in accordance with a custom which permitted the crowd in effect to redeem a chosen convict once a year. But the

crowd, influenced by the priests or by a claque of Barabbas' friends, clamoured for the release of Barabbas instead. Pilate washed his hands of the whole business and let them have Barabbas. Daumier depicted the crucial moment in *We Want Barabbas* (Essen, Folkwang Museum). He is the subject of a modern fable, *Barabbas*, by the Swedish writer Pär Lagerkvist who won the Nobel Prize with it.
(Matthew 27; Mark 15; Luke 23; John 18 )

**Barak**     Son of Abinoam and *Deborah's right-hand man in the destruction of the Canaanites led by *Sisera. See Deborah.
(Judges 4, 5)

**Bar-jesus or**     Jewish sorcerer and false prophet in Paphos in
**Elymas**     Cyprus who tried to prevent **Paul and Barnabas from converting *Sergius Paulus and was struck with blindness – which hastened Sergius Paulus' conversion.
(Acts 13)

**Barnabas**     Also called Joses, one of the chief disseminators, with *Paul, of Christianity to the *Gentiles. He was a *Levite from Cyprus and member of a fairly well endowed community in the Jewish diaspora (see glossary) with continuing connections with Jerusalem. He sold his lands and gave the money to the apostles. He was in Jerusalem at the time of the martydom of *Stephen and proceeded – or fled – to Antioch with other adherents of the new faith whose existence in Jerusalem was being made difficult by orthodox Jewry. He brought Paul to Jerusalem on the latter's first visit to the apostolic nucleus there and became a close collaborator with Paul, with whom he journeyed to Cyprus and there established one of the oldest

Christian churches. (It is the senior member of the group of churches which together constitute the Greek Orthodox Church.) He fell out with Paul over *John Mark, their companion in Cyprus, whom Paul judged to have behaved inadequately. Barnabas therefore set off on his own with John Mark, leaving Paul to undertake with *Silas and others his subsequent journeys through Asia Minor and into Europe.
(Acts 4, 11-15; I Cor. 9; Gal. 2, 13; Coloss. 4)

**Barsabas**  See Joseph Barsabas and Judas Barsabas

**Bartholomew**  One of the twelve apostles, called in *John's gospel *Nathanael. He suffered the most frightful fate of all the apostles if, as later legend related, he was flayed alive in Armenia. He is sometimes portrayed carrying his own skin, e.g. by Michelangelo in the Sistine Chapel in the Vatican.
(Matthew 10; Mark 3; Luke 6; Acts 1)

**Bartimaeus**  A blind beggar of Jericho who hailed *Jesus as the son (i.e. descendant) of *David. Jesus rewarded his insight by giving him his sight: 'Thy faith hath made thee whole'.
(Mark 10)

**Baruch**  Secretary of *Jeremiah. His name has been annexed to a number of works, one of which has found a place in the *Apocrypha. It is a collage which includes a letter supposedly written by Jeremiah; a prophecy of the Return from the *Captivity in Babylon to Jerusalem; and an assortment of exhortations, promises and snatches of wisdom by various hands and originally in various languages.
(Baruch)

**Barzillai**   A man of Gilead who, in spite of advancing years, bestirred himself to succour *David with food and lodging when he was in flight from his son *Absalom's rebellion. After Absalom's defeat David invited Barzillai to recross the Jordan with him and be his guest in Jerusalem, but Barzillai said that he was too old and went back to his own place after David had kissed him. On his deathbed David told *Solomon to show kindness to Barzillai's sons.
(2 Samuel 17, 19; I Kings 2)

**Bathsheba**   Wife of *Uriah the Hittite and of *David, and mother of *Solomon. David caught sight of her from his rooftop and could not wait to get her. He seduced her and had Uriah killed by sending him into the front line of battle. God was vexed by this disgraceful act and made their child sicken and die. But they had a second child, who was Solomon. David promised Bathsheba that Solomon would succeed him as king but as he lay dying another son, *Adonijah, made a bid for the throne with the powerful backing of **Joab and Abiathar. Other great men – particularly **Zadok and Nathan – steered clear of this movement and with Nathan's help and advice Bathsheba secured David's confirmation of Solomon's claim. Rembrandt's picture of Bathsheba having her feet washed by a maid is a portrait of his wife Hendrickje (Paris, Louvre). He also painted her at her toilet with two maids and David on a distant roof (New York, Metropolitan Museum). Cornelius van Haarlem also gives her two maids, one white and one black (Amsterdam, Rijksmuseum).
(2 Samuel 11-12; I Kings 1-2 )

**Bel**   A false god whose rascally priests were exposed by *Daniel. See also Baal. (Bel and the Dragon)

**Belshazzar**    Regent for his father Nabonidus, who was the last
king of independent Babylon before it was taken
by *Cyrus the Great in 538 BC and incorporated
in the Persian empire. (He is in the Bible wrongly
identified with Nebuchadnezzar who may have
been his grandfather.) Belshazzar was feasting
when a mysterious human hand appeared and
wrote on the wall: 'Mene, mene, tekel, upharsin' –
interpreted by *Daniel to mean 'You have been
weighed in the balance and found wanting.' That
night Belshazzar was slain.

Byron judged Belshazzar 'unfit to govern, live
or die' and, in another poem, diagnosed his
downfall more soberly in the lines: 'The Mede is
at his gate. The Persian on his throne.' Heine's
ballad *Belsazar* begins as midnight nears and all
Babylon is at rest except in the king's castle; it
ends with the king brought down by his own men.
Handel's portrayal is of a man more shallow than
wicked. Rembrandt has depicted the prince starting up from his seat at the appearance of the
fateful writing on the wall (London, National
Gallery). Samuel Colman was more interested in
the layout of the cutlery and fine fare as for a
municipal banquet (Oldham, City Art Gallery),
but the full drama of the doom-laden meal was a
natural for the turbulent imagination of the C 19
painter John Martin, whose many Biblical illustrations included also the destruction of Nineveh, of
Tyre, of Sodom and Gomorrah, of the Tower of
Babel, and of the world by the Deluge. The
downfall of Babylon – no longer the splendid city
of Nebuchadnezzar's hanging gardens but the
legendary city of ungodliness and foul living – has
been celebrated in William Walton's oratorio
*Belshazzar's Feast*, one of the choral masterpieces
of this century. Sibelius too wrote music about
him, for orchestra only. See Assyria and Babylon.
(Daniel 5, 7, 8)

**Benaiah**    Son of Jehoiada, one of *David's principal army
commanders. He sided with *Solomon against the

older *Adonijah in the contest for the throne when David died. Solomon used Benaiah to ensure the execution of Adonijah and the chiefs of the opposition and rewarded him with the post of commander-in-chief.
(2 Samuel 20, 23; I Kings I, 2; I Chron. 11, 18, 27)

**Ben-ammi**  One of two sons of *Lot whom his daughters, alarmed by advancing years and their isolation, got their father to father on them when he was too drunk to know what he was doing. Ben-ammi was the ancestor of the *Ammonites, his half-brother *Moab of the *Moabites. The lands of the Ammonites and Moabites were east of the Dead Sea and south of the river Arnon which flowed into it half-way between its two ends. See family tree B.
(Genesis 19)

**Ben-hadad**  There are in the OT two kings of Syria with this name and they were not related, or at any rate not closely related. The first was solicited as an ally by king Asa of Judah against king Baasha of Israel in the early days of these two sister kingdoms when they warred with one another to the considerable advantage of Syria. This Ben-haded was smothered by *Hazael, one of his captains, who was encouraged by the prophet *Elisha to usurp the throne. (I Kings 15, 20; 2 Chron. 16). The second Ben-hadad, Hazael's son, made war on Israel with 32 attendant kings but got drunk before the battle and was defeated. He was defeated the next year and the next.
(2 Kings 13)

**Benjamin**  The youngest of the twelve sons of *Jacob and progenitor of one of the twelve tribes of Israel. His mother was *Rachel, who died giving him birth and was buried at Bethlehem. His one full brother was *Joseph who was sold into Egypt by his other brothers.

Benjamin was so much younger than his brothers – the only one born after Jacob's return home – that when Jacob sent his sons into Egypt to try to find food he kept Benjamin by him. Joseph, by this time a great man in Egypt, demanded of his unsuspecting brothers that they must fetch Benjamin to him before he would give them the corn that they were asking for. Jacob was forced by his economic distress to agree and the brothers returned to Egypt with Benjamin. Joseph was both overcome with emotion and resolved to turn the screws a bit further on his other brethren. He sent them back to Jacob with food but he also had a valuable silver cup put into Benjamin's baggage, sent servants after them and accused Benjamin of theft. Brought once more before Joseph and appalled by the probably deadly effect on Jacob of the news of Benjamin's arrest, his brother *Judah begged Joseph to hold and enslave him in place of Benjamin. Joseph finally revealed his identity and sent for his father and all his brothers to live with him in Egypt.

A Benjamin is traditionally a youngest and doted on son; a Benjamin's mess is a specially large helping, since Joseph directed that Benjamin be given five times as much on his plate as his brothers at the banquet given for them all by Joseph.
(Genesis 35, 42-46, 49)

**Benjaminites**    Descendants of *Benjamin. Their tribal territory lay to the north of *Judah's in Hebron and these two tribes became closely associated, but some time after the conquest and settlement of Canaan by *Joshua a terrible tragedy overtook the Benjaminites. A man of Gibeah in the land of Benjamin took in a stranger. During the night his fellow citizens clamoured for him to surrender the stranger to whom they had taken a lustful fancy.

The host refused and gave them his concubine instead (see the similar story of *Lot in Sodom). The concubine was ravaged all night and left dead. The man cut her body into twelve pieces and sent one to each of the tribes of Israel as a summons to vengeance. The rest of Israel made war on the Benjaminites. In spite of great disparity in numbers the Benjaminites held their own until a third onslaught worsted them and a mere remnant was forced to flee for refuge to a rocky place. The other tribes vowed never to give to a Benjaminite any of their daughters in marriage, but after a bit they regretted having virtually wiped out one of their own twelve tribes. To circumvent their vow they attacked Jabesh-gilead and seized 400 virgins (the rest of the population was slaughtered) whom they gave to the Benjaminites. But these were still not enough and the Israelites counselled the Benjaminites to go to a festival of the *Shilonites and there seize the requisite number of girls as they came out of the city to feast and dance. So the tribe of Benjamin was resuscitated. Historically, however, it faded into a mere appendage of Judah. The most eminent member of the tribe of Benjamin was *Saul. Another was * Mordecai. The Benjamites were the object of *Herod's massacre of the innocents. The tribe of Benjamin is the subject of the stained glass windows designed by Chagall for the Hadassah University Medical Centre in Jerusalem.
(Judges 19-21; Jeremiah 37)

**Bernice**   Or Berenice, daughter of Herod *Agrippa I. She was present with her brother Herod *Agrippa II in Caesarea when *Paul was examined by the procurator *Festus and by his eloquence almost persuaded Agrippa to be a Christian. She rounded off a series of marriages and a bout of incest with Agrippa II by becoming the mistress of the future emperor Titus who, however, was forced to get rid of her because she made herself too unpopular in Rome. Racine made her a great tragic heroine,

which is more than she deserved. See family tree F.
(Acts 25, 26).

**Bethuel**    Father of **Laban and Rebecca. See family tree
B for the complex interlacing of the family of
*Abraham.
(Genesis 22, 24, 25).

**Bezaleel**   Master craftsman and clerk of the works, chosen
to carry out the elaborate instructions given by
God to *Moses on Mount Sinai for the fabrication
of the ark (the receptacle for God's testimony) and
a daunting range of sacred furniture, implements,
ornaments and garments from gold and other
sumptuous materials.
(Exodus 31, 35-38)

**Bildad**     The Shuhite, one of *Job's comforters.
(Job 2, 8, 18, 25, 42)

**Bilhah**     Servant of *Jacob's wife *Rachel and mother of
his sons **Dan and Naphthali. She was seduced
by Jacob's first-born, *Reuben. See also Zilpah
and family tree C.
(Genesis 29-30, 35, 37)

**Boaz**       Husband of *Ruth. Their son Obed was the father
of *Jesse who was the father of *David. Thus the
royal line of the Jews was rooted in Bethlehem,
but also in Moab, since Ruth was a Moabitess.
According to Matthew's Gospel Boaz was the son
of *Rahab, but the OT does not say so. In Victor
Hugo's romantic poem '*Booz endormi*' Boaz, old
and wifeless, is dreaming the impossible, which is

realized when Ruth comes to lie at his feet. See also family tree D.
(Ruth 2-4)

**Buz**  See Huz

**Caiaphas**  High priest in Jerusalem AD 18-36. His term of office embraced the trial of *Jesus. He was the son-in-law of the high priest *Annas and so part of the family which dominated the priestly establishment in Jerusalem. Dante found him in Hell, crucified in a ditch together with Annas and all the members of the priestly council or Sanhedrin. (Inferno, Canto 23). There is a forceful picture of him presiding over the interrogation of Jesus, by Raffaellino da Reggio (Rome, Oratory of the Gonfalone), an artist whose death in his twenties may have been one of history's sadder losses.
(Matthew 26; Luke 3; John 11, 18)

**Cain**  First son of **Adam and Eve. He was a tiller of the soil, his brother *Abel a shepherd. Both made gifts to God of their produce. God accepted Abel's gift but not Cain's. Cain killed Abel. Challenged by God to account for Abel's whereabouts, Cain tried to pretend he did not know what had happened. 'Am I my brother's keeper ?' God cursed Cain and condemned him to fruitless labour and vagrancy. But he also put a mark on Cain so that nobody might kill him. Cain moved to the land of Nod, east of Eden, where his wife bore him a son *Enoch. She appears in a family scene by Veronese (Madrid, Prado), suckling her son. John Steinbeck called his parable on the fall of man 'East of Eden'. Alessandro Scarlatti wrote an oratorio about Cain, Byron a tragedy in verse, and the puzzlingly brilliant Marc Blitzstein a ballet (1930). Legend has given Cain red or reddish-

yellow hair and has attributed his death to a hunting accident.
(Genesis 4)

**Caleb** Son of Jephunneh of the tribe of *Judah, close companion of *Joshua and, with him, the only one of the Israelites who crossed both the Red Sea out of Egypt and the river Jordan into the Promised Land. After the conquest of the Promised Land Caleb was given Hebron, including the *Jebusite city of Jerusalem which he acquired by dispossessing the giant *Anakim.
(Numbers 13, 15, 27; Deuteronomy I)

**Canaan** Son of *Ham and reputed ancestor of the Canaanites who clashed, first with *Abraham coming from the valley of the Euphrates and later with the Israelites emerging from Egypt under the leadership of **Moses and Joshua. See the next entry and family tree A.
(Genesis 9, 10)

**Canaanites** Semites who arrived in what was to be the Promised Land c. 3000 BC or earlier. Together with the *Amorites, later arrivals, they created a considerable power (c. 1800-1600 BC) which extended over Asia Minor and perhaps into the Aegean. This power was defeated and reduced to dependence by the Egyptian New Empire, and by the time the Israelites reached the Promised Land the Canaanites were one among many loosely associated tribes who failed to make effective common cause against the new invaders. Besides Canaanites and Amorites, the Israelites enumerated – but barely distinguished – Perezites, Hivites, Jebusites and Hittites. They regarded the Canaanites as non-semitic aliens descended from *Ham. See also the preceding entry.

**Candace**  Queen of Ethiopia and owner of a eunuch who was converted and baptized by the deacon Philip. (Acts 8)

**Captivity and Return**  In 587 BC *Nebuchadnezzar King of Babylon, having captured Jerusalem for the second time, carried off its king, Zedekiah, and the upper crust of the people of Judah into captivity in Babylon where many of them became forced labourers in that empire's irrigation system: 'By the waters of Babylon we sat down and wept'. The rigours of the Captivity were brought to an end when Babylon was captured in 538 BC by *Cyrus. What happened at this point and in the ensuing hundred years is obscured by the fact that the surviving sources – the Books of **Ezra and Nehemiah – have become hopelessly muddled and are also motivated by something other than historical accuracy. Most of the Jewish exiles did not go back; they became part of the diaspora (see glossary) which, by the beginning of the Christian era, outnumbered the Jews of Palestine. But some did gradually return with the approval and encouragement of Cyrus and his successors. What admits of no doubt is that the walls of Jerusalem and the Temple were rebuilt; and that the Mosaic or Judaic Law was promulgated, by *Ezra in C 4 BC, as a quasi-constitutional code. The champions of these moves may have greatly exaggerated the scale of the Return from Babylon, for their aim was to build up a restored Jerusalem with a substantial and purified population of impeccable descent from the exiles, as distinct from rival Jewish communities which had survived in other parts of the expired kingdoms of **Israel and Judah. This new entity did not become independent again (not, at any rate, for over 2000 years). It was a distinctive Jewish enclave in the Persian and later empires and it was increasingly theocratic with a high priest – an office not heard of before the Captivity – in place of a secular monarch. Its politics degenerated into squabbles between sections of the priesthood and rival interpreters of the Law (see Maccabees). But it ensured the survival of the Jewish race and religion. See also Cyrus, Zerubbabel, Ezra, Nehemiah.

**Cephas**  See Peter.

**Claudius Lysias**  Chief captain of the Roman guard in Jerusalem who, upon learning of a Jewish plot to kill *Paul, hustled him out of the city and to Caesarea with a posse of 200 soldiers and a letter to the procurator *Felix.
(Acts 23)

**Cleopas**  One of the disciples who were on their way from Jerusalem to the village of Emmaus after the Crucifixion, conversing about the extraordinary wonders that had been seen and heard. They were joined by *Jesus, whom they failed to recognize, and were astonished that the stranger professed not to know what they were talking about. At Emmaus they dissuaded their fellow traveller from going on his way and all three sat down to eat together. There it dawned on the two of them who the third was, whereupon he vanished away.

The supper at Emmaus is iconographically second only to the Last Supper among meals: Caravaggio painted it twice (London, National Art Gallery and, his later, less exciting version, Milan, Brera). So did Titian, Veronese and Rembrandt (all Paris, Louvre); Jan Steen (Amsterdam, Rijksmuseum); Pontormo (Florence, Uffizi); Santi di Tito, an altarpiece in S. Croce in Florence with a charmingly irrelevant vignette in the background, testimony to the reviving naturalism of the late C 16 AD; and many more. In a setting characteristically local and sparse Stanley Spencer drew Jesus seated on one side of a table at the

moment when, across it, the two disciples suddenly recognize him. Cleopas' unnamed companion on the road to Emmaus has sometimes been supposed to be Peter.
(Luke 24)

**Cornelius**  A devout centurion of Caesarea who, in obedience to a dream, sent to Joppa to fetch *Peter to Caesarea to preach there.
(Acts 10. II)

**Cozbi**  A Midianitish woman brought into the camp of the Israelites in the wilderness of Sinai by one *Zimri. She was a prostitute and *Phinehas the priest killed them both – but not before 24,000 Israelites had died of the plague with which God afflicted them because of the spread among them of whoredom and Baal-worship.
(Numbers 25)

**Crispus**  Chief ruler of the synagogue in Corinth. Most of the Jews there were hostile to *Paul, but Crispus he converted to Christianity.
(Acts 18)

**Cushi**  One of two runners sent to tell *David that his army had crushed Absalom's rebellion. The other runner was *Ahimaaz, who arrived before Cushi, but was unable to answer David's first question whether Absalom were safe. Cushi brought certain news of Absalom's death.
(2 Samuel 18)

**Cyrus the Great**  One of the world's more astonishing empire-builders, creator of the Persian empire which

lasted from his own day until its overthrow by Alexander the Great (331 BC). Cyrus began as a subordinate king in Persia, which was part of the empire of the Medes. He supplanted his Median overlord Astyages and then added the kingdoms of Lydia and Babylon – in modern terms, Asia Minor and Mesopotamia – to his territories: all this between 550 and 538 BC. Cyrus and his successors adopted a policy of letting Jewish captives in Babylon return to Jerusalem, rebuild their Temple and city, practise their religion and enjoy a degree of autonomy within the Persian empire – whose great extent dictated a policy of controlled devolution. Thus the Babylonian *Captivity of the Jews had an altogether different outcome from the earlier captivity in Nineveh of the people of *Israel who were never heard of again. The initial Return, led by *Zerubbabel, took place in the time of Cyrus himself. The second and third waves, associated with **Ezra and Nehemiah, probably occurred under Artaxerxes I (465-424 BC). This king's father, Xerxes, appears in the Bible as *Ahasuerus, the husband of *Esther, but is even more famous for losing the battle of Salamis to the Athenians in 480 BC.
(Ezra 1-5; I Esdras 2, 5-7; 2 Chron. 36)

**Damaris**  A woman of Athens converted by *Paul.
(Acts 17)

**Dan**  One of the twelve sons of *Jacob and progenitor of one of the twelve tribes of *Israel. He and his brother *Naphthali were the sons of *Bilhah, the servant of *Rachel. Because his tribal territory was in the extreme north of the Promised Land the expression 'from Dan to Beer-sheba' denotes the whole extent of the land of Israel. See also Micah and family tree C.
(Genesis 30, 35, 42-50)

**Daniel**   A hero of Jewish folklore about whom a number of stories were told. They were collected and published, probably during the nationalist revival inspired in C 2 BC by the *Maccabees. The best known of these place Daniel in Babylon during the C 6 BC *Captivity. He is represented as of noble stock and special skills, one of a select few picked out for *Nebuchadnezzar's favour. With three companions – **Shadrach, Meshach and Abednego – Daniel is made free of the king's table but they refuse to eat and drink with non-Jews.

Nebuchadnezzar had puzzling dreams which his native astrologers shrank from explaining, Daniel explained them in a way very agreeable to the king, who heaped more favours on Daniel and hailed the God of the Jews. But Nebuchadnezzar then had a golden image made and commanded all to fall down and worship it on pain of being thrown into a burning fiery furnace. Shadrach, Meshach and Abednego refused; the furnace was heated to seven times its normal temperature; the three were thrown in but were joined by a fourth – an angel. They sang a song (which constitutes a separate Book in the *Apocrypha) and came out safe and unsinged.

In another dramatic scene in the Book of Daniel *Belshazzar, feasting from gold and silver vessels which had once been in the Temple a Jerusalem, suddenly saw a hand writing on the wall. His wise men failed to read the writing but Daniel did, disclosing the doom to fall on Babylon and Belshazzar. That night Belshazzar was slain and his kingdom taken by Darius (an historical error: see Susannah).

Daniel was further exalted. But jealous enemies set a trap for him. A decree had forbidden the presentation of any petition to anybody except the king and when Daniel was seen praying to his God he was accused of disobeying this decree. He was thrown into a den of lions – a scene hardly less familiar to countless children through thousands of years than the nativity of *Jesus or the creation of **Adam and Eve. The next morning Daniel was still there and was released. His accusers, with all their wives and children, were thrown to the lions instead. The second half of the Book of Daniel is quite different. It contains a number of visions which treat in highly obscure language of the rise and fall of empires, from Babylon to Macedon and beyond. It is an early example of the apocalyptic literature which became popular with the Jews.

Daniel is also the hero of the story of *Susanna and the Elders and of two other tales related in the Book of Bel and the Dragon. The 70 priests of Bel (see Baal) tried to prove the reality of their god by providing large quantities of food and drink which the god was supposed to consume during the night. Daniel had ashes spread in the god's temple and was able to show that what happened in the night was that the priests and their families entered the temple secretly and themselves ate and drank this fine fare. They were all executed and Bel's image was demolished. Daniel then proceeded to destroy a dragon or serpent worshipped by the Babylonians: he gave it indigestable lumps of food which made it burst. Daniel was said to have gone to Jerusalem and to have died there, but in the C 12 the relentless Hispano-Jewish traveller Benjamin of Tudela saw his tomb at Susa in south-west Persia.

Rubens did Daniel in the lion's den; the den an open gulley, the lions numerous, Daniel unperturbed (Washington, National Gallery). A window showing the scene in the fiery furnace, designed by Burne-Jones and executed by Morris and co., is one of the high spots of C 19 English stained glass (All Souls, Middleton Cheney, Northamptonshire). The same scene inspired Benjamin Britten's canticle *The burning fiery furnace*. (Daniel: History of Susanna; Bel and the Dragon; Job 14; Ezekiel 28)

**Danites**  Members of the tribe of *Dan. See also Micah. (Joshua 19)

**Dathan**    One of the leaders of the revolt, led by *Korah, against the authority of *Moses in the wilderness of Sinai. These dissidents complained that the Israelites were taking far too long to reach the Promised Land flowing with milk and honey. Their protest cost them their lives. The earth opened and swallowed them up alive with all their kin and cattle. See Korah.
(Numbers 16)

**David**    Seventh of the seven sons of *Jesse, king of Judah c. 1008-1001 BC and king over all Israel c. 1001-968 BC. David's life had three main phases: the first when *Saul was still alive; the second when, for seven and a half years, he was king in Judah but not beyond; and the third when he was king over all Israel for 33 years.

***The boy David***    David was notably handsome: 'ruddy and withal of a beautiful countenance, and goodly to look to.' In his youth he displayed two contrasting characteristics: musicianship and valour. He was brought to Saul when Saul fell into a depression and was looking for a 'cunning man with a harp' who might give him relief. David performed so well that Saul made him his armour-bearer (that is to say, his close personal attendant) and conceived a love for him which, through many violent ups and downs, was never entirely extinguished. David returned to his father but was sent back to Saul's camp with some cheeses for three of his brothers who were serving there. He found Saul's forces confronting the Philistines and scared stiff by the giant *Goliath. David took up the giant's challenge and, with innocent courage, precise skill and a single smooth stone, floored him with his sling (see Goliath). Saul insisted on keeping David by him, but jealousy began to creep in as the people, exhilarated by Goliath's death, hailed David in extravagant terms: 'Saul has slain his thousands, and David his ten thousands ... Saul eyed David from that day forth' and tried to get him killed by appointing him one of his captains.

Saul also gave David his daughter *Michal as wife 'to be a snare to him', first demanding that David fetch him 'a hundred foreskins of the Philistines'. David survived this hazardous test and returned with two hundred foreskins.

At this time began the legendary friendship between David and Saul's son *Jonathan, who warned David that his life was in danger and interceded with Saul for David. Not for the last time Saul relented but then tried to stab David as he was playing the harp. David escaped with the help of Michal who foiled his pursuers by putting a dummy in his bed. When at the new moon king Saul held a special feast David had to decide whether to take his place at it or not. Jonathan agreed to sound out his father's mood; Saul saw through Jonathan's concern and contrivance and angrily warned Jonathan that he would never become king unless David were killed; Jonathan told David to flee beyond Saul's reach. David went first to Nob, where he was succoured by the priest *Ahimelech (for which Ahimelech paid with his life) and collected Goliath's sword. The next stage of his flight took him to the Philistine city of Gath where king *Achish received him hospitably. After pretending to be mad in order to baffle his enemies David moved on again to the cave of Adullam where he was joined by his brothers and by many who where in distress or in debt or dicontented to the number of 400. He became, in reality as well as in Saul's sick mind, a threat to Saul. David tried repeatedly to persuade Saul of his loyalty, while Saul wavered between believing and rejecting him: twice David was in a position to kill Saul but refused to do so. In this period David, having lost Michal whom Saul had taken away from him and given to another man, took two new wives – **Abigail and Ahinoam. He was again harboured by Achish, to whom he attached himself and his following, receiving in return a holding of land at Ziklag near Gath. Achish wanted him to take part in a confederate expedition of the Philistines against Saul, but the other Philistines objected and so David was not present at the battle on Mount Gilboa where Jonathan was killed and Saul committed suicide. David was separately engaged in pursuing and smiting the *Amalekites who had taken the opportunity to raid Ziklag and carry off his womenfolk, including his wives. For David's lament for Saul and Jonathan, the faithless master and the faithful friend, see Jonathan.

**King David**  Saul's death changed David from a fugitive and a vassal of Achish into an independent king. He was acclaimed king by his fellow tribesmen of Judah in Hebron. He was 30 years old. He made an appeal for national unity, but *Abner and other pillars of Saul's court and camp declared Saul's son *Ish-bosheth king over all Israel and there followed seven and a half years of war. Gradually David prevailed, largely thanks to his general *Joab, and when Ish-bosheth and Abner quarrelled (see Ish-bosheth) David established his title to rule over all the twelve tribes of Israel – which he did for another 33 years. He created a new capital city, Jerusalem, which he captured from the *Jebusites and re-built, and to it he brought the ark of the covenant with much celebration and music – and one serious mishap. When the ark, carried in a new cart driven by Uzzah and Ahio, swayed dangerously Uzzah laid a hand on it to steady it and was struck dead by God. David was so upset by this incident that he halted the journey for three months before making the last stage into Jerusalem with more shouting and trumpets and David himself 'dancing and leaping . . . with all his might'. (His wife Michal, watching from a window, depised him for his antics: see Michal). He consolidated the kingdom in wars with the Philistines, Edomites, Moabites and Ammonites to the south and Canaanites to the north. He occupied Damascus and extended Israel's sway to the Euphrates. He exacted retribution from the Ammonites when they humiliated his envoys by cutting off half their beards and half their clothing down to their buttocks (see Hanun). In his long reign he relied on a group of powerful figures who composed a household not unlike that of Charlemagne or other mediaeval European monarchs: his constable *Joab with his other generals **Amasa and Benaiah; the ecclesiastics **Zadok and Abiathar; *Jehoshaphat and Seraiah as heads of his civil administration; his own sons as captains and proconsuls. In Jerusalem he fathered eleven (or thirteen) more sons to add to the six borne to him by six wives during the seven-year war with the Saulites. One of these later sons was *Solomon, whose mother was *Bathsheba. Standing one day on the roof of his house David saw Bathsheba, then the wife of *Uriah the Hittite, and determined to have her. He seduced her and sent Uriah to Joab with a letter instructing Joab to put Uriah in the front line of the fighting. Uriah was killed, David married Bathsheba, but God was vexed and caused their first child to die. But they had a second child who was Solomon.

**Decline and death**    The most critical episode in David's reign was the revolt of his son *Absalom. David and Absalom were first estranged when Absalom murdered his half-brother *Amnon who had raped their sister *Tamar. This breach was healed through the good offices of Joab, but Absalom weaned popular feeling away from David in favour of himself, conspired to seize the throne and succeeded so well that David was forced to flee from Jerusalem eastward. Zadok and Abiathar went with him, taking the ark, but David ordered them to take it back to Jerusalem. David also sent his friend and counsellor *Hushai to Jerusalem to spy out Absalom's intentions and to counter the influence of *Ahithophel, the evil genius of the rebellion. David's fortunes sank so low that he was cursed by *Shimei, an unregenerate Saulite, who threw stones and dung at him and called him 'thou man of Belial' – in spite of which David would not allow his general Abishai to kill Shimei. In Jerusalem Ahithophel urged Absalom to take David's concubines, which he did – an act of defiance and assertion of authority. (After David's return these women continued to be lodged and fed but no longer served their prime purpose.) Ahithophel also wished Absalom to entrust him with the leadership of the army, while Hushai on the other hand pressed Absalom to take command in person. Absalom accepted Hushai's advice, whereupon Ahithophel hanged himself. Two emissaries – **Ahimaaz and Jonathan, sons of the principal priests – were sent secretly to David to divulge Absalom's plans and reached him after an adventurous journey which included being hidden in a well. David withdrew his entire force across the river Jordan and, when Absalom followed, Joab defeated and killed him (see Absalom). David's injunction to see Absalom safe was flagrantly discarded by Joab to David's great grief.

Re-crossing the Jordan in triumph, David was escorted to Jerusalem by the whole of Judah and half of Israel. But he was accompanied too by rumblings of a new rift between Judah and the other tribes, recalling the split on Saul's death and foreshadowing the similar split that was to occur on the death of Solomon. The suppression of Absalom's revolt was followed by a three-year famine which, so God explained, was visited on Israel because in years gone by Saul had mal-treated and killed many of the Gibeonites. The Gibeonites demanded that seven sons of Saul be handed over to them to be hanged, which was done; they included his two sons by *Rizpah. David secured their bones, and also those of Saul and Jonathan (buried at the date of their deaths under a tree in Gilead), and interred them all in the sepulchre of Saul's father *Kish. This was the final act in the history of the ill-fated house of Saul.

David, provoked by Satan, decided to take a census of the people. This took nine months and twenty days and yielded totals of 800,000 adult males ('men that draw a sword') in Israel and 500,000 in Judah. But David recognized that he had sinned and was offered by God the choice of three evils: seven years of famine, or three months of flight before his enemies, or three days pestilence. He chose the last and the angel of death killed 70,000 of his people. Jerusalem, however, was spared. When David saw that the angel paused at the threshing places of Araunah the Jebusite outside Jerusalem he bought it for 50 shekels of silver and built an altar there and so stayed the plague. This was almost his last act. He was old and cold and kept warm in bed only by the Shunamite girl *Abishag. His very last act was to endorse the succession of Solomon in preference to the older brother *Adonijah.

**Achievements and character**

David is the most striking character in the OT – less seminal than Adam, less awesome than Moses, less majestic than Solomon, less profound than Isaiah, but more human and more diverse than any of these. He was a great warrior king who succeeded – almost uniquely in their history – in uniting the tribes of Israel and so creating a kingdom which, in his own and his son's days, dominated the surrounding peoples and attained considerable power and riches. In this achievement he had to contend with the neighbouring kings, with tribal divisiveness and with the philoprogenitive polygamy of his own house – all of which militated against the unity of Israel. His work was inevitably undone when the great empires of the Euphrates/Tigris and Nile valleys were revived in the next century, but his character survived his secular work. He was uncommonly generous, as he showed by his behaviour to Saul and *Mephi-bosheth, to Abner and Shimei and others. He was a religious man whose intense emotions led him to express his religion with an athletic passion and extravagance akin to those of revivalist congregations or whirling dervishes. He was an artist. The psalms were supposed to have been written by him and even if he is no longer credited with their authorship he earned in his lifetime the reputation of being capable of writing them. He organized choirs and bands as well as singing, playing and dancing himself. His eloquence and the depth of his feelings are attested by his laments for Saul and Jonathan, for Absalom and for Abner. He played not only the harp but a number of other instruments too. If his treatment of Uriah stands as a blot on his character it can at least be said that many of his peers, predecessors and successors exhibited little except such blots. The allegation that from his deathbed he recommended Solomon to kill Joab and Shimei is suspect and out of character – although it would not have been bad advice. His contribution to manners was to improve them.

Like other OT figures David has become visually known chiefly through mediaeval and Renaissance eyes. The statues of him by Donatello and Verrocchio (Florence, Bargello), Michelangelo (Florence, Academy) and Bernini (Rome, Villa Borghese) show him as the youthful giant killer. On canvas Titian (Venice, Sta Maria della Salute) and Caravaggio (Madrid, Prado) depict him in the flush of victory; so does Caravaggio's principle disciple Gentileschi (Dublin, National Gallery of Ireland). Anthonio Pollaiuolo (Berlin, Kaiser Freidrichsmuseum) shows him more nonchalant with the giant's head between his feet, while Poussin (Prado) paints him resting after victory. In 1985 David with Goliath's head in Guido Reni's version was sold for £2.2 million. Rembrandt preferred his less militant side – harping for Saul (The Hague, Mauritshuis) or, with Rembrandt's own features, reconciled with Absalom (Leningrad, Hermitage). David at the cave of Adullam is the subject of one of Claude's sweeping landscapes (London, National Gallery). Burne-Jones depicted him lamenting and consoled in a pair of stained glass windows (Newcastle-upon-Tyne, Laing Art Gallery). Three modern views: John Berryman's poem 'King David Dances'; the crowned king in Chagall's best fairy-tale manner, and Stanley Spencer's drawing of two Davids in one frame – his better and his lower nature, the latter in thrall to the seductive captress Bathsheba. For Schumann he was the champion (with the Davids bündler, David's league) of culture and the arts agaist the Philistines in their modern connotation. David and Jonathan are the archetypal examples of inseparable male friends. In English history the Adullamites, or Cave, so called by John Bright because they comprised all those who were discontented or in distress, were those Whigs who disliked Lord John Russell's Reform Bill of 1866 and joined the Tories to defeat it. They ended up in the traditional position of those who try to straddle two stools.

(1 Samuel 16-31; 2 Samuel; 1 Kings 1-2; 1 Chron. 10-29)

**Deborah**   Wife of Lapidoth, prophetess and Judge (q.v.) of Israel who gave judgment under her palm tree on Mount Ephraim. The Israelites having relapsed into evil ways, God sold them into the hands of *Jabin king of Canaan, whose general was *Sisera. Deborah summoned *Barak to go to battle against the Canaanites but he refused to go unless she would go with him. So they went together with an army of 10,000 to Mount Tabor where they confronted Sisera's formidable army of 900 iron chariots. Sisera allowed his forces to be trapped in terrain where they could not manoeuvre and they were routed and killed to a man. Sisera himself, forced to flee on foot, took refuge in the tent of *Jael, wife of *Heber the Kenite, who succoured him and gave him milk to drink and then drove a tent-peg through his head with a hammer. When Barak arrived in hot pursuit Jael showed him Sisera dead. Barak and Deborah then sang the famous song of praise and triumph which is one of the jewels of early Hebrew poetry: 'Blessed above women shall Jael the wife of Heber the Kenite be. . . . He asked water and she gave him milk; she brought forth butter in a lordly dish. . . . At her feet he bowed, he fell, he lay down: at her feet he bowed, he fell: where he bowed, there he fell down dead. . . . The mother of Sisera looked out at a window, and cried through the lattice, Why is his chariot so long in coming? . . .' Yet Deborah failed to stir Handel whose oratorio about her is one of his less successful OT works.

(Judges 4, 5)

**Delilah**  Wife of *Samson and his undoing. She wheedled out of him the secret of his huge strength: namely that his hair had never been shorn. She betrayed his secret to the *Philistines, cut his locks and handed him over to his Philistine enemies, who blinded and enslaved him. Delilah is one of the relatively few women in the OT – **Deborah and Judith are others – who play a primary role and are more than mothers or wives. Fierce, yet with a certain grandness, she has become a symbol of woman's wiles used to trip up good men.
(Judges 16)

**Demas**  One of *Paul's recruits and companions. But he deserted Paul for love 'of this present world' and departed for Thessalonica.
(Coloss 4; Philemon; 2 Timothy 4)

**Demetrius**  A silversmith of Ephesus with a special line in silver shrines of Diana (Artemis). With the slogan 'Great is Diana of the Ephesians' he stirred up a mob against *Paul, whose preaching was inimical to the cult of the goddess and so to his trade.
(Acts 19)

**Dinah**  Daughter of **Jacob and Leah. She was raped by *Shechem, son of Hamor, a neighbouring prince. Hamor, anxious to remain on good terms with Jacob, asked for Dinah as his son's wife. Her full brothers **Simeon and Levi agreed to this proposition on condition that the Shechemites be circumcised. They agreed. While they were still recovering from the after-effects of the operation, Simeon and Levi slaughtered them. Dinah is not heard of again in the Bible but other legends married her to Simeon and to a later husband and transported her to Egypt.
(Genesis 30, 34)

**Dionysius**  The Areopagite, converted by *Paul at Athens. An Areopagite was a member of the Areopagos, the most prestigious court of classical Athens. A freakish tradition has equated him with Dionysius or Denys, bishop if Paris in C 3, patron saint of France, founder of the abbey that bears his name and holds the tombs of many French kings, and the martyr of Montmartre – whence he carried his own severed head to the site of his abbey. A third Dionysius, a C 5 mystic, has also been conflated with these two, giving to the original Areopagite a spurious place in visionary theology as well as in French history.
(Acts 17)

**Doeg**  An *Edomite and governor of Nob where the priest *Ahimelech succoured David in his flight from *Saul. Doeg reported Ahimelech's action to Saul and at Saul's command killed Ahimelech and 85 other priests.
(I Samuel 22)

**Dorcas**  See Tabitha

**Drusilla**  Daughter of Herod *Agrippa I and wife of the procurator of Judaea, Antonius *Felix. See family tree F.
(Acts 24)

**Edomites**  Descendants of Edom, alias *Esau. Of all the peoples or tribes with whom the Israelites contended the Edomites were nearest to them in kin and their love-hate relationship was the most acute. To the Romans Edom was Idumaea. See also *Herod the Great and family tree F.

**Eglon**   An exceptionally fat king of *Moab who, with the help of **Ammonites and Amalekites, defeated the *Israelites and ruled over them for 18 years. They were rescued by *Ehud, who killed Eglon by plunging a dagger into his belly.
(Judges 3)

**Egypt**   By the time that *David became king in Jerusalem there had been a king in Egypt for over 2000 years. Egypt was at the beginning of a long slow decline but it still loomed large: the shadow of a great name and capable of spurts of vigour.

The crucial element in Egyptian power was union of the Nile Valley and the Delta. This union was first achieved by Dynasties I-VI which, besides building the pyramids, created the Old Kingdom and ruled for a thousand years: c. 3200-2200 BC. After a gap when the union was broken the Middle Kingdom (Dynasties XI and XII) revived Egypt's power and extended it north and south into Asia and Nubia. This power dissolved c. 1786 BC. Egypt then fell apart again and parts of if were ruled by foreign invaders. It was reunited by Ahmosis I. c. 1580-1557, the first king of Dynasty XVIII which created the powerful New Empire which reached the Euphrates. Early in this period *Abraham trekked from Ur on the lower Euphrates to what was to become the homeland of the children of *Israel. His great-grandson *Joseph was one of the many who were drawn into Egypt from far and wide by its affluence and stability. The number of Israelites led out of Egypt by *Moses testifies to the numbers who had migrated there in preceding generations. In spite of ups and downs in the great power struggles of the day, in spite of the neglectful rule of a pharaoh more interested in ideas than conquests, and in spite of a spate of invasions from the north-west by 'Peoples of the Sea' (who included the *Philistines), the New Empire flourished for several hundred years: by deflecting the Philistines Egypt created a problem for the Israelites, who lost control of the Asian coastline to these newcomers. By c. 1100 BC – that is to say, shortly before *David formed a new kingdom and captured the fortress of Jerusalem to make a new capital for it – the empire of Egypt was losing its grip in Asia and in C 10 BC the Delta was ruled by Libyan intruders, one of whom – called *Shishak in the Bible – looted Jerusalem. This time there was no sustained revival. In the chaotic C 7 BC Egypt was occupied for 20 years by Assyria; staged a recovery when Assyria was assailed by Medes and Scythians from one quarter and Babylon from another; defeated and killed king Josiah of Judah at Megiddo and put a puppet on his throne; switched to helping Assyria against a Babylonian-Median alliance; but was finally routed at Carchemish in 605 BC by the rising star of Babylon. Its empire gone, it remained nevertheless prosperous. It became part of the Persian empire in 525 BC, was annexed by Alexander the Great and, after being ruled by his successors the Ptolemies, by Rome. In the NT period it was one of the richest of Rome's provinces.

**Ehud**  A left-handed Benjaminite and one of the earliest *Judges of Israel. The Israelites were smitten by *Eglon king of Moab who, with the **Ammonites and Amalekites, reduced them to servitude for 18 years. Ehud was chosen by God to bring this servitude to an end. Eglon was a very fat man. Ehud armed himself with a two-sided dagger about two feet long, took presents to Eglon, professed to have something secret to tell him, and when the two were alone plunged his dagger – blade and shaft – into Eglon's belly so far that the fat closed over the blade and Ehud could not pull it out again. Ehud escaped while Eglon's servants, thinking that he was relieving himself, were slow to discover his death. The Israelites, encouraged by this deed, turned out in force and killed 10,000 Moabites at the crossing of the Jordan. They had no more trouble from this quarter – the east – for

80 years but a single verse in the Bible (Judges 3, 31) shows that about the same time they were being harassed from the west by the *Philistines, since Ehud's successor Shamgar, about whom nothing else is known, delivered Israel by killing 600 Philistines with an ox-goad.
(Judges 3)

**Eleazar**  Priest, son of *Aaron, and his successor. Aaron's elder sons Nadab and Abihu were killed by God when they 'offered strange fire' (that is to say, sacrificed in the wrong way) in the wilderness of Sinai. Their places were taken by Eleazar and his younger brother Ithamar. Eleazar was the senior priest at *Joshua's side when the Israelites crossed the river Jordan and when the Promised Land was divided among the twelve tribes and the *Levites at Shiloh. Eleazar's son Phinehas continued Aaron's line in the priesthood but must not be confused with another *Phinehas, unsatisfactory son of *Eli.
(Numbers 20, 27, 31, 32; Joshua 14, 24)

**Eli**  Prophet and priest at Shiloh and exemplar of the venerable man whose offspring are no good. His sons **Hophni and Phinehas, also priests, corruptly appropriated more than their due share of the offerings in the temple and whored after women. So God cursed Eli's house and condemned his descendants to die young. Eli's servant was the child *Samuel, chosen by God to take Eli's place. God spoke to Samuel in the night. Samuel thought that the voice was Eli's until the call was twice repeated. Eli, however, realized that God was speaking to Samuel and persuaded Samuel to tell him what God was saying: that Eli and his house would be destroyed and Samuel become priest in Shiloh. This transpired when the Philistines defeated the Israelites in a series of battles and captured the ark of the covenant (see glossary) which was in Shiloh. Hophni and Phinehas were killed in battle and when Eli, 98 years old and blind, learned of these disasters he fell off his seat backward and broke his neck, 'for he was an old man, and heavy'.

The ark of the covenant was a richly ornamented wooden box made to God's design to hold the tables of stone on which the laws and Ten Commandments were written by the finger of God on Mount Sinai and given to *Moses. It was about 45 feet long, 3 feet wide and 3 feet high. The Philistines took the ark to the temple of their god Dagon in Ashdod but the image of Dagon fell down before it and broke and the Ashdodites, afflicted with haemorrhoids, sent the ark on to Gath, whose citizens, likewise smitten, sent it on to Ekron. The priests of the Philistines advised its return to the Israelites in a new cart and with appropriate offerings and images and this advice was followed. It rested for 20 years in the house of *Abinadab in Gibeah and was eventually taken to Jerusalem by *David after he made it his capital. The return of the ark with an escort of Philistines was painted by Sebastien Bourdon (London, National Gallery).
(1 Samuel 1-4; Exodus 25, 37 ; 2 Kings 6)

**Eliezer**  The servant sent by *Abraham to find a kins-woman to be the wife of his son *Isaac. Eliezer found *Rebecca by waiting at a well for a girl to offer him a drink. Murillo painted the scene (Madrid, Prado).
(Genesis 24)

**Elihu**  Tried to impress *Job with the impropriety of inquiring into the ways of God to man.
(Job 32-37)

**Elijah**     The Tishbite, prophet of the C 9 BC. Elijah was
the champion of the Jewish religion against its
rivals and so the scourge of *Ahab who imported
the heathen cult of *Baal into Israel along with his
wife *Jezebel. Elijah lived in danger from the king
and queen and also from the drought and famine
which were afflicting the country at this time, but
he was protected and provided for by God. At
God's bidding he hid by the brook Cherith, where
he was fed by ravens (this is a small tributary east
of the Jordan about half-way between the Sea of
Galilee and the Dead Sea), and was then directed
to and mysteriously fed by a widow near Sidon on
the coast: he retrieved the widow's child from
death. His most dramatic moment came when he
persuaded Ahab to assemble 450 priests of Baal
on Mount Carmel and staged a competition in
igniting a sacrificial bullock. In spite of much
capering and self-mutilation the priests of Baal
were totally unsuccessful. Elijah on the other hand
was immediately successful, Ahab was abashed,
and Elijah was so elated that he ran before the
king's chariot all the way to Jezreel. (Carmel may
have been disputed territory, ceded to Ahab by his
marriage contract but not transferred from the
priests of Baal to the God of Israel until Elijah's
triumph).

Jezebel vowed vengeance on Elijah and he fled
to Beer-sheba and into the desert beyond. There
God came to him in a 'still small voice' and
despatched him to find and anoint *Elisha as his
successor and also to anoint *Hazael and *Jehu as
kings-to-be in Syria and Israel who would between them kill Ahab and his brood and all the
worshippers of Baal. Elijah performed the first of
these tasks but left the others to Elisha. Elijah did
not die but was whirled up to heaven in a great
wind by a chariot and horses of fire.

Many mountains are named after him. The
choruses in Mendelssohon's *Elijah* are a not ignoble
attempt to recapture the glorious moments on Carmel.
Ford Madox Brown painted Elijah descending from
the widow's loft with her reived child in his arms
(Birmingham, City Art Gallery). His ascent to

heaven by Palma Giovane is in Helsinki. 'Elijah and the Wheel' is one of the more popular Negro spirituals. Elijah's exploits on Mount Carmel made him a favourite with the Carmelite Order, in whose churches and cloisters he is frequently depicted.
(1 Kings 17-19, 21; 2 Kings 1; 2 Chron. 21)

**Elimelech**   Born in Bethlehem and husband of *Naomi. He went with her and their two sons to Moab and died there. *Ruth was his daughter-in-law.
(Ruth 1, 2)

**Eliphaz**   The Temanite, one of *Job's comforters.
(Job 2, 4, 5, 22, 42)

**Elisha**   Prophet, son of Shagpat. He was a ploughman upon whom *Elijah cast his mantle while Elisha was guiding his oxen. After Elijah's assumption into heaven Elisha performed the task laid upon Elijah to anoint **Hazael and Jehu as kings-to-be in Syria and Israel who would between them kill king *Ahab of Judah and all his evil brood and all worshippers of *Baal. Elisha cured *Naaman of his leprosy; miraculously replenished a widow's cruse of oil; rewarded a *Shunammite woman who had given him board and lodging with a child even though her husband was old, and brought the child back to life when it died. Elisha was bald. Pestered by cheeky children who teased him with his baldness, he cursed them and had the satisfaction of seeing 42 of them carried off by she-bears.
(1 Kings 19, 2 Kings 2-9, 13)

**Elizabeth**   Wife of *Zacharias and mother of *John the Baptist. The archangel Gabriel appeared to Zacharias while he was officiating as a priest in the Temple and promised that although he and Elizabeth were both beyond the normal child-bearing age they would have a son, a new *Elijah. Five months later Gabriel visited Elizabeth's cousin *Mary and announced to her the birth of her child, who was to be called *Jesus. Mary went to visit Elizabeth and as soon as Elizabeth heard Mary's voice her child stirred in her womb. Mary answered her greetings with the words of praise to God since known as the Magnificat. At the circumcision of Elizabeth's son her friends and neighbours assumed that he would be named after his father Zacharias, but Elizabeth said that he should be called John, and Zacharias – who was still dumb because of his incredulity at the angel's message – confirmed this choice by writing the name on a tablet. Mary's visit to Elizabeth, known as the Visitation, is one of those scenes combining great events with domesticity which characterize the NT and have appealed to children and to artists through the ages. The Visitation was a popular theme for mediaeval sculptors and painters: for example, on the west front at Rheims and a touching painting by Raphael (Madrid, Prado). (Luke 1)

**Elymas**   See Bar-jesus.

**En-dor**   Witch of. She was consulted by *Saul, whom at first she did not recognize because he came to her in disguise as well as in despair. She raised for him the spectre of *Samuel, who revealed to Saul his coming defeat by the Philistines and death on the next day. Overwhelmed by his predicted fate and weak from want of food, Saul fell to the ground. The witch urged him to eat and with help from his servants got him to do so. In two short poems *'Saul unter den Propheten'* and *'Samuels Erscheinung vor Saul'* Rilke told, first of Saul in his days of confidence and, secondly, of Samuel's ghostly appearance followed by Saul's last meal. (I Samuel 28).

**Enoch**   One Enoch was the son of *Cain. Another, father of *Methuselah, 'walked with God' without, so it appears, suffering death. See family tree A.
(Gen. 5)

**Epaphras**   A companion of *Paul when he was in prison and seemingly a leading light in the Christain communities of Colossae and of others in the valley of the Lycus in Asia Minor.
(Coloss. I, 4; Philemon)

**Epaphroditus**   A 'fellow soldier' of *Paul and special link between Paul and the Christians of Philippi.
(Philippians 2, 4)

**Ephraim**   Younger but more favoured of the two sons of **Joseph and Asenath. When presenting his sons to his father *Jacob, Joseph took Ephraim by his right hand and *Manasseh by his left, but Jacob laid his right hand on Ephraim's head and his left on Manasseh's. Joseph, displeased, tried to get Jacob to do the opposite but Jacob refused, saying that the younger would be greater than the elder. Both Joseph's sons became progenitors of separate tribes among the twelve tribes of Israel. Jacob's preference for the younger brother was taken by mediaeval Christians to betoken the superiority of Christianity over the older Judaic religion. See family tree C.
(Genesis 41, 48, 50)

**Ephraimites**   Descendants of *Ephraim. Their tribal territory was in the centre of the Promised Land, west of the Jordan and north of Benjamin and Judah. The Ephraimites were only dubiously loyal to their tribal cousins. They quarrelled with *Jephthah and were defeated by him; they incurred the special wrath of *Isaiah for their idolatry; and they were suspected of making secret deals with the Syrian enemy. They escaped destruction at the

hands of the Assyrians in 734 BC but became one of the Lost Ten Tribes when the Assyrians came back twelve years later.
(Joshua 21; Judges 12, 14, 16)

**Ephron**  Son of Zahor, a Hittite from whom *Abraham bought for 400 shekels the cave of Macpelah at Hebron and the field and trees which went with it as a burial place for his wife *Sarah. He himself was buried there and so were **Isaac and Rebecca, Jacob and Leah.
(Genesis 23, 25, 49, 50)

**Esau**  Twin brother of *Jacob and son of **Isaac and Rebecca. The conflict between the brothers, who were their parents' only children, lay at the root of much later history. Esau and Jacob, renamed Edom and Israel, personified the feud between Edomites and Israelites which was healed only when – over a millennium later – the Edomite (Idumaean) *Herods were forced by the *Maccabees to become Jews. Esau was the victim of trickery which, here as elsewhere in the Bible, was frowned upon without being forthrightly condemned or penalized. The struggle between the twins began in their mother's womb. Rebecca was told by God that she had conceived two nations and that the elder should serve the younger. The firstborn was Esau who was followed by Jacob, clutching Esau's heel. Esau became a hunter, Jacob a plainsman living in tents. Esau was his father's favourite, Jacob his mother's. Some years on, Esau, faint and dying of hunger, begged Jacob for food a mess of pottage which Jacob gave him in return for the sale of his birthright – which, since he believed himself to be dying, Esau valued lightly. More years on, Isaac, now old and blind, told Esau to go and kill venison and make him a savoury meal so that he might bless Esau before he died. Rebecca overheard this conversation and told Jacob to go and kill two kids with which she would make Isaac a savoury meal for Jacob to

give him, so that he would then bless Jacob
instead of Esau. Jacob was afraid that Isaac, in
spite of being blind, would detect the trick since
Esau was a hairy man and he himself was smooth;
and that Isaac would then curse him instead of
blessing him. But Rebecca overruled Jacob's
doubts, dressed him in Esau's clothes and covered
his hands and neck with the kids' skins. Everything went as planned and Jacob got his father's
blessing; when Esau came just too late Isaac's
blessing had been irrevocably bestowed on Jacob.
Esau hated Jacob and resolved to kill him as soon
as Isaac died, but Rebecca saved Jacob by getting
him to flee for a while to *Laban, her brother.
Jacob stayed away for 20 years, returning only
when Isaac was near death. Alarmed by a report
that Esau was coming to meet him with a retinue
of several hundred, Jacob sent Esau a present of
550 animals of all kinds, but Esau embraced him
warmly, refused the gift and went back peacefully
to Edom. They met again when Isaac died and the
brothers together buried him. Esau's wives were
Canaanites – which grieved his parents. He also
married a daughter of Ishmael. In non-Biblical
stories Esau met his end by making war on Jacob,
who killed him. See family tree B.
(Genesis 25-28, 32, 35, 36; Hebrews 12)

**Essenes**    Judaic sect. See under Pharisees etc.

**Esther**    Otherwise Hadassah, wife of *Ahasuerus, king of
Persia. She was the niece and adopted daughter of
*Mordecai, a Jew. When the king put away his
disobedient wife *Vashti he organized a search for
young virgins. Esther was one of these and she so
pleased the king that he made her his wife and
queen. Her uncle nearly brought catastrophe upon
her and the entire Jewish population of Ahasuerus' realms by refusing to bow down to the
king's favourite, *Haman. In revenge for this
slight Haman planned to have all Jews killed and
obtained the king's careless endorsement. But

Esther took her courage in both hands and, although nobody – not even the queen – was allowed to approach the king unbidden, she entered his presence fainting with apprehension and, when he held out his sceptre in token of condoning her intrusion, invited him to a banquet where, with Haman in attendance, she revealed what Haman was planning. Haman, distraught by fear, threw himself on Esther's mercy and on her bed – an action which was misinterpreted by the king and made Haman's position even worse. He was hanged on a gallows which he had prepared for Mordecai, while the excellence of the imperial posts, operated by horseback, mules, camels and young dromedaries to all the 127 provinces of the empire, saved the Jews and authorized them to kill instead of being killed. 75,000 non-Jews were massacred – not a happy ending to an otherwise moral tale. The Jewish feast of Purim has been traced back to these events.

Esther became one of the most celebrated heroines of antiquity. When the Palazzo Vecchio in Florence was turned inside out to become the home of Duke Cosimo I of Tuscany, a suite of rooms was fashioned for the Duchess and decorated with the exploits of famous females. Esther was one of these (the tapestries are still in what was once the Duchess' dining room), along with Penelope, the raped Sabine women, and a girl who won fame and a place in Dante's *Paradiso* for refusing to kiss a mediaeval emperor. Rilke's poem 'Esther' delineates the immensity of her daring in soliciting her husband-king. So does Tintoretto's painting of her fainting with agitiation at the audacity of her act. (This picture was once part of the magnificent collection made by Charles I and, unlike most of it, is still in England – at Hampton Court. A second version is in the Prado in Madrid.) Rembrandt's Esther is at Raleigh, North Carolina. Handel's *Esther,* originally entitled *Haman and Mordecai,* was conceived primarily as a clash between good and evil. (Esther; The Rest of Esther)

**Eutychus**   A young man of Troas who, during a long sermon by *Paul, fell asleep and out of a third-floor window but was revived by Paul. (Acts 20)

**Eve**   First woman, created by God by putting *Adam into a trance and taking from him a rib which He built up into a woman. Eve's name was given her by Adam, "because she was the mother of all living" (*havvah* in Hebrew = life, lifegiving). In the garden of Eden the serpent ridiculed Eve's belief that if she ate the fruit of a certain forbidden tree she would die. The serpent persuaded her that, on the contrary, she would become like a god and know good and evil. Since in addition the fruit of the tree looked appetizing Eve took some and ate it and gave some to Adam, who also ate it. Their eyes were opened but their innocence was lost and therewith their place in Eden. Interrogated by God, Eve blamed the serpent but God condemned all her sex to bear children in pain and to be dominated by the male and drove her and Adam out of the garden. She bore Adam three sons: **Cain, Abel and Seth.

Representations of Eve are innumerable but one cannot forbear to mention the capital in the cathedral at Autun on which Eve is hiding round the corner in the undergrowth while, on the front face of the column, God is admonishing Adam. Rodin's bronze Eve is in the Museum of Arts, Toledo, USA. Her days of innocence and nudity have inspired a host of pictures of feminine beauty, particularly of the kind – lithe rather than rounded – favoured by German artists: Dürer (Madrid, Prado), Cranach (Florence, Uffizi), Altdorfer (Washington, National Gallery). Milton's voice, far and away the most influential in English in re-telling the story of the Fall of Man, put most of the blame on Eve and so provided antediluvian sanction for man's scorn of women. (Genesis 2-4)

**Ezekiel**  Prophet and the oddest of the prophets. He was the son of a priest and lived in Babylon during the Exile, probably among the victims of *Nebuchadnezzar's deportations from Jerusalem in 597 and 587 BC. Ezekiel flew through the air more than once. He suffered periods of speechlessness and physical immobility. His Book contains imagery which is original as well as strange: for example, his vision of the valley of dry bones which are re-assembled and clothed with flesh, a symbol maybe of the redemption of both Judah and Israel and their reunion. He was not so much a leader of the Return from Babylon to Jerusalem as a focus for the thought of that difficult period. He anticipated further trials and tribulations for the Israelites but left room in his pedantic way for tentative hope.

Ezekiel, although at first sight an unlikely subject for popular art, inspired the American Negro song 'Dem Bones' which turns the prophet's vision of resurrection into a lively reconstruction of the human skeleton bone by bone. Laurence Binyon seeks a deeper meaning: his 'Ezekiel' foresees a reanimation of the detritus of a material civilization which is at once a monument to human creativity but a menace to the diversity of God's creation. In painting the prophet's vision Raphael shows him strangely suspended above the world (Florence, Pitti). Ezekiel's name stands at the head of the papal Bull with which, in 1463, Pius II made the papacy's last desparing and futile bid to reflate the crusading spirit and rescue Jerusalem – which Ezekiel had judged more harshly than Sodom and Gomorrah – from the infidel. See also Prophets. (Ezekiel)

**Ezra**  Or Esdras, priest, scholar and one of the foremost architects of the survival of the Jewish people's religion and identity. The restoration of the Jews in Babylon to Jerusalem, initiated by *Cyrus and led by *Zerubbabel in the late C 6 BC, had proved hesitant and incomplete. Ezra was the leader of a second, more emphatic wave c. 458 BC. He was an almost fanatical believer in the supreme importance of the letter of the Law and gave the restoration a specifically religious twist. He created in the city of \*\*David and Solomon a high priesthood in place of a monarchy and promulgated the Mosaic or Judaic Law as its quasi-constitution. To later generations he was the second \*Moses.

Ezra is the Greek form of Esdras whose name is attached to a variety of writings, including two Books in the Apocrypha. 1 Esdras is a mainly historical work covering the same ground as 2 Chronicles, Ezra and Nehemiah and is the oldest Greek version of these passages. It contains also the delightful tale of the three soldiers who, upon being challenged to show what was the most powerful force in the world, responded with eulogies on wine, the monarch and women. The last speaker (alleged in a late marginal interpolation to be Zerubbabel) was declared the winner. 2 Esdras, a much later compilation, consists of a vision of the Son of God and a series of nightly discussions with the archangel Uriel, who explains the author's fantastical dreams. It is a futuristic essay in apocalypse, or revelation, particularly of the Eschata or Four Last Things at the End of Time: Death, Judgment, Heaven and Hell. See also Cyrus, Zerubbabel, Nehemiah,
(Ezra 7-10; 1 Esdras 8-9; 2 Esdras; Nehemia 8)

**Felix**  Antonius, procurator (governor) of Judaea AD 52-60, an obnoxious freedman whose powerful brother Pallas was among other things the lover of Agrippina, Nero's wife. Felix married \*Drusilla, daughter of Herod \*Agrippa I. His governorship saw mounting disorder, crime and corruption. From AD 58-60 he kept \*Paul in prison at Caesarea, vacillating between Paul and his enemies in Jerusalem.
(Acts 24)

**Festus**  Porcius, procurator (governor) of Judaea AD 60-62. He died in office, having despatched *Paul to Rome.
(Acts 24-26)

**Gad**  One of the twelve sons of *Jacob and progenitor of one of the twelve tribes of Israel. He and his brother *Asher were the sons of *Zilpah, the servant of *Leah. His tribal territory was east of the Jordan. See family tree C.
(Genesis 30, 35, 42-50; Joshua 4, 13, 22)

**Gallio**  L. Junius, Roman proconsul of Achaia AD 51-52 (or perhaps a year earlier) and friend of Ovid. He was the brother of the Stoic philosopher and playwright Seneca and uncle of the poet Lucan: they were from Spain. He was an educated mandarin posted to a city which should have appealed to him but whose citizens did not. He refused to be drawn into the disputes between *Paul and his Jewish adversaries in Corinth, for he 'cared for none of these things'. According to his brother his ambition was to win fame with a thesis on natural history.
(Acts 18)

**Gamaliel**  A learned and respected *Pharisee who spoke against the rough handling of the apostles on the grounds that, if they were doing only men's work, it would come to nothing but that, if they were doing God's work, opposition to them was futile. He was credited in later legend with having retrieved the body of *Stephen after he had been stoned to death.
(Acts 5)

**Gedaliah**  A native of Judah who was made governor in Jerusalem by *Nebuchadnezzar after his first capture of the city in 597 BC. Gedaliah was almost immediately assassinated and this deed, by

raising fears of exemplary reprisals, caused a
wholesale flight into Egypt. Among these refugees
was *Jeremiah.
(2 Kings 25)

**Gehazi**    Servant of the prophet *Elisha. He tricked *Naaman out of silver and garments and was smitten
with Naaman's leprosy by Elisha. He has become
a symbol of turpitude. Elisha's first question to
him on his return from cheating Naaman,
'Whence comest thou, Gehazi?' was used by
Rudyard Kipling as the first line of his blistering
attack on Rufus Isaacs (later Lord Reading) for his
dealings, when Attorney-General, in Marconi
(telegraph) shares immediately the wreck of the
Titanic dramatized the value of Marconi's invention.
(2 Kings 5)

**Gentile**    A Latin adjective meaning 'belonging to a people
or nation' but in that sense obsolete. Restricted to
meaning 'belonging to a people other than the
Jews'. This meaning derives from the earliest Latin
translations of the Bible, notably the Vulgate (for
which see the Introduction to this book).

**Gideon**    Son of Joash and one of the Judges of Israel. He
delivered Israel from the *Midianites who, with
the *Amalekites, were ravaging the country. The
Midianites had seeped north along the far side of
the Dead Sea and then across the river Jordan.
They had become a severe nuisance to settled
people like the *Israelites, particularly at times
when drought drove them westward in search of
pasturage. They had penetrated Galilee and the
valley of Jezreel and many Israelites spent seven
years hiding from them in dens and caves. Gideon
was threshing wheat and hiding it from the
Midianites when an angel came and sat under his
father's oak and told him that he would defeat the
Midianites and rescue Israel. Gideon asked for a

sign, which the angel gave by conjuring fire out of a rock. At God's command Gideon then overturned an altar of *Baal during the night, cut down Baal's sacred grove and built an altar to God on which he sacrificed a bullock with the felled wood. When the men of the city called on Joash to hand over his son to be executed for these acts of defiance Joash turned their arguments against them by telling them to leave it to Baal to look after himself.

Gideon blew a trumpet and sent out messengers and assembled a large host, but he still wanted signs of God's support. God consented to perform two miracles with a fleece. On one night a fleece was drenched with dew while the ground round about remained dry; on the next night the reverse happened and Gideon asked no more questions. God did not want a victory over the Midianites to be achieved by mere numbers. So the timid were told to stand down: 23,000 out of 32,000 did so. But the remaining 10,000 were still too many. They were divided into two groups by a water test at a stream. Those who leaned over and lapped – a stupid thing to do if enemies were lurking – were dismissed, while those who squatted and brought the water up to their mouths in their hands were retained. These, the more alert and quicker-witted, were a mere 300 against the Midianites and Amalekites who were as numerous as grasshoppers, but Gideon and his few companies staged a surprise night attack in which, after blowing trumpets and shouting the slogan 'The sword of the Lord and of Gideon', they terrified and routed their foes. Oreb and Zeeb, princes of Midian, were killed. Zebeh and Zalmunna, kings of Midian, fled with Gideon and his 300 in hot pursuit. Gideon caught the kings and killed them with his own hands and then returned on this tracks to take vengeance on the men of Succoth and Penuel who had refused to give the pursuers food to help them on their way. The Israelites offered Gideon an hereditary kingship over them but he replied: 'The Lord shall rule over you.' One of Gideon's sons, *Abimelech, took a different view and had himself declared king after his father's death, with unhappy consequences.

Stanley Spencer, one of comparatively few modern painters to draw extensively on the Bible (and almost always on the NT, not the OT), has depicted the startled Midianites roused from their sleep by Gideon's trumpets in *The Sword of the Lord and of Gideon* (London, Tate Gallery). The Gideons are a modern international proselytizing association which provides free Bibles to hotels and hospitals.
(Judges 6-9)

**Gog and Magog**    Vaguely Satanic beings located somewhere in the north. They are perhaps related to the giants of the race of Gogmagog who were extirpated by Brute (Brutus), a descendant of Aeneas and eponymous ancestor of the British, who is extolled in Geoffrey of Monmouth's *History of the Kings of Britain,* Spenser's *Faerie Queen* and Drayton's *Polyolbion.* Effigies of them, several times replaced, have stood on the site of London's Guildhall since the reign of Henry V.
(Genesis 10, Ezekiel 30, 39; Revelation 20)

**Goliath**    Famous giant of Gath, six cubits and a span tall – rather more than 13 feet. He had a brass helmet, a coat of mail, greaves of brass, a shield of brass between his shoulders and a huge spear. He issued a challenge on behalf of the *Philistines to personal combat with any champion of the *Israelites, but there were no takers until the boy *David appeared armed only with five smooth stones, a sling and his faith in the God of Israel. One stone was enough. It struck the giant's forehead and sunk in and killed him. David then cut off his head. A brother and four sons of Goliath – one of them had twelve fingers and twelve toes – appeared in David's last wars with the Philistines but made little impact. For some Goliath is just a lumbering lout, yet before he encountered David he had an excellent record. A

more sophisticated view makes him a hide-bound conservative undone by inattention to technological advance and by vainglorious conceit. Arnold Toynbee has an erudite disquisition on these lines in *A Study of History* Part IV C III (c) 2. J.M. Barrie's play *The Boy David* tells Goliath's story.
(I Samuel 17; 2 Samuel 21)

**Gomer**  Wife of the prophet *Hosea, formerly a whore; a symbol of the inextricability of passion and disappointment. See Hosea.
(Hosea)

**Habakkuk**  Prophet. Like *Obadiah he spanned the period of the Babylonian conquests. The sayings ascribed to him in the Book that bears his name are an outpouring of social indignation and a passionate appeal to God to chastise the oppressors who make the people miserable. He is pessimistic about an escape from the Babylonian yoke but allows a glimmer of hope. A commentary on Habakkuk, probably of C 1 BC, was one of the most valuable of the Dead Sea Scrolls discovered in 1947. See also Prophets.
(Habakkuk)

**Hadad**  An *Edomite who was in his childhood a refugee from a comprehenisve razzia conducted in Edom over six months by *Joab, *David's general. Hadad fled to Egypt where he was made welcome by the pharaoh and married the queen's sister. When he heard that both David and Joab were dead he returned to Edom and was used by God to harry *Solomon in the years when Solomon was losing favour with God.
(I Kings II)

**Hadassah**  Otherwise Esther *q.v.*

**Hagar**   An Egyptian servant of *Sarah, *Abraham's wife.
When she was still childless Sarah gave Hagar to
Abraham as a concubine. This change of status
destroyed the relations between the two women
and Sarah so ill used Hagar that she ran away. An
angel comforted Hagar and she returned and bore
*Ishmael. When Sarah later bore *Isaac she
persuaded Abraham to evict Sarah and Ishmael.
Claude painted Hagar at least twice. His picture
of her eviction at Sarah's behest makes this
episode look more polite than it can have been
(Munich, Alte Pinakothek). In another painting
(London, National Gallery) Hagar is shown with
the angel in a broad and agreeable landscape. See
family tree B.
(Genesis 16, 21)

**Haggai**   Prophet of the late C 6 BC who lived and may
have been born in Babylon. He was, with
*Zechariah, a cheerleader for the Return from the
Exile which was led by **Zerubbabel and the
high priest Jeshua. His central concern was the
rebuilding of the Temple as the essential element
in the rehabilitation of the *Israelites, in which,
unlike most of the prophets, he saw the priesthood
as no less significant than the royal house of
*David. To a considerable degree the force of his
message came from the narrowness of his purpose. See also Prophets.
(Haggai; Ezra 5)

**Ham**   Son of *Noah. He saw his father lying drunk and
naked in his tent, for which offence Noah cursed
Ham's son *Canaan and decreed that his progeny
should be the slaves of the sons of **Shem and
Japheth. Ham is the eponymous progenitor of the
Hamites, who spread over the northern part of
Africa from Morocco to Ethiopia. A Hamite was
by definition not a semite and so an enemy of the
Israelites, who traced their descent from Shem.
The doughtiest Hamite in the OT is *Nimrod. See
family tree B.
(Genesis 5-11)

**Haman**     Favourite of king *Ahasuerus. He planned to kill all Jews in revenge for a slight put upon him by the Jew *Mordecai. His plans were defeated by *Esther and he was hanged on a gallows which he had perpared for Mordecai. Haman became a prime hate object for Jews and his name might not be mentioned without being reviled. To hang as high as Haman is proverbially to be well and truly hanged, to be hoist with one's own petard.
(Esther; The Rest of Esther)

**Hamites**     See Ham.

**Hannah**     Mother of *Samuel. Her husband Elkanah had children by another wife but for many years none by her. She was noticed by *Eli as she prayed in the Temple at Shiloh. Seeing her moving her lips but soundlessly, Eli thought at first that she was drunk but, perceiving his mistake, he blessed her. Back home she bore a child and in gratitude devoted it to God as servant to Eli. She visited the child regularly, bringing him each year a new little coat.
(I Samuel 1-2)

**Hanun**     King of the *Ammonites whose deplorable ill manners and perverted sense of humour ruined him. His father had been on good terms with *David and when Hanun succeeded to the Ammonite throne David sent him a mission of goodwill. But Hanun thought that this was a moment to assert himself. He had half of the beards of David's emissaries shaved off and their clothes cut off down to their buttocks. David sent his generals to trounce Hanun, which they did. Hanun's father was *Nahash.
(2 Samuel 10; 1 Chron. 19)

**Haran**     Son of *Terah and brother of *Abraham. He died in Ur before Terah and Abraham led the migra-

tion out of that city. Haran had two children: *Lot, who migrated with Abraham, and a daughter *Milcah who married *Nahor, her uncle. See family tree B.
(Genesis II)

**Hazael**  A senior personage at the court of king *Ben-hadad of Syria. Learning from *Elisha that he was destined to succeed his ailing master, he gave destiny a shove by suffocating Ben-hadad. He had numerous victories over Israel, Judah and the Philistines but suffered devastating Assyrian invasions in 842 and 839 BC, a foretaste of the Assyrian annihilation of Syria a century later. See Syria.
(2 Kings 8, 10-13; 2 Chron. 22)

**Heber**  The Kenite, husband of *Jael who slew the fleeing Canaanite general *Sisera with a nail through the head. Heber is represented as betraying to the Canaanites the pre-battle dispositions of the Israelites, but in view of the part played by his wife after the battle it is permissible to surmise that, consciously or unconsciously, he planted on Sisera information which the Israelites wanted Sisera to have. See also Deborah.
(Judges 4, 5)

**Hebrews**  A name for the *Jews. Hebrew is a language, one of the many within the *semitic group. The Hebrews to whom the NT Epistle to the Hebrews was addressed were probably Christians of Jewish origin. This Epistle is no longer ascribed to *Paul whose authorship of it was suspect from early times.

**Herod the Great**  Governor of Galilee from 47 BC and king of Judaea 40-4 BC. His father Antipas was an Edomite or Idumaean who was appointed by Julius Caesar to govern Judaea, and Herod himself saw clearly that fortune and power lay in the gift of the Romans. He became a familiar figure in high Roman society and made friends with Mark Antony and, more closely and enduringly, with Augustus. The Romans made him a king. Through one of his wives he was connected with the *Maccabees and so had a family claim to kingship in Jerusalem – a claim fortified by the reconciliation of the Edomites and Israelites (the children of **Esau and Jacob) in his father's time and his family's conversion to Judaism. He was an observant Jew, even an enthusiastic one; he followed Jewish dietary rules and spent lavishly on refurbishing the Temple. But, unlike the Maccabees, he was also a cosmopolitan. His ten wives included women of different races and religions and by them he had numerous sons, some of whom he murdered. He is the Herod who despatched the wise men to locate the infant *Jesus and, when they failed to report their find, ordered the massacre of the innocents – that is to say, of all children of two years or under, in and around Bethlehem. Herod's grounds for this massacre, for which *Matthew is the sole source, were his fears that among these infants was one who would claim his place as king of the Jews. Upon his death Herod's kingship was abolished by Augustus and his kingdom partitioned among three of his sons, the ethnarch *Archelaus and the tetrarchs Herod *Antipas and Herod *Philip. Another son, also called Philip, was the father of *Salome. Herod's line was continued through yet another son, Aristobulus, father of Herod *Agrippa I, last king of Judaea. This king's children – **Herod Agrippa II, Berenice and Drusilla – marked the end of a line which lost in them its glories but not its vices. Most of the Biblical references to Herod are to Herod Antipas, tetrarch of Galilee. Herod the Great's legendary excesses (frequently depicted in mediaeval mystery plays) led Hamlet to coin the phrase to 'out-Herod Herod' in his directions to the actors not to overplay their parts. Advancing years aggravated his violence and eccentricities and by the time he died at the age of 68 he was to all intents and purposes mad. The massacre of the innocents, always a lively, if grisly scene, has been famously painted by Peter Breugel the Elder (Vienna, Kunsthistorisches Museum) and by Guido Reni (Bologna, Pinacoteca). See family tree F.

(Matthew 2, 14; Mark 6; Luke 1)

**Herodias**  Mother of Salome, sinful wife of Herod *Antipas and lethal enemy of *John the Baptist. See under Antipas.

**Hezekiah**  King of Judah c. 715-687 BC. He inherited a kingdom in a hopeless dilemma and bought for it an extended lease of a doomed life. The revival of Judah under king *Uzziah had proved a flash in the pan and Hezekiah's father, Ahaz, had left him a kingdom which was no more than a satellite of *Assyria. Hezekiah rebelled against this thrall but unsuccessfully. Forced into direr and direr straits, he turned in despair to *Isaiah for advice. Isaiah promised him that God would not allow the Assyrian king Sennacherib to take Jerusalem – a promise which was redeemed when 185,000 Assyrians encamped about the city died in one night. In his poem 'The Destruction of Sennacherib', Byron calls him the Assyrian who 'came down like a wolf on the fold'. As Hezekiah lay dying with his face to the wall Isaiah told him that God had granted him another fifteen years of life. Incredulous, Hezekiah asked for a sign, which was vouchsafed him when the sun's shadow on the dial moved backwards ten degrees. But the repulse of Sennacherib had been no more than a reprieve. Hezekiah's son *Manasseh, king c. 687-642 BC, was taken captive by Assyria. While in captivity he wrote the Prayer of Manasses, a Book of the Apocrypha which is a confession of sin and a plea for forgiveness this side of eternity, a glimpse of the state of mind of C 7 BC Judah. See also Shebna, Josiah.

(2 Kings 18-21; 2 Chron. 29-33; Jeremiah 15, 26; Hosea I)

**Hilkiah**   Priest in Jerusalem in the reign of *Josiah. During repairs to the Temple c. 621 BC he discovered a book of the Law, probably the Book of Deuteronomy, and with the king's enthusiastic support launched a movement which was both a reassertion of traditional beliefs and manners and also a foretaste of the strict ritual and priestly constitution which Israel was to adopt in later centuries. He was the father of *Jeremiah.
(2 Kings 22; 2 Chron. 34)

**Hiram**   King of the Phoenician city of Tyre, friend of *David and ally and business partner of *Solomon. He supplied Solomon with cedars and firs for the building of the Temple in Jerusalem in a barter deal in which he received in exchange food and oil. Hiram contributed also to the building of palaces for Solomon and his wife and to their sumptuous decoration. His navy and Solomon's sailed together to Ophir at the far end of the Red sea to fetch gold and timber and precious stones. These two kings were partners in luxury.

Tyre was in ancient times an island, connected to the mainland by a causeway possibly constructed by Hiram. With its excellent harbour it was one of the principal centres of Mediterranean commerce and survived until destroyed in AD C 12 by the Muslims engaged in repulsing the Christian crusades. Tyrian purple, an indigo dye made from the Mediterranean sea-snail *murex brandaris*, was the symbol of Tyre's successful exploitation of the luxury trade.
(I Kings 5, 7, 9; I Chron. 14; 2 Chron. 2, 4, 8, 9)

**Hittites**   In Biblical times the supposed remnant of the ancient and expired Hittite empire. See *Uriah and the historical note in the Introduction to this book.

**Holofernes**    Captain of the hosts of Nebuchadnezzar. He was decapitated by *Judith.
(Judith 2-7, 10-15)

**Hophni**    One of *Eli's two disappointing sons.
(I Samuel 1, 2, 4)

**Hosea**    Prophet. He lived under the shadow of the threat from *Assyria whose downfall he foretold. Hosea struck a comparatively compassionate note even though inveighing strongly against idolatry, luxury, debauchery and the irresponsibility of rulers who betrayed their trust. He urged Israel to concentrate on religious and moral reform and stop dabbling in international politics (whether by courting Assyria or *Egypt). He believed that God's function was to punish but also to show mercy; that God was pulled two ways by Israel's sins and by its sufferings. Hosea himself was not a happy man and, uncharacteristically for a Hebrew prophet, his private life was entangled with his prophecy. He was ordered to marry a harlot, *Gomer, (by whom he had three children) and later to redeem a fallen woman who may have been Gomer lapsing again or another adultress. Whether or not he knew of Gomer's past before marrying her, he became bitterly hostile to sexual irregularity and developed a parallel between earthly marriage and the relationship – compounded of passion and disappointment – between God and his chosen people.
(Hosea)

**Hur**    One of the chief lieutenants of *Moses after the Exodus. In their battle with the *Amalekites the *Israelites prevailed so long as Moses held up his arms. When he got tired Hur and *Aaron held them up for him.
(Exodus 17, 24)

**Hushai**　The Archite, a friend of *David who played a key role in restoring David's rule in Jerusalem in the face of the rebellion of his son *Absalom. David had been forced to flee eastward to the river Jordan, leaving the initiative to Absalom. Hushai was despatched back to Jerusalem to discover Absalom's intentions and to try to induce him into error. In particular Hushai's task was to undermine the influence of *Ahithophel who had deserted David for Absalom. Ahithophel wanted Absalom to give him the command of the army; Hushai urged Absalom to take command in person. Absalom took Hushai's advice, Ahithophel hanged himself and Absalom marched across the Jordan to defeat and death.
(2 Samuel 16, 17; I Chron. 27)

**Huz and Buz**　Two of the eight children of *Nahor, *Abraham's brother.
(Genesis 22)

**Ichabod**　So called by his mother because 'the glory has departed' with the capture by the Philistines of the ark of the covenant in Shiloh. He was the grandson of *Eli and his mother was the wife of Eli's unworthy son *Phinehas. When her child was born and she was told that it was a son she said nothing and refused to look at it. Nothing more is known about Ichabod.
(I Samuel 4)

**Isaac**　Son of **Abraham and Sarah, born to his parents in their old age by miraculous intervention. When God chose to test Abraham by demanding the sacrifice of Isaac, Abraham prepared to obey and led his beloved son to a mountain-top. The boy was puzzled by the absence of a sacrificial animal but Abraham told him that God would provide one. Having built an altar, Abraham laid Isaac, bound, on it and raised his knife, but an angel called to him not to touch his son but to sacrifice instead a ram caught by its horns in a nearby thicket.

Abraham was determined that Isaac's wife should be one of his kin and not a Canaanitess. He sent a trusted servant *Eliezer, to the country of his brother *Nahor where he himself had come from. Waiting at evening by a well outside the city, Eliezer decided that the right girl would be the one who would give him a drink and then offer also to water his camels. In this way he found *Rebecca, put a gold ring on her nose and gold bracelets on her wrists, and was taken to the house of her brother *Laban where he disclosed himself and his mission. Rebecca went back with him the next day. She bore Isaac twin sons, **Esau and Jacob, the one his father's favourite and the other his mother's. In old age Isaac was tricked by Rebecca into bestowing his blessing and inheritance on the younger Jacob. He was buried by Esau and Jacob in his parents' tomb at Macpelah in Hebron.

'Isaac's Marriage', a poem by Vaughan, describes Isaac as 'first, a young patriarch, then a married saint'. The greatest pictures of the sacrifice of Isaac are by the greatest, but sometimes anonymous, artists: a C 6 mosaic in S. Vitale, Ravenna; Titian (Venice, Santa Maria della Salute) and Rembrandt (Munich, Alte Pinakothek), the latter showing Abraham in the act of dropping the knife. Sodoma's Isaac is a shivering nude, but the urgent angel and lurking ram are firmly contrasted (Pisa, Duomo). The deluded Isaac blessing Jacob is depicted by Girolamo da Treviso (Rouen, Musée des Beaux Arts) and Govert Flink (Amersterdam, Rijksmuseum) – the latter shows an obviously worried Jacob with Rebecca hovering in the background. Wifred Owen's poem 'The Parable of the Old Man and the Young', and Benjamin Britten's use of it in his *War Requiem*, commemorate the awful scene on the mountain-top, but Owen, poet of the horror of war, drastically changed the story: 'But the old man would not do so, but slew his son, And half the seed of Europe, one by one'. See family tree B. (Genesis 21, 22, 24-28)

**Isaiah**    Prophet, statesman and counsellor of kings in Judah. His alleged royal kinship cannot be proved but he seems to have enjoyed considerable licence for unpopular views and activities. He lived through four reigns, issuing warnings of the need for reform and also giving political advice. He possessed exceptional poetic eloquence and imagination. No less impassioned than other prophets, Isaiah had also something of the noble Roman – principled, unflinching in the face of disaster and the certainty of more to come, sustained by his belief in the ultimate triumph of righteousness (which he would not live to see). There is a heroic streak in Isaiah's pessimistic patriotism and his personal self-control. He was seldom vindictive, although he had some difficulty in restraining his language about the old enemy *Edom. He foretold the destruction by Assyria of Judah's sister kingdom of *Israel and foresaw for Judah such horrors that the women would be left in a majority of seven to one over the men. His central concern was the sinfulness of his own people – idolaters, moral perverts (drink and sex), over-rich landowners. He saw the cruel empire of Assyria as something which had to be endured, which it was fruitless to resist, whose cruelties were merited by its sinful victims and which would come to an end in the foreseeable future. After its fall God would establish general peace and make a new beginning for the world, almost a second Creation, in which the God of Israel would govern a universal empire from Jerusalem. In this picture there figured a personage from the royal line of *David who was later magnified into the Messiah. The Book of Isaiah therefore acquired associations with the mission of *Jesus although Isaiah's Messiah was credited with neither divinity nor immortality.

In the practical sphere Isaiah was firmly opposed to foreign entanglements in spite of Judah's inherent weakneses and need for allies. Thus he opposed alliance with *Syria to check the power of Assyria: Syria was no fit ally because it was wicked and in any case Assyria, he foretold, was to meet its nemesis. Trust in God, said Isaiah, not in Assyria. Later he counselled *Hezekiah against joining a grand anti-Assyrian coalition which was initiated by the *Philistine city of Ashdod and supported by Egypt (713 BC), advice which was justified when Assyria once more defeated all its enemies. His faith in God enabled him to promise Hezekiah that the Assyrian king Sennacherib would not take Jerusalem and he was again proved right when Sennacherib's army besieging Jerusalem melted away in the night, whether stricken by the angel of death or – as Herodotus believed – driven away by a plague of mice, or simply paid to go away.

The Book of Isaiah contains sayings of at least two other prophets who, since their names are unknown, are called Deutero-Isaiah and Trito-Isaiah. Deutero-Isaiah (chapters 40-55) lived in exile in Babylon c. 550 BC. His message of hope to his fellow-exiles contains many of the most inspiring passages of the OT (and of Handel's *Messiah*). He offered comfort: 'Comfort ye, comfort ye my people' are his opening words. Through the 'voice of him that crieth in the wilderness' he promised the advent of one who would trace a high road from Babylon back to Jerusalem. More than that: Jerusalem would be rebuilt resplendently, God himself would be king, the children of Israel would reoccupy a central position in the world and hold it for ever, and all rival religions would wither away. Deutero-Isaiah belongs to the category of dreams which are too good to be true but he has also four passages of more abiding influence. These concerned a mysterious servant who was, as it were, God's viceroy on earth, who would irradiate the whole world and who – in terms readily made to apply to Jesus

– would be killed and buried and come again.
Trito-Isaiah (chapters 56-66) was more sober. He
was a slightly later prophet of C 6 BC who may
have been part of the first contingent of Jews to
return to Jerusalem from the *Captivity in Babylon. He kept up the prophetic tradition of moral
censure and deplored the lavish restoration of the
Temple on the grounds that that was not what
God wanted. See also Prophets.
(Isaiah; 2 Kings 19-20)

**Ish-bosheth**  Son of *Saul and the focus, after Saul's death, for
the party opposed to *David's succession to the
kingship. In the ensuing seven-year war the
leading generals on either side were **Abner and
Joab, but Ish-bosheth quarrelled with his general,
Abner, over one of Saul's surviving concubines,
*Rizpah, and both then made their peace with
David. David insisted that Ish-bosheth give back
*Michal – the daughter whom Saul had first given
to David as wife and had then taken back and
given to another man. Ish-bosheth was killed by
two of his own men while he was taking his
noontide siesta. Hoping to curry favour with
David, the murderers took his head to the king,
who berated them and had them executed.
(Samuel 2-4)

**Ishmael**  Son of **Abraham and Hagar, his Egyptian
concubine. After the birth of her own son *Isaac,
*Sarah persuaded Abraham to evict Hagar and
Ishmael. But God promised that although Isaac
and his offspring should inherit Abraham's patri-
mony, Ishmael and his twelve sons would become
a great people. The Ishmaelites were circumcised –
Ishmael himself at the age of 13 – and so not as
alien as the *Canaanites. When Abraham died
Ishmael returned to perform the burial rites with
Isaac. Ishmael is the archetype of the outcast.
When the narrator in Melville's *Moby Dick* opens

his story with the words: 'Call me Ishmael', he is recalling the description of the Biblical Ishmael as 'a wild man; his hand will be against every man, and every man's hand against him.' See family tree B.
(Genesis 16, 17, 21, 25, 28)

**Ishmaelites**   Descendants of *Ishmael, outcasts.

**Israel**   The name of both an individual and a kingdom. The individual was *Jacob, alias Israel, whose sons sired the twelve tribes of Israel which, hundreds of years later, conquered the Promised Land and settled there (see Moses, Joshua and family tree C). In time the tribes were united as the kingdom of Israel, ruled by **Saul, David and Solomon. On Solomon's death this kingdom split, the larger part becoming Israel, the smaller *Judah. This Israel, whose first king was *Jeroboam, lasted for 200 years and was extinguished by Assyria in 722 BC when its inhabitants became the Lost Tribes of Israel. Unlike neighbouring Judah it had no long-lived dynasty. See further under Jerboam, Omri, Ahab, Jezebel, Jehu.

**Israelites**   Descendants of *Israel, alias *Jacob. The protagonists of the OT.

**Issachar**   One of the twelve sons of *Jacob and progenitor of one of the twelve tribes of Israel. His mother was *Leah. He was noted for animal strength. His tribe and that of his brother *Zebulon were located west of the Sea of Galilee in the northern part of the Promised Land. See family tree C.
(Genesis 30, 35, 42-50; Joshua 17, 19)

**Jabal**    Son of *Lamech by his first wife Adah. He was a herdsman. His brother was *Jubal. See family tree A.
(Genesis 4)

**Jabin**    King of Hazor. He put together a league of Canaanite kings to oppose *Joshua and the Israelites after their successes against Jericho and other cities and peoples to the south. They were completely defeated, all the kings were killed, but their cities – except Hazor – were spared together with their flocks and herds. A second Jabin was similarly routed by *Deborah and Barak. These are probably two different accounts of the same event.
(Joshua 11, Judges 4, 5)

**Jacob**    Son of **Isaac and Rebecca. He was the younger of twins. They began fighting in the womb and Jacob merged cluthing *Esau's foot. Jacob was his mother's favourite, Esau his father's; Jacob a pastoralist, Esau a hunter. When Isaac was old and blind he sent Esau to make a kill for a savoury stew, so that he might bless Esau before dying. Rebecca overheard this conversation and told Jacob to counterfeit his brother by killing a kid, of which she would make a similar stew for Jacob to give his father and so get his blessing in Esau's place. Jacob was afraid that Isaac would detect the fraud since Esau was a hairy man and he a smooth one, but Rebecca put the kid's skin on Jacob's arms and neck and Isaac was deceived. When Esau came with his offering the deed had been done and Isaac's blessing irrevocably bestowed on Jacob. Esau resolved to kill Jacob as soon as Isaac died. Rebecca decided to send Jacob out of harm's way. She told Jacob that she could not bear the idea of Jacob marrying a local girl of the *Canaanites and so Isaac sent Jacob away to his uncle *Laban with instructions to get one of

Laban's daughters as a wife. On his way to Harran, where Laban lived, beyond the upper Euphrates, Jacob rested the night with his head on a stone and saw in a dream a ladder set between earth and heaven and angels going up and down it. On waking he made his head's stone into a pillar, poured oil over it and called the place Bethel: the Lord's house.

**Years of exile**  He was effusively received by Laban, promptly fell in love with the younger daughter *Rachel and engaged himself to work for Laban for seven years before marrying her. At the end of that time Laban got his elder and less attractive daughter *Leah into Jacob's bed, so that Jacob had to engage himself for another seven years in order to get Rachel too. He spent in all 20 years with Laban, during which time Leah bore him six sons and a daughter (*Dinah), Rachel one son (*Joseph), and the sisters' maids **Bilhah and Zilpah two sons each (see family tree C.). Jacob's wages accumulated without being paid, in spite of the fact that he proved an excellent shepherd and immeasurably increased Laban's flocks and herds. He made a fresh deal with Laban. Instead of taking his wages in money he would take all Laban's black lambs and spotted goats. Laban agreed but surreptitiously removed all the striped he-goats, all the spotted she-goats and all the black rams and then went on a journey, leaving Jacob to look after the remainder. Not to be outdone, Jacob devised ingenious schemes for multiplying his share of the flocks. He cut and peeled strips of white-wooded trees and stuck them upright by the watering places, facing the females which were on heat. These females so longed for the rods that their young were born striped. At the same time Jacob let the ewes run only with striped or black rams and so ensured that the new lambs should belong to him and not to Laban. He also had the notion of separating the stronger from the weaker she-goats and displayed his rods only to the stronger when they came on heat, adding the weaker kids to Laban's share and the stronger to his own. Laban and his sons came to the conclusion that they were being cheated and Jacob decided that he had better leave. This he did secretly with his wives, children and much besides. Rachel went so far as to steal her father's household gods. Laban pursued them, reproached Jacob for flitting in the night after such a long stay and demanded his gods back. Jacob, not knowing of the theft, vowed that if Laban dicovered any stolen property the thief would be put to death, but Rachel succeeded in obstructing Laban's searches of her things by pretending that she was menstruating. Jacob and Laban parted on reasonably good terms and Jacob continued homeward.

**Return home**　Hearing that Esau was coming to meet him with a large retinue, Jacob became understandingly nervous and sent Esau valuable presents. During the night before their encounter Jacob wrestled all night alone by the brook Jabbok with a man who did not throw him and refused to tell his name. The man told Jacob that he was thenceforward to be called Israel, and Jacob perceived that he had been wrestling with God. His only hurt was a limp from a blow on his hip. With day he went towards Esau, who gave him a warm welcome and refused Jacob's proffered gifts. So Jacob returned to the land of Canaan and settled first at Shechem and then at Bethel. He had one more son when Rachel bore *Benjamin and died at Bethlehem. Jacob's later years were beset by the loss of Joseph and by a famine which eventually drove him and his people to Egypt, where he lived 17 years and died: for which events see under Joseph. Jacob's body was embalmed in Egypt and carried to the family burial gound of Macpelah in Hebron by his sons and their families and the chief men of Egypt. Through his twelve sons Jacob, alias Israel, was the forebear of all the *Israelites: the twelve tribes and the *Levites. Of his sons Joseph was far and away the most successful in his lifetime, becoming a great man in an altogether different society; but in the light of history the most successful was *Judah.

Jacob dreaming peacefully has been painted by Ribera (Madrid, Prado); his journey back

home – a pell-mell migration of men, women and beasts – by Bassano (H.M. the Queen). Jacob meeting Rachel at the well is one of the scenes designed by Raphael for the Vatican and executed after his death by his pupils. Stanley Spencer drew Jacob and Rachel in modern dress and in an English setting (London, Tate Gallery). Epstein's Jacob wrestling with God, two massive interlocked alabaster figures, caused much tut-tutting when first exhibited. Jacob's ladder and the angels going up and down it can be seen on the west front of Bath abbey. In nature Jacob's Ladder is a small water-loving wild flower *(polemonium caeruleum)* which was one of the plants chosen by Burne-Jones for the charming Flower Book in which he illustrated a number of flowers with scenes suggested by their names. Jacob's sheep are a carefully nurtured primitive breed which still survives. Jacob wrestling with God provided Charles Wesley with the theme for one of his finest hymns, 'Come, O thou traveller unknown'; and his grandson S.S. Wesley wrote for it the tune called 'Wrestling Jacob'. Schoenberg's oratorio (like his opera *Moses and Aaron*) was left unfinished, largely because nobody would give him the money he needed to escape the grind of teaching.
(Genesis 25-37, 42-50)

**Jael**  Wife of *Heber the Kenite. she succoured the fleeing Canaanitish *Sisera and then drove a tent-peg through his head. See Deborah.
(Judges 4, 5)

**Jairus**  A synagogue elder who appealed to *Jesus to save his twelve-year old daughter who was at the point of death. When Jesus came to the house where she was he was met with the news that the girl was dead. With **Peter, John and James he went in, saying that she was not dead but sleeping. The

bystanders laughed but Jesus, having ordered them out of the house, brought the girl back to life and commanded her parents and his three disciples to keep what he had done secret. Stanley Spencer painted a triptych whose central panel shows Jesus reviving the girl in her bedroom; the side panels show more general resurrections in a street and a cemetery. (Southampton, Art Gallery).
(Mark 5; Luke 8)

**JAMES**  Two of *Jesus' twelve apostles were called James: James, son of *Zebedee (James the Great) and James, son of Alphaeus. There is a third James, called the Less, speculatively identified with James, a supposed brother of Jesus.

**James**  Fisherman, son of *Zebedee and one of the twelve apostles, called James the Great to distinguish him from *James the Less. With his brother *John and with *Peter, James belonged to an inner circle among the twelve. He was executed in AD 43 by command of King Herod *Agrippa I. Jesus gave the sons of Zebedee the nickname Boanerges – sons of thunder – because they offered to call down fire from Heaven on the Samaritans. In C 7 a story gained wide credence that James had gone to Spain – or alternatively that his body had somehow got there – and his shrine in his church of Santiago at Compostela became one of the most popular and venerated objects of pilgrimage in the Middle Ages. He was believed to have helped the Christian reconquest of Spain from the Muslims, notably at the battle of Clavijo in C 9 (but historians now doubt whether this battle ever took place). His emblem is the scallop-shell which mediaeval pilgrims sewed into their clothes as a talisman. Sir Walter Raleigh's poem 'The Pilgrimage', written the night before he was beheaded, begins 'Give me my scallop-shell of quiet'. Shaw

gave the name Boanerges to the booming President of the Board of Trade in his play *The Apple Cart*.
(Matthew 4, 10, 17; Mark 1, 3, 5, 9, 10, 13, 14; Luke 5, 8; Acts 1, 12; I Cor. 15)

**James**     Son of Alphaeus and one of the twelve apostles. He is not named by *John.
(Matthew 10; Mark 3; Luke 6; Acts I)

**James the Less**     Frequently but dubiously identified with James, described as brother of *Jesus. In what way a brother is uncertain. A suggestion, more ingenious than well grounded, has it that he and his brothers – **Joses, Judas and Simon – and various sisters were children of *Joseph by an earlier marriage. In another version they were the children of a certain Mary who was a daughter of *Anne (the mother of the Virgin *Mary) by a later marriage and so half-cousins of Jesus. Whether or not a relative of Jesus, James the Less became a highly respected member of the Christian community in Jerusalem. In the dispute over whether the Christians must be circumcised Jews, and in particular at the crucial meeting with *Paul in Jerusalem in AD 46, James was a protagonist of the narrower, anti-Pauline party but also an influence for moderation and accommodation, insisting only on the observance of dietary and sexual rules. The Epistle of James, probably written in this period, may be from his correspondence: it is an unprovocative statement of the case for seeing Christianity as a brand of Judaism and limiting it to its Jewish origins. When Paul visited Jerusalem again some ten years later James succeeded in getting the apostle of the Gentiles, who was himself a Jew, publicly to perform Jewish rituals and avow his Judaism. He failed, however, to prevent Jewish purists from stirring up trouble for Paul, who had to be rescued by the Roman authorities (see Paul), and a few years later James was himself attacked for refusing to denounce Jesus and was stoned and clubbed to death at the instigation of the high priest *Ananias.

(Matthew 13; Mark 6, 15, 16, 24; Acts 15, 21; Gal. 1, 2)

**Japheth**  The third of *Noah's three sons. He and his brother *Shem managed, by walking backwards with a cloak, to cover their father's drunken nakedness without seeing it. In the legendary reaches of Anglo-Saxon history Japheth, renamed Seth, became the ancestor of the kings of Wessex and England, thus giving King Alfred (for example) a clear descent from Adam. See family tree A.

(Genesis 5-11)

**Jason**  A Christian of Thessalonica with whom **Paul and Silas stayed. His home was assaulted by an anti-Christian mob.

(Acts 17)

**Jebusites**  A semitic people loosely associated with the *Canaanites and others with whom the *Israelites had to contend when they entered the Promised Land. Their territory included Jerusalem.

**Jehoiada**  Priest in Jerusalem in the days of the heathen queen *Athaliah who seized the throne of Judah on the death of her son Ahaziah. Jehoaida had family as well as religious reasons for hating Athaliah, since he was married to Ahaziah's sister. He organized the overthrow of Athaliah, destroyed the altars and images of *Baal and installed Ahaziah's seven-year-old son Joash as king. All went well until Jehoiada died, when king and court relapsed into heathen ways. They were reprimanded by Jehoiada's son Zechariah, but the king had Zechariah stoned to death. God loosed the Syrians upon Judah in requital for this wickedness.

(2 Kings 11-12; 2 Chron. 22-24)

**Jehoshaphat**  Fourth king of Judah, c. 873-849 BC. His father Asa, who ruled for 40 years, had put an end to the strife between Judah and Israel which had been going on since the founding of the two sister kingdoms by **Rehoboam and Jeroboam. Jehoshaphat's reign in Judah covered roughly the same years as *Ahab's in Israel. He decided to become an active ally of Israel against *Syria and visited Ahab, who proposed a joint campaign against Syria. When the two kings consulted a number of prophets, all – except *Micaiah – egged them on. Jehoshaphat was simple enough to agree to go into battle wearing Ahab's robes while Ahab disguised himself. Nevertheless Ahab was killed and Jehoshaphat escaped. He subsequently inflicted defeat on **Moabites and Ammonites. He also cleared out of Judah such *Sodomites as had escaped a purge by Asa. See under Athaliah, Uzziah, Hezekiah, Josiah for later rulers of Judah. The valley of Jehoshaphat was expected to be the scene of the central events on the Day of Judgement. Holman Hunt's travelling and painting companion Thomas Seddon painted a picture of *Jesus in the valley.

(I Kings 15, 22; 2 Chron. 17-20; Joel 3)

**Jehu**  King of Israel c. 842-815 BC. He was a general of *Ahab and famous for his furious chariot-driving. After Ahab's death he joined the nationalist and religious opposition congregated round *Elijah, led a successful coup against Ahab's line and slaughtered Ahab's widow *Jezebel, all his sons and all the worshippers of the heathen *Baal. He

thus purged Israel of Ahab's sins – but not of *Jeroboam's original offence of partitioning *Solomon's kingdom and setting up Bethel and Dan as centres of worship in competition with Jerusalem. The dynasty which Jehu founded, much the longest in Israel's choppy history, lasted 100 years. He was succeeded from father to son by four generations of kings, of whom the last was killed c. 745 BC, fulfilling the prophecy that the house of Jehu would reign for only four generations after its founder. Jehu's descendants continued to war against Judah and Syria under the thickening cloud of the spreading power of *Assyria. By the time his line ended Israel was under Assyria's thumb, and five kings and 21 years later the kingdom inaugurated by *Jeroboam ceased after 200 years to exist. In 722 BC the last king *Hoshea was taken captive, his capital destroyed and his people carried off to Nineveh. They disappeared from history and so became the ten Lost Tribes of Israel. The Compagnons de Jehu, creations of the hyperprolific Alexander Dumas (father), were noble bandits who seized money to finance the counter-revolution in France: Jehu standing for the Bourbon king in exile, Ahab for the grisly and infidel revolutionary regime. In C 19 coachmen and cabbies were called Jehus, especially if they drove fast.
(2 Kings 9-11)

Another Jehu, son of Hanani and a very minor propet, was a mouthpiece of God's adverse judgement on Baasha, king of Israel, for whom see under Jeroboam.
(1 Kings 16; 2 Chron. 20)

**Jemima**  The eldest of the three daughters born to *Job after the recovery of his fortunes. The others were **Kezia and Keren-happuch. Job made them co-heirs with their seven brothers.
(Job 42)

**Jephthah**  Son of Gilead by a harlot and one of the principal *Judges of Israel. After two relatively obscure Judges, Tola and Jair, had judged Israel for half a century the *Israelites lapsed into sinfulness more comprehensive than ever before, worshipping *Baal and Ashtaroth and the gods of Syria and Sidon and Moab and Ammon and the *Philistines. Jephthah had been thrust out of his family, but when the Ammonites mustered against Israel elders went to find him and offered him the captaincy over them. After some persuading Jephthah struck a bargain with the elders. He also made a vow to God that if God should give him victory he would sacrifice to him whatever came out of his house to greet his return. He then made a very great slaughter of the *Ammonites. On his return his daughter and only child came out to meet him with timbrels (tambourines) and dances. After a respite of two months spent in the mountains bewailing her virginity she was sacrificed and thereafter the daughters of Israel made a lament of four days every year for the daughter of Jephthah.

The tribe of Ephraim was furious with Jephthah for not inviting them to join his expedition against the Ammonites. They came to blows, the Ephraimites were defeated and Jephthah, occupying the crossings of the Jordan, killed all Ephraimites (42,000 of them) trying to cross the river. He identified them by forcing all comers to say the word 'Shibboleth', which the Ephraimites could not do, dropping the 'h'. Jephthah was followed by three obscure Judges – Ibzan, Elon and Abdon – between his death and the advent of *Samson.

Handel's oratorio *Jephtha*, his last, longest and most sombre, contains some of his most famous arias: 'Waft him, angels' and 'O had I Jubal's harp', as well as one of his most tremendous, choruses: 'How dark, O Lord, are thy decrees'· In his poem 'Jeptha's Daughter' Byron dresses her in the high heroic and patriotic mode, concluding her last song to her father with the words: 'Forget not I smiled as I died'. The modern word shibboleth is derived from this incident. In Hebrew, shibboleth means an ear of wheat or a stream. (Judges 11, 12)

**Jeremiah**  Prophet who lived through the upheavals that accompanied the decline of the kingdom of *Judah in C 7 BC. He was born near Jerusalem and lived most of his life in that city. He was a countryman with an observant affection for country things, and also a member of a distinguished priestly family, his father *Hilkiah being a descendant of *Solomon's chief priest *Abiathar. In quieter times he could have been a sort of Gilbert White of Selborne, but the combination of his circumstances and his temperament rendered him miserable and made him exceedingly unpopular. He was frequently in personal danger from his own people, physically assaulted and for several years in hiding. Increasingly obsessed with Judah's dangers from without and within – from external enemies and the nemesis of its own sins – he adopted attitudes towards Babylon which were difficult for the average Jerusalemite to accept. He saw *Nebuchadnezzar as God's chosen instrument for chastising Judah and so not only foretold but welcomed the coming destruction of Jerusalem by Babylon. He incurred the wrath of his own class by arguing that good behaviour was more important than ritual observances, which he regarded as by themselves spiritually and ethically empty. He lived through the religious and moral revival of *Josiah's reign only to experience the backsliding and incompetence of that king's ephemeral successors. He proclaimed that after 70 years a purged Judah would recover its independence and past glories, but his contemporaries, more concerned with the present than the future, dubbed him a traitor and he was being suffocated in mud in prison when Nebuchadnezzar's capture of Jerusalem saved his life. He remained in Jerusalem for another ten years, but when Nebuchadnezzar's governor *Gedaliah was assassinated he fled with other refugess in fear of exemplary reprisals to Egypt, where he died.

Pessimism and persecution, only partially relieved by his personal communion with God, drove Jeremiah to an extremity of despair – for which his name has become a synonym – a jeremiad. The Book of Lamentations was ascribed to him (wrongly, it is now believed). These lamentations are a series of sincere and complicated poems on the theme of *Captivity. They provide the nine texts for the three lessons at Tenebrae (Matins) on the last three days before Easter Sunday and have inspired plainsong and polyphonic settings by the greatest composers of church music: Okeghem, Tallis, Byrd, Palestrina. Haydn's Lamentation Symphony (no. 26) got its name from its use of echoes from the plainsong chant. More recently Stravinsky used the Greek equivalent *Threni* as the title for his own setting. Jeremiah, the most tragic of the Hebrew prophets, evoked from Rilke a poem about the tragic need to be for ever lamenting. Rembrandt's study of him lamenting the destruction of Jerusalem has the same dark poignancy (Amsterdam, Rijksmuseum). See also Prophets.
(Jeremiah; Lamentations; Baruch; 2 Chron. 36)

**Jeroboam**   Son of Nebat, first king of the partitioned kingdom of *Israel, c. 922-901 BC. Jeroboam was a servant of *Solomon whose rule became in his later years harsh and unpopular. One day Jeroboam was accosted by the prophet *Ahijah the Shilonite, who seized from him his new coat and tore it into twelve pieces and delared that God would make him king over ten of the twelve tribes of Israel. Jeroboam, who was involved in conspiracy against Solomon's line, fled to Egypt to be out of Solomon's reach, but when Solomon died he returned and was present when the Israelites questioned Solomon's son *Rehoboam about how he intended to treat them. Rehoboam's tough and insensitive answers caused a revolt – 'To your tents, O Israel' – and Jeroboam was made king over all except the lands of Judah and Benjamin, which Rehoboam retained. Israel was the larger and more fertile of the two kingdoms but did not include the hallowed city of Jerusalem. Jeroboam created new centres of worship at Bethel and Dan, in the far south and far north of his realm: these had echoes of a reversion to the worship of the golden calf or bull which so outraged *Moses in the Sinai wilderness. Jeroboam and his successors were never forgiven by the strict guardians of Judaism for creating this competition with Jerusalem or for partitioning the kingdom of *David and Solomon.

The history of Israel and Judah has been recorded by chroniclers who were on Judah's side and ascribed all Israel's troubles to the sinfulness of its kings, beginning with Jeroboam. Israel was a state with some strategic importance because the coastal road from Egypt to Syria and on to the Euphrates passed through or close to its territory. Judah by contrast was a small landlocked state, cut off from the sea by the cities of the *Philistines and only sporadically valuable as a make-weight in alliance politics. Whether from sinfulness or other causes Israel's history was chaotic. Unlike Rehoboam, Jeroboam founded no lasting dynasty. His son Nadab ruled for a mere two years and his line was then slaughtered by Baasha (king c. 900-877 BC), whose son and line were in their turn slaughtered by Zimri, who ruled for a week before being killed by *Omri. Jeroboam – a mighty man of valour – has given his name to a mighty measure of champagne equal to six standard bottles or about three quarters of a gallon. (Jeroboam II, king of Israel c. 786-746 BC, was no relation of Jeroboam I but a great-grandson of *Jehu.)
(I Kings 11-15; 2 Chron, 10, 13)

**Jesse**    Father of *David. He was descended from **Adam and Seth through **Shem and Boaz and became the ancestor of the royal and messianic line of *Judah. Jesse trees, depicting the generations of Jesse through David to *Jesus, were a

favourite pictorial theme of mediaeval illustrators, particularly in stained glass, known as Jesse windows. Although much has been destroyed over the centuries, the cathedrals of Chartres and Wells and the church of St. Stephen at Beauvais present splendid surviving examples.
(I Samuel 16)

**Jesus** Called Christ, whence Christians. The dates of his birth and death are uncertain. He was born in Bethlehem in Judaea in the reign of *Herod the Great (who died in 4 BC) and in a year when a census was being taken throughout the Roman empire. Recent scholarship points to 12 BC as the year in question and this date coincides well enough with one other piece of historical evidence, the appearance of Halley's comet. But other dates are seriously supported. Jesus was condemned to death by crucifixion at Jerusalem during the governorship of *Pontius Pilate (AD 27-36). The date of his crucifixion lies between AD 30 and 35.

*His beginnings* Jesus' mother *Mary, the virgin wife of *Joseph of Nazareth in Galilee, was told by the archangel Gabriel that she would conceive and bear a child of the Holy Ghost and call him Jesus. For the census Joseph, who was descended from the royal line of *David, had to go to Bethlehem, where the child was born in a manger because there was no room at the inn. From Bethlehem Joseph and his family fled to Egypt to escape the murderous designs of Herod against all children born at that time. They remained in Egypt until Herod's death made it safe for them to return to Galilee. The records of Jesus' childhood and early manhood are sparse and are regarded by many Christian scholars as legendary, but there is the ring of truth in the story of how, having been taken to the Temple in Jerusalem, he was so engrossed that he could only with difficulty be brought away. This religious bent was a prelude to a career entirely devoted to religious teaching, mainly in Galilee but also in adjacent parts and in Judaea to the south, where it ended. Jesus was baptized by his cousin *John the Baptist, already famous for his eccentric fervour although only a few months older than Jesus. After his baptism Jesus retreated into the desert and remained there for forty days, during which he rebuffed a threefold temptation by Satan, a temptation promising magical powers and wordly dominion. He became rapidly famous as an itinerant preacher in Galilee and attracted large crowds. He picked a select band of followers who became the twelve apostles (see glossary), the spearhead of his expanding mission. His natural eloquence was reinforced by the cures he effected and the miracles he performed. From Galilee he ventured west to the Phoenician coast and east to the Decapolis (the area straddling the Jordan south of the Sea of Galilee), leaving Galilee either under the spur of his missionary purpose or from a prudent fear of sharing the fate of John the Baptist who had been beheaded by order of the tetrarch (see glossary) of Galilee. His closest followers, particularly *Peter, divined that he was the Messiah, the promised redeemer who would restore the power and temporal fortunes of the Jews under the aegis of their one God. Jesus acknowledged to them that he was the son of God but enjoined them to keep quiet about it. Confirmation, if such were needed, was provided when, accompanied by three of the twelve, Jesus retired to a secluded place where they saw him dazzlingly transfigured into a brilliant whiteness and conversing with **Moses and Elijah.

*His teaching*

During his public career Jesus made a big impact in a short time. He did so by what he said and what he did. His favourite way of teaching was in parables, more than 30 of which have been recorded. The parable is a brief story composed out of everyday material, with one or two characters only, designed to make a point by drawing a homely but unexpected parallel. It is initially puzzling or disturbing and so demands attention and invites further explanation. As used by Jesus the parable is a moral tale: although the ingredients are commonplace, the message is moral. Jesus was brought up in the Jewish tradition – he probably knew no other – and reverenced the Law and the *Prophets but he taught insistently and even subversively that the Law and the Prophets were not enough. Like some of the Prophets themselves he demanded something more than a meticulous knowledge of the Law and observance of its rules, which he subordinated to an overriding moral code of behaviour. He was therefore, in the eyes of the Priests and the learned, a dangerous man and the more he prospered in popular acclaim the more these guardians of the Law became convinced that he must be put away. While his popularity was largely due to what he did (above all, his miracles ) it was what he said that gave the greatest offence to the authorities, Jewish and Roman. By treating the Law as a starting point or springboard rather than a static and self-sufficient set of ordinances, he challenged not only established beliefs but also the authority of the interpreters and upholders of those beliefs – the *Pharisees and Sadducees – and the peace of mind of the Roman administration which was concerned above all to avoid trouble. Moreover Jesus shocked the conventions of his time and place in other ways. He went out of his way to speak well of outcasts: harlots, lepers, taxmen, *Samaritans. His enemies frowned on the company he kept as well as on what he said. He did not belittle conventional sins but he pointed out that an individual sinner might also have virtues which might outweigh his sins. Akin to this unfashionable outlook was his championing of the lowlier sort of person, to whom he gave hope, even to the extent of saying that their superiors in the hierarchies of property and power might find their love of riches incompatible with salvation.

No less original was his denunciation of violence. He was sharp in his rebuke to Peter for cutting off *Malchus' ear at the moment of his arrest, and he comprehensively condemned any resort to the sword. He was no eremite; he did not, like John the Baptist, spend his time in the desert; but he was strikingly out of step with that part of the Jewish communal tradition which glorified the martial deeds of the *Judges, the kings of **Israel and Judah, and the *Maccabees. His radical idealism – still regarded as impractical after 2000 years but still alive and debated – is best studied in his Sermon on the Mount. This sermon may never have been delivered in the form in which it appears in the Gospel of *Matthew (who probably collated and edited various sayings of Jesus) but its authenticity is guaranteed by its departure from both conventional teaching and standard prophetic protest. Peace, love, justice and prayer: these were to be the distinguishing features of the Kingdom of God which was coming. Jesus, although a herald of this Kingdom, did not say when it was coming – he said that he did not know – so that the urgency of his message stemmed not from the imminence of this vague transformation of society but from the uncertain fact that it might happen at any moment. But that this transformation was coming was the centre-piece of his teaching.

*His miracles*   Jesus' popular following came from acts more than words. People flocked to him because of what he did and was reported to be able to do. Miracles were not then so very amazing, but Jesus' miracles were numerous and sometimes spectacular. Many of them were cures: healing diseases, restoring sight and, in the language of the day, driving out the devils which were at once the cause and manifestation of illness. In a few cases this healing power was believed to extend to death itself and the bringing of dead persons back to life: *Jairus' daughter, the widow's son in Nain, *Lazarus. There were also miraculous stories which had nothing to do with illness or death: walking on the water, stilling a storm, feeding thousands of people with a trifling number of loaves and fishes, turning water into wine at a marriage feast at Cana. All four evangelists give details of a number of miracles and refer in general terms to many more. Their purpose was to make clear that Jesus was not only no ordinary man, nor even an ordinary prophet, but the

Messiah. All the Gospels culminate in the trial and death of Jesus and the writers lead up to these tremendous events by harping on miracles which, besides drawing the crowds, demonstrated the uniqueness of the career – and therefore the death – of Jesus. The miracles were not just bizarre stories but an essential part of the messianic claim and, after the Resurrection, of the Christian claim – claims which made it difficult for Jewish Christians to come to terms with the rest of the Jewish community whose leaders the Christians accused of deicide. (This charge, originally levelled against the priests of Jerusalem at the time of the Crucifixion, was subsequently extended by the Christian Church to the Jews generally and became a prime ingredient in Christian anti-semitism).

*His Passion*  The last scenes in Jesus' life took place in Jerusalem. The evangelists disagree on how often Jesus went to Jerusalem before his final visit but they all give the greatest prominence to this last occasion. They were right to do so, not only because of the obviously dramatic nature of what ensued but also because Jesus' death anywhere else would have been an event of far less significance. Judaea and its capital Jerusalem were at the centre of a society in which Galilee, where Jesus spent most of his life, counted as no more than a provincial offshoot. Galilee was reasonably prosperous, thanks mainly to its fisheries and olive groves, but it was neither a religious centre nor the seat of Roman administration and power. Jesus went to Jerusalem with foreboding and fortitude, putting his head into a lions' den. His entry into the city was a triumphal procession and so a challenge, enhanced by uncharacteristally violent behaviour in the Temple, where he castigated those engaged in normal, if unholy, buying and selling and money-changing. In private discourse with his disciples he was at pains to prepare them for life without him, to charge them with their future duties and – particularly at their Last Supper together – to solemnize the bonds between him and them and the future Christian community. The Temple authorities and the Romans briefly held their hands. Then one of the twelve – *Judas Iscariot – went to the priests to betray Jesus and duly did so by identifying him by a kiss in the garden of Gethsemane where he had gone to pray in evident anxiety. This was done at night, perhaps because the priests were afraid to arrest Jesus in broad daylight.

Jesus was apprehended by an armed posse sent by the priests but he was eventually executed by order of the Roman governor. In the Gospels and in Christian tradition the governor, Pontius Pilate, is represented as acting under pressure from the priests who were keener to get Jesus out of the way, but the Romans too had their reasons for fearing Jesus since, however uninterested they might be in his teaching or his disputes with the Pharisees and Sadducees, they could not help observing that he was making some sort of claim to be a king in a province which they had only recently annexed and were finding troublesome. Jesus was first taken before the Council of the Sanhedrin (see glossary), presided over by the high priest *Caiaphas – with, according to *John, a preliminary and secret appearance before *Annas, the ex-high priest and father-in-law of Caiaphas. The priests tried to trap him into making blasphemous statements but it is not clear that their claim that he had done so was at all sound. In any event they had no power to condemn an accused to death and they transferred Jesus to the governor's tribunal. Pilate prevaricated. He may have felt himself trapped between pressures from the priests and popular support for Jesus. He offered to release Jesus in accordance with a custom which allowed him to release one prisoner to popular demand at the feast of the Passover. He gave the crowd a choice between Jesus and a convicted criminal called *Barabbas, but the crowd – influenced either by the priests or by a pro-Barabbas clique – chose Barabbas, whereupon Pilate washed his hands of the matter and the grisly and protracted procedures of a Roman execution ensued: scourging, vilification, the living death by crucifixion. Jesus was crucified at a place near Jerusalem called Golgotha, 'the place of the skull'. A passer-by, *Simon of Cyrene, was pressed into helping to carry the cross, on which Jesus was mockingly described as King of the Jews. Two thieves were crucified with him, one on either side. As he died extraordinary and super-natural phenomena occurred such as could be explained only by supposing that Jesus was God's son. There were also great crowds which alarmed Jesus' followers. One of these, *Joseph of Ari-mathea, asked Pilate for Jesus' body so that he might bury it in a cave in a nearby garden. Here it was protected by a large stone placed across the cave's entrance; by one account the stone was the idea of the priests who feared the body would be stolen and then declared to have been miraculous-ly resurrected. At this tomb, at the end of the Sabbath, some women made a momentous discov-ery. These women (they are variously named in the Bible – see Mary) had followed Jesus to his execution and had remained at the foot of the cross while he died; his male followers seem all to have fled. When two days later the women came to the tomb they found the stone removed and the tomb empty. According to the most vivid account (*John's) the discovery was made by *Mary Magdalene, who summoned two of the apostles and then saw Jesus himself, first mistaking him for a gardener. Jesus also appeared to others – on the way to the village of Emmaus (see Cleopas) or in Galilee – and having shown that he had risen from the dead ascended into heaven.

During his active life on earth Jesus appeared to most of those who encountered him to be either the Messiah, a figure in a well established Jewish tradition, or alternatively an impostor. But the two poles of his life – the Incarnation at the beginning of it and the Resurrection at the end – had no place in that tradition. The Jewish Messiah was not a divine incarnation nor was he expected to rise from the dead. When, shortly after Jesus' death, these became firmly established beliefs they formed a new religion.

**Jesus**  Son of Sirach, author of the Book of Ecclesiasticus, a C 2 BC moral guide whose epilogue is the splendid invocation: 'Let us now praise famous men, and our fathers that begat us...'
(Ecclesiasticus)

**Jethro**  Midianite priest and father-in-law of *Moses. Sometimes called Reuel or Raguel.
(Exodus 2-4, 18)

**Jews**  A sub-group of the *Semites; in the NT contrasted with *Gentiles. The word 'Jew' comes from the Latin name for the inhabitants of the Roman province of Judaea which roughly occupied the area of the OT kingdom of *Judah. The word was extended to all followers of the religion of the *Israelites, as practised at Jerusalem. See also Samaritans.

**Jezebel**  Wife of *Ahab, king of Israel. She was the daughter of Ethbaal of Sidon and her marriage with Ahab was an essay in dynastic politics and a catastrophe. Alien in race and religion, Jezebel gave enormous offence to the stricter elements in Israel who branded her an idolatress and harlot. After Ahab's death in battle this opposition, led by *Elijah, was joined by Ahab's general *Jehu. Jezebel tried to seduce Jehu, painting her face and looking out of her window in Jezreel. But Jehu commanded that she be thrown out of the window, and when later his servants came to collect her body for funeral they found only her skull and the soles of her feet and the palms of her hands. So was fulfilled Elijah's prophecy that the dogs would eat the flesh of Jezebel in Jezreel. She has become a symbol of female wickedness, evinced in particular by a painted face. See also *Naboth.
(I Kings 16, 18, 19, 21; 2 Kings 9)

**Joab**  Son of *Zeruiah, *David's sister. He was David's most successful general and staunchest (although not always obedient) henchman both before and after the death of *Saul. The foundation of Joab*s career was his capture of Jerusalem for David. It was consolidated by his victories over the Ammonite king *Hanun and over a Syrian league. These successes extended David's power northward to Damascus and the Euphrates and enabled him to turn against Edom and the Philistines in the south. Joab was to David what *Abner was to Saul and their rivalry dominated the military history of a whole generation. This rivalry was personal as well as professional, for Joab had a feud with Abner over the killing by Abner of Joab's brother *Asahel, and when David made peace with the Saulite party Joab – in defiance of David's more generous intentions – enticed Abner back to David's headquarters and murdered him. Joab engineered the reconciliation of David with his son *Absalom after Absalom killed *Amnon for the rape of their sister *Tamar. He fought for David at the lowest point in David's reign, the rebellion of Absalom, and with his own hand killed Absalom when he was caught defenceless in a tree: a deed which flagrantly defied David's express order to see Absalom safe. Joab also murdered his cousin *Amasa who had gone over to Absalom. As David lay dying Joab backed *Adonijah against *Solomon for the throne and was subsequently killed on Solomon's orders in spite of taking refuge by the altar in the Lord's tabernacle. Joab was one of the most eminent of the OT's mighty men of valour and one of the harshest, as inflexible in his feuds as he was skilled in the field.
(2 Samuel 2-3, 10-11, 14, 17-21, 23; I Kings 1-2; I Chron. 11, 18-21, 27)

**Job**  A prosperous and blameless man who had the misfortune to become the object of a wager between God and Satan. Job was a God-fearing man afflicted by God and he wanted to know why he was so ill used and why God behaved in so seemingly unjust fashion. He never found out that he was the object of a wager but he did recover all his prosperity and more.

The action in this profoundly puzzling story begins when a deputation, which includes Satan, appears before God and in the course of discussions Satan provokes God into making a bet on whether Job can be made by misfortune to revile God. His flocks and herds and his sons and daughters are destroyed and then Job himself is afflicted with horrible boils and pains. But he refuses to curse God. Three friends turn up to comfort him. They are simple men, each presenting a different simplified answer to the question why God should so assail a good man. To Eliphaz the Temanite it is impossible to suppose that God could do such a thing and therefore Job must have done something wrong. Bildad the Shuhite tries to persuade Job that his suffering, deserved or underserved, will do him good in the end. Zophar the Naamathite, equally devout and even more of a simpleton, says it is all a mystery that will be cleared up one day. Job gets no comfort from these comforters. He remains sure of his blamelessness and, his conundrum unresolved, his friends' arguments merely drive him into terrible doubts about a God who can plague him with such pains and perplexities and refuse to commune with him about why.

From this point in the story the drama is twice intensified by the successive appearane on the stage of two new interlocutors. Unlike the comforters they do not argue with Job about his problem. They make assertions which sidestep it. The first, Elihu, proclaims the sovereign attributes of God and implicitly condemns Job for prying into the way God works. The second is God himself. He arrives in a whirlwind and delivers a tremendous speech on the omnipotence of His creativity with a barrage of crushing rhetorical questions designed to emphasize the gulf between Himself and Job — or any other man — who could never imagine or create such marvels as Behemoth, Leviathan (hippopotamus, crocodile) etc. What God does not attempt is to answer Job's question. Two conclusions are possible. The one is that by ignoring Job's question and concealing the wager God is admitting covertly that there is something not quite nice about the wager. Alternatively, however, God's display of the immensity of his powers may be taken to show that he is beyond questioning and demands unquestioning faith. On this interpretation the comforters are wrong: God is not just and Job has not sinned. God is beyond justice, no more just than unjust. Job is not entitled to ask questions. He must have total faith. After God's monologue the story concludes with Job restored to health and wealth. He becomes even richer that before – more camels, sheep, oxen and asses – and gets a new family of sons and daughters and lives to a great old age: some *ex gratia* compensation perhaps for having been used as a guinea-pig. The Book of Job is one of the most profound in the OT and one of the most profoundly unsatisfying. Job's passivity is something less than heroic, while God fails to make His case, whatever it may be.

An English edition of the Book of Job, published in 1825, contained eighteen illustrations 'invented and engraved' by William Blake, whose bizarre genius demonstrated the hopelessness of trying to make sense of the Book. Blake's drawings inspired Vaughan William's masque *Job* in which elemental strains of folk music are combined with 20th-century harmonies to create paradoxes which, if not the same as those in the Book of Job, are further testimony to the Book's power to disturb. In a baroquely expressive picture by Andrea Sacchi (Wilton, Wilton House) Job is shown, almost naked and almost despairing, with his wife and – curiously – two of the three friends. In 'Job Visited by his Wife' Georges de la Tour shows that Job's wife was a true comforter in dark times (Epinay, Musée Departmentale des Vosges). See also Jemima.
(Job)

**Joel**   A prophet exceptionally hard to date – perhaps one of *Isaiah's principal successors in the late C 7 BC but possibly post-Exilic (mid C 4 BC). If the latter, he exceptionally transcended the blustering Jewish nationalism of that period. Cultivated and rational, he was a utopian rather than a reformer, and although he warned of the disasters in store for the ungodly and the unjust he did so without gloating. His message was mildly optimistic, for he believed that disaster turns people to repentance and unlocks God's mercy. See also Prophets. (Joel)

**JOHN**   The Johns noted below are John the Baptist; John, son of *Zebedee, apostle; John the evangelist; John, author of the Book of Revelations; and John Mark, companion of **Paul and Barnabas. John has been the most popular name for Christian boys throughout the centuries, and more Popes have taken it than any other.

**John the Baptist**   Son of **Zacharias and Elizabeth in their old age. He was born six months before Jesus – who was his cousin – and became a prophet in Judaea, living wild on locusts and honey, roughly clad in a hair shirt, preaching the coming of the Messiah and urging repentance through baptism with water. Jesus came from Galilee to be baptized by John, who objected at first that it ought to be the other way round. After leaving Judaea to preach east of the Jordan John was thrown into prison by the tetrarch of Galilee, Herod *Antipas, whom he had denounced for marrying his sister-in-law *Herodias; and the tetrarch had him beheaded to please his step-daughter *Salome.

John was both a typical figure and original. His was a troubled age which produced many vagrant preachers with wild imaginings; he himself had a special urgency and a special offer, insisting on the imminence of the advent of the

Messiah and introducing the idea of baptism by water as a step on the road to salvation which the Messiah would complete by baptism with the Holy Spirit. John earned the hostility of the priests and Pharisees as a religious subversive and of Herod as a political subversive. When he left Judaea for Galilee he jumped out of the frying-pan into the fire. Later legend carried his severed head to Constantinople in C 4 and thence to King Pepin in Gaul: an early example of Western tuft-hunting. In the Orthodox Church John is called the Forerunner (of Jesus) rather than the Baptist. (To baptize is to sanctify or initiate by pouring on water or by total immersion.)

John the Baptist has been portrayed countless times – in infancy, in action and in death. He figures in pictures of the Holy Family, happily playing with Jesus about the feet of their elders. He figures too as a preacher, roaming the desert wild and ragged and often alone (as, for example, by Domenico Veneziano in the National Gallery in Washington); but also, by Pieter Breughel the Elder, in terms and dress and landscape of a sedate Netherlandish Protestant gathering (Budapest, Museum of Fine Art). His severed head has been a popular, if gruesome theme: Giovanni Bellini's version best combines the dignity and horror of his end (Pesaro, City Museum). Caravaggio presents the actual decapitation – a sombre scene pierced by flashes of light and observed by two surreptitious onlookers through a grill (Valetta, Cathedral). His sculptured figure may be seen throughout Christendom, most famously by Donatello (Siena, Cathedral and in the Bargello in Florence, which contains a delightful head and shoulders in low relief as well as two stirring statues); and by Rodin (New York, Museum of Modern Art).
Matthew 3, 4, 9, 11, 14, 21; Mark 1, 2, 6, 11; Luke 1, 3, 5, 7, 9, 20; John 1, 3, 5, 10; Acts 1, 13)

**John**    Son of Zebedee, fisherman and one of the twelve apostles. He has been identified with *John the

evangelist but the identification is shaky. With his brother *James and *Peter, John belonged to an inner circle among *Jesus' disciples, was himself the 'beloved disciple' and was charged by Jesus with the care of his mother *Mary after the Crucifixion. See under Peter for the special prominence of John and Peter.
(Matthew 4, 10, 17, 26; Mark I, 9-14; Luke 5, 6; John 20, 21; Acts I)

**John**  Author of the Fourth Gospel, probably of the three Johannine epistles in the NT, but not – in spite of an early and long tradition – of the Book of Revelation. His contribution to the formation of Christianity is hardly less powerful than *Paul's, but his personality is much less clear and so is his meaning. He lived to a great old age, probably in Ephesus where he is said to have died. His Gospel is both different from the other three and yet like them. The structure is the same: a narrative account of Jesus' trial, death and resurrection, preceded by selected vignettes of his doings, sayings and teachings before these culminating events. It is different in detail and in its intelletual scope and style. Some of the differences of detail are striking: Jesus' ministry is not confined, as in the other three Gospels, almost entirely to Galilee; John refers to visits to Jerusalem some time before the Passion; he says nothing about the transfiguration or the agony in the garden or the Last Supper; he alone tells of a preliminary appearance of Jesus before the ex-high priest *Annas; and he puts the Crucifixion one day earlier than the other evangelists. These differences are striking because only four canonical Gospels exist and John's is odd-man-out; but they are much less significant than John's altogether different and wider range of reference.
**Matthew, Mark and Luke set Jesus' Passion in the context of Jesus' life on earth and (Matthew particularly) Jesus' position in Jewish messianic genealogies, prophecies and expecta-

tions. John's frame of reference is much wider and his language more sophisticated. Just as Paul widened the Christian message from Jews to Gentiles, so John widened it yet further by taking as his setting God's plan: 'In the beginning was the Word . . . ' The Word, or *Logos,* is God's plan which preceded the creation, and John's account of Jesus' ministry and passion is related to his place in God's scheme from before the creation until the end of the world. Far more than his fellow evangelists John, in his thought and his literary style, tackled the immensely awesome story of Jesus *sub specie aeternitatis* and with the aid of philosophic notions, Judaic and Greek, which were current among educated people of the age and were to some extent percolating into commoner currency. John differs from the other evangelists not only in his view of Jesus' place in God's scheme, but also in his view of Jesus' own nature: all the texts supporting Jesus' belief in his own divinity are to be found in the Fourth Gospel, all the texts pointing the other way in the other Gospels. John has never been easy to understand and, as Robert Browning rightly discerned, it was touch and go whether his explanations and vision – so much more remote from ordinary people's understanding than the writings of Matthew, Mark and Luke – would survive him. In 'A Death in the Desert' Browning poses the poignant question how the teaching of Jesus may survive after the death of John, the last of those who 'saw, heard, knew' Jesus. Browning's purpose in this poem was to counter contemporary attacks on Christian beliefs; its abiding impact, however, is its picture of the last survivor of a generation of incomparable blessedness dying as his companions melt away.

**John**  The recipient from an angel of the Revelation which constitutes the last Book in the Bible. A tradition almost as long as the Christian era has made him out to be the same as *John, apostle and evangelist, but scholarly opionon has veered strongly away from this conclusion. By his own account he was exiled to the island of Patmos in the Dodecanese. Gide, at his most malicious, said that John's visions came from eating a book on Patmos – like a rat getting indigestion from gnawing books.

**John Mark**  A Jew from Cyprus and cousin of *Barnabas. He joined *Paul and Barnabas in Jerusalem and accompanied them back to Antioch and on part of their joint missionary journey to Cyprus. Paul and Barnabas quarrelled over John Mark, Barnabas wishing to take him on their next journey but Paul objecting on the grounds that he had failed to stay the course on the first. Paul and Barnabas went their separate ways, the former with *Silas and the latter with John Mark. Later Paul and John Mark made friends again.
(Acts 4, 12, 13; Coloss. 4, Philemon; 2 Timothy 4)

**Jonadab**  Friend, cousin and and evil counsellor of *Amnon, son of *David. Jonadab devised the plan which enabled Amnon to rape his half-sister *Tamar. Amnon was murdered two years later by her full brother *Absalom. The allurements of this domestic melodrama have stimulated literary imaginations down to the present day, the latest example being the play *Yonadab* by Peter Shaffer.
(2 Samuel 13)

**Jonah**  Unwilling prophet, hero of perhaps the earliest unforgetable short story. Jonah is commanded by God to go to Nineveh and denounce its vices. Understandably fearing what the people of Nineveh will do to him he takes ship for Tarshish in the opposite direction. But God is not so easily foiled and stirs up a great storm. Jonah sleeps through this storm but his shipmates have a terrible time and attribute it to Jonah after casting lots to discover who is the culprit in their company responsible for this bad luck. They throw him overboard, the storm subsides and Jonah is swallowed by a huge fish. After three days and three nights in the belly of the fish Jonah is cast up on dry land, apparently none the worse for his singular adventure. God then repeats His command and Jonah carries it out. The people of Nineveh repent and God spares them. Jonah is angry that they are spared. He has built himself a hut just outside the city in the expectation of enjoying the spectacle of divine vengeance upon them. God causes a gourd to grow up and shield Jonah from the sun and wind, but a day later He sends a worm which kills the gourd, leaving Jonah so exposed to the weather that he wants to die too. He reflects on these things, feels sorry for the defunct gourd and so arrives at feeling sorry for the Ninevites and approving God's revocation of the sentence of perdition upon them. This moral tale is a mixture of parable and magic and above all a very good story. The English pamphleteer and worthy Francis Quarles published in 1620 a paraphrase of the Book of Jonah, entitled *A Feast of Wormes*. Lennox Berkeley wrote an oratorio about Jonah. A Jonah is a person whose mere presence brings misfortune upon his companions. (Jonah)

**JONATHAN** Three Jonathans are noted below: the son of *Saul; the priest's son who served *David; and Jonathan Maccabaeus.

**Jonathan** The oldest of the three sons of *Saul. After Saul's installation as king over all the tribes of Israel, he and Jonathan made war on the *Philistines. Jonathan, thinking to stage a private success of his own, set off secretly with his armour-bearer and so did not hear Saul's order imposing a one-day fast to prevent any slackening in the Israelites' attack and pursuit. He ate some wild honey which he found in a wood. He was condemned to death by his father but was reprieved by popular clamour. Jonathan became the devoted friend of

*David, took David's side when Saul turned against him, interceded for him and warned him of threats to his life – all this in defiance of his father, the king, and in spite of the fact that David's existence threatened his own prospects as Saul's heir. Jonathan and his brothers were all killed in the last of Saul's battles with the Philistines, when Saul himself committed suicide. Their bodies were recovered by men of Jabesh-gilead, were cremated there and their bones buried under a tree but removed many years later by David for reburial in the sepulchre of *Kish, Saul's father. David's lament for Saul and Jonathan has the piercing throb of deep sorrow, loyalty and devotion. 'The beauty of Israel is slain upon thy high places: how are the mighty fallen! Tell it not in Gath, publish it not the streets of Askelon; lest the daughters of the Philistines rejoice, lest the daughters of the uncirumcised triumph....thy love to me was wonderful, passing the love of women.' (1 Samuel 14, 18-31; 2 Samuel 2; 1 Chron. 10)

**Jonathan** Son of the priest Abiathar. Jonathan and *Ahimaaz (son of the priest *Zadok) were chosen to take intelligence about *Absalom's intentions from Jerusalem to *David who had fled from his capital in the face of Absalom's rebellion. Before reaching David they had to hide in a well, but they succeeded in delivering their vital information which caused David to withdraw across the Jordan and so entice Absalom to his doom. (2 Samuel 15)

**Jonathan** Brother of *Judas Maccabaeus and his successor as ruler of the Maccabee principality from the death of Judas in 160 BC to his own death in 142 BC. He secured the office of high priest in 153 BC. See Maccabees and family tree E. (1 Maccabees 9-14; 2 Maccabees 8)

**JOSEPH** The Josephs noted below are *Jacob's son; the

husband of *Mary mother of *Jesus; Joseph of Arimathea; and Joseph Barsabas, a follower of Jesus.

**Joseph**   Son of *Jacob and great lord in Egypt. He was the elder of *Rachel's two sons, a special favourite of his father and a dreamer – all of which made him disliked by his half-brothers. He did nothing to appease them by relating to them two dreams which indicated that he would become greater than they and that even his father and mother would bow down to him. Jacob's love for Joseph was evidenced by a coat of many colours which Jacob made for him. Joseph was wearing this coat when Jacob sent him out to find his brethren who were feeding the family flocks at a distance. When they saw him coming they plotted to kill him but *Reuben, the eldest, jibbed at this extreme crime and suggested instead that they throw him into a pit without food or water. They did so. When a band of Ishmaelites appeared the brothers decided, at the suggestion of *Judah, to sell Joseph, for whom they got 20 pieces of silver. Reuben was absent during this transaction and was distressed when he returned to find Joseph missing. The brothers took Joseph's coat and daubed it with the blood of a kid and took it back to Jacob as proof that Joseph had been killed by a wild animal.

*Sold into Egypt*   Joseph's captors carried him to Egypt and resold him to a prosperous captain of the pharaoh's guard called *Potiphar, who treasured and promoted him in his household. But Potiphar's wife wanted to sleep with Joseph and when he refused she accused him of trying to seduce her. He was thrown into prison where he won favour with the governor and was put in charge of the other prisoners. To this prison was consigned the pharaoh's chief butler and chief baker who had given offence to their master. Both dreamed dreams and asked Joseph to tell them what the dreams meant. Joseph told the butler that he would be restored to his office in three days and the cook that he would be hanged. So it was. The butler promised to tell the pharaoh about Joseph and get him out of prison but he forgot his promise for two years. What reminded him of it was a series of disturbing dreams by the pharaoh. When nobody could interpret these dreams – in which seven fat cattle were devoured by seven lean cattle, and seven good ears of corn were devoured by seven rank ears – the butler remembered Joseph. Joseph explained to the pharaoh that his dreams betokened seven years of plenty to be followed by seven years of famine, and he proposed a scheme of famine control by which the surplus of the good years would be stored against the coming famine. Joseph was put in charge of the entire programme, became the pharaoh's chief minister, was given the daughter of an Egyptian priest as wife (*Asenath), and when the famine duly came was sitting on a comfortable store of a scarce commodity at rising prices.

*Reunited with his brethren*

The famine affected Jacob and his people and, hearing that there was corn in Egypt, he sent ten of his sons to buy some. He kept with him only *Benjamin, Joseph's young full brother, for fear that he might come to harm on the long journey. When the ten arrived in Egypt Joseph recognized them and decided to play a game with them. He pretended to believe that they were spies come to see Egypt's plight in the famine and refused to sell them corn or let them go again unless they proved their good faith by producing the youngest brother,whom they had mentioned. They returned to Jacob having left *Simeon behind as a hostage, but Joseph was so far touched by family feelings that he had their sacks filled with corn and also with the money which they had brought to pay for it. Jacob refused at first to let Benjamin go, but the famine forced his hand and he relented when *Judah gave personal assurances for Benjamin's safety (their two tribes were to be specially linked in later history). Joseph was overcome with emotion at the sight of Benjamin but he had not yet finished tormenting his other brothers. Sending them back with the corn they sought, he had a precious silver cup put into Benjamin's sack and sent servants in pursuit who arrested Benjamin as a thief. Judah pleaded to be allowed to take Benjamin's place in prison, but at this point Joseph broke down and revealed himself.

At the pharaoh's invitation Jacob and all his people moved into Egypt. As the famine continued Joseph traded corn for the cattle of the starving people of Egypt and Canaan and for their lands and exacted from them a gift, to the pharaoh in perpetuity, of one fifth of the produce of all lands (except those of the priests). When Jacob died after 17 years in Egypt Joseph and all his brothers and the chief men of the pharaoh carried his enbalmed body to the family burial ground of Macpelah in Hebron and then returned to Egypt. Joseph died in Egypt and was embalmed and 400 years later his remains were carried away by *Moses on the Exodus.

Whatever Joseph represents in history (echoes of economic pressures in a pastoral world), he stands in human terms for two things above all: the triumph of magnanimity over fraternal ill will, and the capacity of a man of virtue and wisdom to rise to the greatest heights even in a foreign land. He had also a good business head. His largest monument in the modern world is Thomas Mann's huge novel – or rather three consecutive novels in one frame – *Joseph and his Brethren,* where Mann uses Joseph's story for an extended disquisition on the reconciliability of opposites – body and spirit, nature and culture – as the necessary condition for a humanist civilization. The coat of many colours is the centrepiece of paintings by Velasquez (Madrid, Prado) and Ford Madox Brown (Liverpool, Walker Art Gallery); in the latter, four of the brothers are showing the coat's bloody remnants to the horrified Jacob. Pharaoh with his butler and baker was painted by Pontormo (London, National Gallary); Potiphar's wife by Titian (Prado), as naked as she wanted Joseph to be. Lanfranco (early C 17 ) painted the dreams which Joseph interpreted (Rome, Palazzo Mattei) and the same period produced a magniloquent depiction by Mola of Joseph revealing his identity to his agitated brethren (Rome, Quirinal). Méhul's opera *Joseph* is the work of a gifted composer, more respected in his own time than later, a transitional figure between the artifices of C 18 AD and the new naturalism of the romantics, but one of those artists who hover on the verge of greatness without ever getting to it: his inspiration was more religious than musical. Andrew Lloyd Webber's musical, *Joseph and the Amazing Technicolour Dreamcoat* may have a longer life. (Genesis 30, 35, 37, 39-50; Exodus 13)

**Joseph**   Husband of *Mary, mother of Jesus. He was a carpenter in Nazareth but also a descendant of the royal line of *David and so of **Abraham and Adam. Joseph discovered that his wife was pregnant before they had slept together. As he pondered what he should do, an angel told him in a dream that her pregnancy was the doing of the Holy Ghost. During her pregnancy there was a census of tax-payers and Joseph had to go to his home city which, since he was of David's house, was Bethlehem. There Mary's child was born. After the birth Joseph was once more visited by the angel who told him to flee with his family to Egypt to escape the murderous designs of king *Herod. When Herod died the angel appeared a third time to tell Joseph that it was safe to go back to Israel. Nevertheless Joseph was careful to avoid the realm of Herod's son *Archelaus as he returned to Nazareth. Joseph died some time before Jesus began his ministry in Galilee. (The flight into Egypt and return are narrated by *Matthew only, the journey to Bethlehem for the census and Jesus' birth there by *Luke only.) (Matthew 1, 3; Luke 1-2; John 6)

**Joseph of Arimathea**   A rich follower of *Jesus who petitioned *Pilate for the body of Jesus after the crucifixion and wrapped it in a clean cloth for burial. According to *John, who gives the most detailed account of this episode, Joseph acted as he did because he

was afraid of what the Jews might do and was helped by *Nicodemus to anoint the body and put it in a new, unoccupied tomb in the garden where the crucifixion had taken place; they chose this tomb because it was nearby. Joseph's alleged visit to England, in particular to Glastonbury, is an invention of the late Middle Ages. In C 14 a linen shroud, alleged to be the one provided by Joseph for Jesus' body, was put on display in France by a knight's widow who was in need of money. In the next century it was bequeathed to the Duke of Savoy and it has continuted to belong to his heirs – the kings and ex-kings of Italy. In C 16 it was placed in a special chapel in the new Savoyard/Piemontese capital, Turin. It may have reached France after being looted in Constantinople during the Fourth Crusade (1204). Whether it is also the same as the Mandylion – a cloth bearing an alleged likeness of Jesus, first found in Ephesus and moved to Constantinople in C 6  – is a question even more difficult to answer than others concerning this intriguing relic. George Moore's *The Brook Kerith* is a fictionized biography of Joseph of Arimathea.
(Matthew 27; Mark 15; Luke 23; John 19 )

**Joseph Barsabas**   One of the candidates to fill the place among the twelve apostles made vacant by the treason of *Judas Iscariot. But the lot fell not on him but on *Matthias.
(Acts I)

**Joses**   One of the supposed brothers of *Jesus. See under James the Less.

**Joshua**   Son of Nun, was second only to *Moses in the saga of the Israelites' trek out of Egypt and into their Promised Land. After Moses had led the generation of the Exodus through 40 troubled years from the Red Sea to the east bank of the Jordan, Joshua led the second generation across the Jordan, conquered kings, peoples and cities, and divided the Promised Land between the twelve tribes of Israel and the *Levites. After the death of Moses it was to Joshua that God spoke, telling him to take possession of all the country between the 'great sea' (the Mediterranean) and the Euphrates.

**The conquest of the Promised Land**

The tribes of Reuben and Gad and half the tribe of Manasseh had been allocated lands east of the Jordan but their fighting men accompanied their brethren when Joshua crossed the Jordan not far north of the Dead Sea and began the first of his campaigns. This main phase comprised the capture of Jericho in the valley west of the river; the capture of Ai in the hills further west; then, southward along the hilly spine, the subjugation of the Gibeonites (people of Gibeah) by a mixture of diplomacy, force and deceit; the defeat of a league of kings headed by the king of Jerusalem; and finally miscellaneous cleaning-up operations which carried the Israelites down into the lowlands and as far south as Gaza. The second phase of Joshua's work took place in the northern area to the west of the Sea of Galilee where he defeated a Canaanite league.

All these lands were theoretically still part of the Egyptian empire but in practice Egypt's power had lapsed and Joshua's adversaries were a variety of loosely connected peoples. His more serious weaknesses were his lack of siege apparatus and chariots. He had, however, a substantial counter advantage: the defeat by Moses of kings **Sihon and Og on the east of the river had spread alarm and despondency westward and morale was low among Joshua's enemies before he got to grips with them. Before crossing the river Joshua sent two spies to Jericho. They found lodging with a harlot called *Rahab who, sensing that the Israelites were the wave of the future, decided to secure her safety by first hiding the spies on the roof of her house and then helping them to escape by letting them down by a rope from her window, which conveniently was in the city's wall. The spies, having promised her protection when the city fell (which she duly got), returned to Joshua with encouraging intelligence. Joshua set his force in motion. The ark of the convenant, escorted by the *Levites, was carried to the river, which immediately dried up – 40,000 fighting men crossed over. As they did so one man from each tribe picked up a stone from mid-stream and with these Joshua raised a memorial at Gilgal. On the west bank he performed an essential preliminary by ordering the circumcision of all his host. The Israelites who left Egypt had been circumcised but no circumcision took place during the forty years in the wilderness and since Joshua and *Caleb were the only Israelites who crossed both the Red Sea and the Jordan all their companions were at this latter point uncircumcised. After remedying this defect Joshua advanced on Jericho. For six days the Israelites, with the ark and trumpets made of rams' horns, paraded once round the walls of the city. On the seventh day they circled them seven times, blew the trumpets and shouted. The walls fell down flat. This miraculous victory gave the Israelites a boost and further depressed the morale of their enemies. But the conquest of the next stronghold – Ai – was not so easy and was preceded by a reverse caused by over-confidence. A first attack was defeated. It transpired that an Israelite had sinned by helping himself to the communal spoils of war. He was identified as *Achan and he and his sons and daughters were all stoned to death and burned. The assault on Ai was resumed and the city taken when the defenders were lured away by a stratagem. It was sacked, its king hanged, and 12,000 persons killed. Turning southward, Joshua came to the cities of the Gibeonites with whom he had already been in correspondence – perhaps even before the siege of Ai. By making a compact with them he detached them from their neighbours and then, claiming that they had deceived him by pretending that they lived far away, denounced the compact and reduced them to being second-class citizens, 'hewers of wood and drawers of water' for ever. The kindred peoples, incensed by the defection of the Gibeonites, assembled a coalition to punish them – a league of five kings led by *Adoni-zedek of Jerusalem. But Joshua confronted and defeated this league in a long battle in which Joshua won extra time by commanding the sun to stand still; all the kings were killed and Joshua completed his conquest of the highlands with more slaughtering of peoples and razing of cities. Thenceforward he was able to move south to the cities of the *Philistines or north to Samaria and Galilee. He did both. He overran the southern lowlands as far as Gaza, stopping short however of the principal coastal cities of the Philistines. In the north he met a Canaanite league led by *Jabin, king of Hazor, and was again massively successful, enticing the Canaanite chariots into a narrow place where they could not manoeuvre and then descending on them. This victory won him control over the lands between the Sea of Galilee and the coast but not possession of the main coastal cities of the Phoenicians. The number of kings defeatd by Joshua after crossing the Jordan was 31.

In broad historical terms Joshua and the Israelites conquered and reduced to servitude most of the peoples who had entered these lands in C 17 and C 16 BC, only the coastal strip remaining beyond their grasp. The history of the next two centuries was punctuated by the attempts of the defeated to turn the tables and by the campaigns of the *Judges of Israel, who maintained or retrieved Israel's dominion.

***The settlement of the tribes of Israel***
Joshua's conquest was followed by settlement. At Shiloh, (which became the Israelites' most sacred place until *David took the ark of the convenant to his new capital at Jerusalem) Joshua and *Eleazar, the son of *Aaron, divided the conquered lands by lot between the nine and a half tribes – Reuben, Gad and half Manasseh being already accommodated east of the Jordan. The Levites got no tribal territory but 48 cities and their suburbs scattered throughout the twelve

tribes 'for their cattle and for their substance'. Six sanctuaries were designated, three on either side of the river, where a man who had killed might take refuge from vengeance until he was duly tried. Joshua himself was given the city of Timnath-serah on Mount Ephraim where he died and was buried at the age of 110 after reminding the Israelites of God's gifts to them, adjuring them to remain faithful, and warning them that the peoples among them – subjugated but not exterminated – would be snares for them. His last address and dignified departure are the subject of a poem by Rilke. He is the hero of one of the numerous OT oratorios with which Handel filled his later years and the new Covent Garden opera house; of John Martin's huge and melodramatic pictures *Joshua commanding the Sun to stand still over Gibeon* and *Joshua Spying out the Land of Canaan* (Manx Museum); and of the Negro spiritual *Joshua Fit the Battle of Jericho*.
(Exodus 17; Numbers 11, 13-14, 26-27 34; Deuteronomy 31-34; Joshua)

Josiah    King of Judah c. 640-609 BC. He was the great-grandson of *Hezekiah. Caught between **Assyria and Egypt he tried to save his kingdom from the first by alliance with the second. This policy was an ill-timed failure. He was killed in battle against Egypt, and Judah became an Egyptian puppet. *Jeremiah's lament for Josiah is in the apocryphal Book of Esdras.

During Josiah's reign a notable discovery was made in Jerusalem. The priest *Hilkiah found in the Temple, which was being repaired, a book of Judaic Law – probably the Book of Deuteronnomy. Josiah warmly adopted this code, supposed to be the work of *Moses, and gave it a quasi-constitutional status. Although his immediate successors reversed this innovation, after the *Captivity the leaders of the Return (**Ezra and Nehemiah) and the later prophets (**Haggai, Zechariah, Malachi) created a new Israel founded on the authority of the mosaic Law and the

Mosaic Books (the Pentateuch). Josiah's early enthusiasm for the Law makes him a precursor of this theocratic state. He is cited by Robert Burton in his *Anatomy of Melancholy* as an exemplar of kingship – along with Rome's legislator-king Numa Pompilius and the emperor Augustus.

Judah itself did not long survive Josiah. From being an Egyptian puppet it became a province of Babylon. *Nebuchadnezzar looted Jerusalem in the reign of one king and deposed the next. The last king, Zedekiah, was taken captive to Babylon (587 BC) where he was blinded and all his sons were killed. The kingdom of *Rehoboam ceased to exist but its royal line — the house of *David — went on and returned to Jerusalem in the person of Zerubbabel some fifty years later (2 Kings 22, 23 ; 2 Chron. 34, 35; Jeremiah I; Zephaniah I)

**Jubal**      Son of *Lamech by his first wife Adah. He was the first harpist and organist, the ancestor of those who make music and musical instruments. His brother was *Jabal. See family tree A. (Genesis 4)

**Judaeus**    One of the twelve apostles. See under Thaddeus.

**Judah**      The name of an individual, a tribe and a kingdom. Judah was one of the twelve sons of *Jacob, the fourth of his sons by Leah and the most successful. He far surpassed his full brothers – Reuben, Simeon, Levi, Issachar, Zebulon – in the annals of the Israelites. The royal line which he engendered descended from his seduction of his daughter-in-law *Tamar, a Canaanitess; their son Perez was the forebear of *David. Judah's tribal territory lay to the west of the Dead Sea and included the cave of Macpelah at Hebron, the burial place of **Abraham, Isaac and Jacob, and also the city of Jerusalem, built by David. From being one of twelve tribal territories this area became one of two kingdoms when, after the death of *Solomon,

his kingdom split into *Israel and Judah. The latter's first king was *Rehoboam, its capital Jerusalem. It was the smaller and poorer of the two, a landlocked state cut off from the sea by the cities of the *Philistines; only sporadically valuable as a make-weight in alliance politics; less cosmopolitan than the sister kingdom and fiercer in it religious and nationalist exclusiveness. But it lasted a century and a half longer and, when overthrown, revived. Although destroyed in 586 BC by *Nebuchadnezzar its people were not annihilated, as were the people of Israel who became after 722 BC the Lost Tribes. In time Judah became the Roman province of Judaea and gave the Jews their name. See also Jehoshaphat, Athaliah, Hezekiah, Josiah.
(Genesis 29 35, 37, 38, 42 -50)

**JUDAS**    The more famous bearers of this fairly common name are Judas Maccabaeus and Judas Iscariot. Also noted below are a supposed brother of Jesus, and Judas Barsabas, an associate of **Paul and Barnabas. *Luke called one of the twelve apostles Judas; he appears to be identical with *Thaddeus. The epistle of Jude, which is probably of AD C 2 and overlaps the epistle called 2 Peter, has been ascribed to Judas, brother of Jesus. This seems to be one of several cases where a name has been appropriated to give weight to somebody else's work.

**Judas Maccabaeus**    The most eminent member of the heroic family which, in revolt against the Seleucid empire, created the mini-state which, with Jerusalem as its capital, subsisted for a hundred years before the arrival of the Romans. Handel chose Judas Maccabaeus as the subject for the oratorio with which he celebrated the defeat of the Young Pretender at Culloden in 1746. It provided him with the greatest popular success of his career and included the march-chorus: 'See the conquering hero comes' – on which Beethoven wrote a set of variations for cello and piano. For Sir Thomas Malory, writing the preface to his *Morte Darthur* in C 15 England, Judas Maccabaeus was one of the three great men of the Jews – with Duke Joshua and King David. See Maccabees and family tree E. (I Maccabees 3-9; 2 Maccabees 2, 5, 8, 10-15)

**Judas Iscariot**    Judas of Kerioth, a place in Judaea – the apostle who betrayed *Jesus to the priests for (according to *Matthew) 30 pieces of silver. Jesus had finished washing his disciples' feet and had sat down again to eat with them when he told them that one of them would betray him. *John, prompted by *Peter, asked Jesus whom he meant. Jesus replied that it was he to whom he would give a piece of bread dipped in the dish before them. He gave it to Judas, telling him to do quickly what he had to do, but none of the others followed his meaning. This is John's account of the prologue to the betrayal. The other evangelists tell a similar story within their more elaborate accounts of the Last Supper. Judas brought a posse of soldiers and police to the garden called Gethsemane, a place frequented by Jesus on the Mount of Olives. In John's version of the events Judas played no further part, but according to the other evangelists he betrayed Jesus with a kiss. All agree that there was a short scuffle in which one of Jesus' party, identified by John as *Peter, cut off the ear of one of the servants of the high priest. After Jesus had been condemned by the priests Judas repented, threw away the pieces of silver and hanged himself. The Judas tree (*cercis siliquastrum*) is the tree on which he is said to have done this. The priests, his paymasters, recovered their money and used it to buy a field for the burial of strangers: from being known as the Potter's Field it became the Field of Blood. Legend allows Judas one night a year out of hell to cool himself on an iceberg: see, for example, Matthew Arnold's poem *St*

*Brendan*. Dante places him in Satan's mouth in the lowest circle of hell with those other betrayers of benefactors, Brutus and Cassius. His betrayal has been a perennial theme for artists as well as moralists, as witness its representation from Giotto – an affectingly human kiss (Padua, Arena) – to Stanley Spencer (Belfast, Ulster Museum). Rembrandt shows him throwing away the pieces of silver. In *The Lost Leader* Robert Browning gave great offence by implying that Wordsworth had betrayed the liberal cause: 'Just for a handful of silver he left us'. A Judas is a spyhole.
(Matthew 10, 26, 27; Mark 3, 14; Luke 6, 22; John 6, 12, 13, 18; Acts I, 3, 4, 8)

**Judas**    One of the supposed brothers of *Jesus (for whom see under *James the Less). This Judas has been dubiously identified with *Thaddeus, also called Judaeus, one of the twelve apostles. As Jude he later became the patron of persons in despair and of lost causes, but why nobody seems to know.

**Judas Barsabas**    Sent with *Silas by the Christians of Jerusalem to Antioch with **Paul and Barnabas. After a while Judas returned to Jerusalem but Silas remained in Antioch and became one of Paul's chief missionary companions.
(Acts 15)

**Judges**    The Judges were rulers appointed periodically by God to rescue the Israelites from the consequence of their sins. They were heroes who took power in a crisis and proved themselves worthy of it. They functioned in the period – c 1200-1000 BC – between the conquest of the Promised Land under *Joshua and the consolidation of a single kingship under **Saul and David. The Israelites who took and partitioned the Promised Land constituted a loose federation of tribes settled in territories whose previous rulers had been neither exterminated nor expelled. The consequence was an alternation of co-existence and conflict: on the one hand economic commerce, fraternization and intermarriage; on the other hand political rivalry exacerbated by the exclusive monotheism which the Israelites opposed to the laxer polytheism of everybody else. From time to time one or more of the tribes of Israel lapsed into heathenism by worshipping the god or *Baal of a neighbouring people. This dereliction was punished by the God of Israel who delivered the backsliders into the hands of those whom they had subjected when taking possession of the Promised Land. But after varying periods of servitude God chose a deliverer in the shape of a Judge, the tables were turned once more, the heathen were defeated and killed in large numbers, and the repentant Israelites prospered again under the eye of the Judge. When the Judge died the circle began again. It was broken only when the loose federation of this age was transformed into the centralized kingdom of Israel which, under David's son *Solomon, became a rich regional power.

The heathen peoples with whom the Israelites alternately consorted and warred were regarded by them as distant cousins who had remained in these lands when the children of Israel (alias *Jacob) went down into Egypt. The Canaanites, for example, were the descendants of Canaan, son of *Ham; the Moabites and Ammonites the descendants of **Moab and Ben-ammi, sons of Lot; the Edomites the descendants of Edom or *Esau. Only the *Philistines were alien in race as well as religion. For these relationships see family trees B and C; and for the more famous Judges see under Ehud, Deborah, Gideon, Jephthah, Samson, Samuel.

**Judith**  A widow in comfortable circumstances in Bethulia in Judah. She cut off the head of *Nebuchadnezzar's general *Holofernes in order to save her compatriots. Nebuchadnezzar, incensed by the refusal of neighbouring states to help him in his war with the Medes, sent Holofernes to devastate their lands. This he did, ending with an expedition against the comparatively insignificant land of *Judah. Learning that her city could hold out for only five days, Judith made her way with a maid to the enemy camp, pretending to be a deserter. After three days of well judged prevarication she consented to eat and drink with Holofernes, exchanging her widow's weeds for more gorgeous clothes, and contrived to end the evening alone with him. He was drunk and she cut off his head with his own scimitar and put it in a bag which the maid carried as the two made their escape. She gave the maid her freedom.

There is something disturbing about the popularity of Judith's bloody story with Renaissance artists and patrons – and the equal popularity of the decapitation of *John the Baptist. There are three Judiths by Tintoretto in one gallery alone (Prado) and he does not hesitate to depict the gruesomeness of the act. Nor does Caravaggio (Rome, Casa Coppi). Botticelli, however, shrank from such enormities. The nearest he got to them was in his picture of Judith emerging from Holofernes' tent with the head; he also painted a pair of pictures showing Judith hurrying back to Bethulia and the discovery of Holofernes' dead body the next morning (all these in the Uffizi). On the ceiling of the Sistine Chapel in the Vatican Michelangelo shows a decapitated Holofernes sprawled on a bed in the background as the ladies hurry away. By the rococo age Judith gets a whole ceiling to her glorification – Luca Giordano (Naples, S. Martino). Titian made the maid black (Detroit, Art Gallery). Giorgione painted a wonderfully beautiful picture of a serene girl who happens to have her foot on a severed head (Leningrad, Hermitage). Judith was a favourite with Mantegna as the National Galleries in Dublin and Washington can show and Rembrandt's drawing of her triumphant return (London, British Museum) echoes Mantegna. By C 16 public purpose and heroic patriotism are overshadowed by something else: Cavallino's Judith is pursuing a private vengeance (Stockholm, National Museum) while the younger Allori is simply showing his own mistress holding his own head (Florence, Pitti). But for the most stirring combination of the dignity and indignity of the deed turn from paint to Donatello's bronze (Florence, Palazzo Vecchio). In C 19 the German stage saw her from two angles: Hebbel wrote a play about her on the theme of good *versus* evil and Johann Nestroy wrote a parody of that play. Arnold Bennett also wrote a play about her and operas have come from Honegger and Alexander Serov, Wagner's chief Russian champion and imitator. In Rilke's 'The Return of Judith' the heroine is making for home exalted and yet sobered. Meyerbeer toyed with a theme well suited to his flashy talent but abandoned it.

**Julius**  A courteous centurion charged to take *Paul by sea from Caesarea to Rome. The full complement of the vessel in which they sailed was 276. (Acts 27)

**Justus**  *Paul's host in Corinth. (Acts 18)

**Keren-happuch**  Daughter of *Job. See Jemima

**Keturah**  Wife of *Abraham after the death of *Sarah. She had six sons whom Abraham endowed with gifts but sent eastward out of range of *Isaac, his heir. Many peoples, from Greece to southern Arabia, including the Midianites, later claimed

descent from Abraham through this dispersed progeny.
(Genesis 25)

**Kezia**  Daughter of *Job. See Jemima

**Kish**  A *Benjaminite and father of *Saul. Kish sent Saul to search for his asses which had got lost, but after three days Saul and his servant still could not find them. The servant suggested consulting a local man of God, Saul was dubious because he had no present to offer, but the servant had a quarter of a shekel. The man of God was *Samuel and in this way God brought Saul to Samuel, who made him king over all the tribes of Israel.
(I Samuel 9)

**Korah**  A Levite and the leader of the most serious cabal against the authority of *Moses in the desert. With *Dathan and Abiram he voiced the discontents of those who felt that the Israelites were taking too long to reach the land flowing with milk and honey. The earth opened and swallowed them up alive with their families and fellow dissidents. The imminence of this punishment was one of the scenes chosen by Botticelli for the side wall of the Sistine Chapel in the Vatican devoted to the life of Moses. Beccafumi depicted the same scene in the cathedral at Pisa.
(Numbers 16)

**Laban**  Brother of *Rebecca and so brother-in-law of *Isaac. Laban belonged to that part of the family which had remained in Mesopotamia when *Abraham migrated to the west, but he had moved from Ur on the lower Euphrates to Harran between the upper courses of the Euphrates and the Tigris. Laban was somewhat tight-fisted. When Abraham sent a servant with rich gifts to find a wife for his son Isaac, Laban was more than happy to despatch his sister Rebecca with only one day's delay. Many years later Rebecca sent her son *Jacob to Laban in order to get him out of the way when she feared that his life was in danger from his brother *Esau whom he had defrauded (see under Jacob). Rebecca persuaded her husband Isaac to tell Jacob to go and woo one of Laban's daughters, **Leah or Rachel. Jacob stayed with Laban for 20 years and came back with both daughters and a large family. On first arriving he had immediately seen and fallen in love with Rachel. Laban, having welcomed Jacob effusively, offered to give him Rachel at the end of seven years and proposed that Jacob should meanwhile work for him and – in spite of being a kinsman – receive a wage for his work. When the seven years were up Laban slipped Leah, who was not nearly as attractive as Rachel, into Jacob's bed, and in order to get Rachel too Jacob had to promise to work for Laban for another seven years, during which he slept with both sisters and with their servants. He shepherded Laban's flocks so well that they were immeasurably increased and eventually he told Laban that he wanted to leave. Laban, who had not yet paid any of the promised wages, asked how much he owed and offered to settle up. But Jacob proposed a revised deal whereby he would take payment in kind – a share of Laban's flocks. Each tried to cheat the other (again see under Jacob) and when Laban and his sons saw that they were doing badly they became so hostile to Jacob that he sensed that it was time to be gone. He departed secretly with his wives, children and animals. Rachel added insult to injury by stealing her father's household gods. Laban gave chase and reproached Jacob for running away secretly after so many years and for stealing his gods. Jacob, who knew nothing about the gods, promised that if Laban could find them the thief would be put to death but Rachel

obstructed Laban's search by pretending that she was menstruating. Laban and Jacob, who had much to forgive one another for, made it up and parted. See family tree B. Pietro da Cortona painted Laban searching in vain for his gods while his deceitful daughter looks on (Bristol, City Art Gallery).
(Genesis 24)

**Lamech**  There are two Lamechs in Genesis, the one descended from *Cain and the other from *Seth. The sons of the former were **Jabal, Jubal and Tubal-cain. They represented respectively nomad herdsmen, music and musical instrument makers, and smiths. The second Lamech was the son of *Methuselah and father of *Noah. See family tree A.
(Genesis 4)

**Lazarus**  There are two, the one a proverbial symbol of poverty, the other an actual example of sickness healed. The first was a beggar at the gates of a rich man who was over-dressed and over-fed (commonly called Dives, Latin for rich). The beggar lived in hope of crumbs fallen from the rich man's table and was covered with sores which the dogs licked. Both died. The rich man went to hell and Lazarus to *Abraham's bosom. The rich man espied Lazarus and pleaded with Abraham to send Lazarus to dip the tip of his finger in water and cool his burning tongue. But Abraham refused: their fates in death justly reversed their fates in life. The rich man asked Abraham to warn his yet surviving brothers but again Abraham refused, saying that the brothers had Moses and the Prophets to go by. In his setting *Vater Abraham* the C 17 composer Heinrich Schütz gives the rich man music of such dignified pleading that one feels unexpectedly sorry for him. A lazaret is an asylum for the destitute. (See also next entry.)
(Luke 16)

**Lazarus**  The second Lazarus appears only in John's Gospel, where he is described as the brother of **Martha and Mary and living with them in Bethany. *Jesus, says John, specially loved all three. It was reported to Jesus, who was not then in Bethany, that Lazarus was ill but, since he was sleeping, on the road to recovery. Jesus, however, said that Lazarus was not sleeping but was dead. Approaching Bethany Jesus learned that Lazarus had been dead for four days. Martha went to meet Jesus and said that if Jesus had been there her brother would not have died. Jesus replied that he would rise again. Martha supposed that Jesus was referring to the general resurrection of the dead at the last day, but Jesus said that he would bring Lazarus back to life. Mary then came to meet him with the same doleful tale that Lazarus would not have died if Jesus had been by, and they came on a large concourse of weeping mourners. 'Jesus wept' (this is the shortest of the verses into which the Bible was divided in a later age). Jesus told them to roll away the stone in front of the tomb, to which Martha objected that since Lazarus had been dead for four days he would stink. But it was done and Jesus called to Lazarus to come out, which he did in his grave clothes. On a later occasion, when Jesus was eating with Lazarus and his sisters, one of these poured precious ointment over his head: see Martha and Mary.

The raising of Lazarus is the miracle by Jesus which most strains modern credence. In the Middle Ages, however, Lazarus was revered as a saint, and after the Christian conquest of the Holy Land by the first Crusade his home village of Bethany was bought by Queen Melisande of Jerusalem who established there a convent in his honour. His dramatic story has attracted dramatic painters: both the more traditional drama of Sebastiano del Piombo (London, National Gallery) or Caravaggio (Messina, Museo Nazionale), and the more idiosyncratic view – foretaste of Edvard Munch – by Rembrandt's friend Jan Lievens (Brighton). Epstein's sculpture of Lazarus, seen from behind and swaddled in his grave-

clothes, is in New College, Oxford. Less grim, even homely, is the version (now in The Prado, Madrid) by Queen Isabella of Castile's court painter, Juan de Flandes, painted for the Church of St Lazarus in Palencia. In Rilke's poetic imagination Jesus raised Lazarus to satisfy the crowd but inwardly regarded the episode as a ghastly experiment. One of Schubert's many unfinished works is a cantata about Lazarus: the composer seems to have got stuck as he came to the crucial culmination.
(John 11, 12)

**Leah**   Elder daughter of *Laban and, with her sister *Rachel, wife to their cousin *Jacob. Leah bore six of Jacob's twelve sons and their daughter *Dinah. Claude painted the two sisters with Jacob in one of his luscious landscapes (Leningrad, Hermitage). See further under Laban and Jacob, and family tree C.
(Genesis 29-33)

**Levi**   The third of the twelve sons of *Jacob. His mother was *Leah. With his brother *Simeon he wreaked cruel and deceitful vengeance on *Shechem and the Shechemites in retaliation for the rape of their sister *Dinah. On his deathbed Jacob cursed Levi and Simeon. Unlike his brothers Levi founded no tribe. His descendants became a functional caste instead of a territorial tribe. See *Levites, family tree C, and the next entry.
(Genesis 29, 34, 35, 42-50)

**Levi**   Son of Alphaeus. See Matthew, apostle, and the foregoing entry.

**Levites**   The descendants of *Levi, the third son of **Jacob and Leah, through his three sons Gershon, Kohath and Merari – Kohath being the grandfather of **Aaron and Moses. God claimed the Levites for himself in place of the firstborn of all the Israelites and their animals, to which he was entitled. God then gave the Levites to Aaron to serve, between the ages of 25 and 50, as a priesthood with specified functions. They forfeited the right of the other sons of *Jacob (alias Israel) to a territorial area in the Promised Land and were given instead 48 cities, with suburbs extending 1,000 cubits from the city walls, to sustain themselves and their flocks and herds. Before the crossing of the Jordan into the Promised Land (see Joshua) they were numbered separately from the rest of the Israelites: the Levite males of all ages beyond one month came to 22,000. In later times Aaron's descendants monopolized the higher functions of the priesthood in Judah with other levitical families as their associates. The main centre of their cult was at Shiloh, where *Eli was priest until the *Philistines seized and sacked it and carried off the ark enshrining the covenant between God and *Abraham. Senior priests acquired political influence. Thus *Ahimelech and 85 of his colleagues supported David against *Saul, who had them all killed with the sole exception of *Abiathar who managed to escape. When David died Abiathar supported *Adonijah for the throne while *Zadok supported the successful *Solomon and so secured the chief priestly offices in Jerusalem for his descendants until the extinction of the kingdom of Judah in 586 BC. After the Exile in Babylon the power of the priests increased until the high priest became in effect the secular as well as the religious head of the nation. In C 2 BC the priests disgraced themselves by bribery, corruption and even murder, thus giving rise to the reform movement led by the *Maccabees. The Maccabees established a 100-year independent religious state with themselves as high priests and kings. Deprived of their kingship by the Roman general Pompey, the later Maccabees continued as high priests until the last of their line was put to death by *Herod the Great in 37 BC. The office of high priest survived with diminished effect and respect until the destruction of Jerusalem by the Romans in AD 70.

**Longinus** The name attached in the Middle Ages to the soldier at the Crucifixion who, according to *John, thrust his spear into Jesus' side. He became the patron of Mantua.
(John 19)

**Lot** Son of *Haran and nephew of *Abraham. During Abraham's long years of childlessness Lot was his closest male relation of the next generation. Together they travelled arduously but also fruitfully until their flocks and herds were more than their lands could support without danger of friction and strife. Abraham proposed that they part and gave Lot the choice between going one way or the other. Lot chose the well watered plain of Jordan and went to live in Sodom, leaving Abraham the land of Canaan further west. Lot became involved in the wars of Chedorlaomer and other kings (including the kings of Sodom and Gomorrah), was taken captive and saved by a punitive expedition led by Abraham. Lot returned to Sodom. There two angels came to him disguised as men. He entertained them and protected them when some *Sodomites surrounded his house and clamoured to see them (for a purpose not specified in the Bible). Lot offered the Sodomites his virgin daughters instead but they persisted until the angels came to his rescue by making the rowdies blind. The angels told Lot to collect his relations and belongings and leave the city since God was going to destroy it. As God rained brimstone and fire on Sodom and Gomorrah Lot escaped towards Zoar with his wife and daughters, but along the road Lot's wife looked back and was turned into a pillar of salt. Lot was afraid to stay in Zoar and went to live in a cave with his daughters. Cut off from the world, the daughters feared they would never get a man and so they plotted to make their father seduce them when he was drunk. Each bore a son, **Moab and Ben-ammi, the ancestors of the Moabites and Ammonites. Guido Reni painted Lot and his daughters leaving Sodom (London, National Gal-

lery) – three fine faces, although not particularly
Biblical. Bonifaccio packed his version of the same
event with moral ambiguities and, in the background, the catastrophic destruction of Sodom
and Gomorrah (Norfolk, Virginia, Chrysler
Museum). The daughters' seductiveness is stressed
by Francesco Furini (Madrid, Prado), a forgotten
C 17 priest and naturalist painter who figures in
Robert Browning's *Parleyings with People of
Importance in their Own Time* as a peg for the
poet's argument that painting the nude is promp-
ted not by lust but by a love of beauty (or may be).
Lot's wife, larger than life and in marble, is caught
in her fateful turn by W.H. Thornycroft (London,
Leighton House). See family tree B.
(Genesis 11, 14, 19)

**Luke**  Physician, evangelist and saint. He was a Greek
Gentile who was born probably in Antioch and
died possibly in Greece. He was the author of the
third Gospel and its continuation, the Acts of the
Apostles, which is a little about *Peter and a lot
about *Paul. Without Luke we should know
practically nothing about Paul's activities
(although his letters would still testify to his
beliefs and character). Luke is the most stylish of
the evangelists. He seems, like Matthew but less
so, to have used Mark as well as other sources for
his account of Jesus' ministry and passion – but
scholars are not unanimous on this matter. From
Luke alone do we learn of the birth and infancy of
*John the Baptist, Jesus' early appearance in the
Temple, the Good *Samaritan, the *Prodigal Son,
*Lazarus and the rich man in Hell, and *Zac-
chaeus who climbed the sycamore to get a good
view of Jesus. If – which is contested – Luke
accompanied Paul on some of his journeys and is
the Luke whom Paul in Rome called the last of his
companions, then Luke's main sources for his
later work will have been Paul himself and his
own personal experiences. Tradition relates that
Luke settled in Greece and died there at a great
age. He wrote his Gospel in the early 80s or a little

later. He was reputed to have painted pictures of the Virgin Mary. In C 5 the Byzantine empress Eudocia Augusta, who had retired to Jerusalem to get away from her sister-in-law, sent back to Constantinople a portrait of Mary by Luke and there is another such in Santa Maria Maggiore in Rome, but there are insuperable technical and stylistic objections to the authenticity of these ascriptions. Nonetheless Roger van der Weyden painted Luke painting the Virgin (Leningrad, Hermitage – the best of several versions by him). Luke's emblem is a bull.

(Coloss. 4; 2 Timothy 4; Philemon)

**Maccabees**   A family of rebels, high priests and kings who dominated Palestine for five generations and 100 years (164-63 BC) with Jerusalem as their capital. They created an independent state out of the disintegration of the Seleucid empire in Syria and lost it to the Romans in the person of Pompey.

Under the successors of Alexander the Great Palestine was debatable ground between the dynasties founded by two of his generals – the Seleucids based in Damascus and the Ptolemies in Alexandria. The former prevailed (198 BC). Under Antiochus III, who visited Jerusalem, and his sons Seleucus IV (187-176 BC) and Antiochus IV (176-164 BC) Palestine was governed by priests whose feuds with one another, sometimes murderous, gave the Seleucid monarchs ample opportunity for intervention and manipulation. In 167 BC the corruption of these priestly cliques, the humiliations which they brought upon Israel and the increasingly unbearable behaviour of the mad Antiochus IV (who believed himself to be Zeus, desecrated the Temple by putting in it a statue of himself as Zeus, and pillaged it because he was short of cash), caused a revolt which was led by Mattathias, the founder of the Maccabee dynasty. Although not of the royal line of *David, Mattathias inspired a movement of national regeneration and liberation which set his grandson on a throne.

Of Mattathias' sons the most famous, *Judas –
nicknamed Maccabeus or Hammer – took Jerusalem in 164 BC and ruled there until his death in
battle four years later. He was succeeded by two
brothers: **Jonathan, who continued the war
against Syria until he was killed in 142 B C, and
*Simon, who ruled after him until 134 B C. Both
secured the office of high priest which they made
hereditary in their family, thus displacing the line
of *Zadok which had monopolized it since the
time of *Solomon. Simon's son John Hyrcanus
(134-104 BC) fought Israel's ancient *Edomite
enemies as well as Syria and took the title of king,
but the decline of Maccabee power and character
began with him. His elder son Aristobulus pursued the Maccabee policy of territorial expansion,
coupled with forcible conversion to Judaism, but
died after a year and was followed by his brother
Alexander Jannaeus (103-76 BC), in whose time
foreign wars became crossed with civil conflict
and sectarian feuds. One sect, the *Pharisees,
turned for help to Syria – the recurring factor in
the life of Israel and Judah for a thousand years.
Alexander and the rival sect of the *Sadducees
survived reverses at the hands of this coalition and
counter-attacked sucessfully against Syria to the
north and Edom (Idumaea) to the south. Alexander was the builder of the fortress at Masada by
the Dead Sea which, strengthened by *Herod the
Great, was the last refuge of the Jewish revolt
against the Romans in AD 66-70; it did not
surrender until, AD 74 when all its inmates except
five women and two children died in a mass
suicide. (Explored in 1963-65, Masada yielded
ancient texts of Biblical Books, supplementing the
equally exciting discoveries at Qumran in 1947-
56.) Alexander was succeeded by his widow
Alexandra as monarch and by his feeble son
Hyrcanus as high priest. A younger son, Aristobulus II, displaced Hyrcanus as high priest and
succeeded his mother on the throne in 67 BC. He
was the last Maccabee king. Four years later
Pompey extinguished the Maccabee kingdom and
restored the accommodating Hyrcanus as a pup-

pet high priest. Palestine entered on a long stretch as part of the Roman empire, ruled either by satellite princes (like the *Herods) or by Roman governors. Four Books of the Maccabees have survived. 1 Maccabees is a history of the years from the accession of Antiochus IV to the death of Simon (175-134 BC). 2 Maccabees covers the earlier part of the same period. 3 and 4 Maccabees are later works, not included in the Bible. See also Judas Maccabaeus and family tree E.
(I and 2 Maccabees).

**Magdalene, Mary**   See Mary.

**Magog**   A son of *Japhet. See Gog.
(Genesis 10)

**Maher-shala-hash-baz**   A son of *Isaiah.
(Isaiah 8).

**Malachi**   The name of the last Book in the OT but not the name of a man – *malachi* means messenger. The author shared the concern of the later Prophets to keep the Israelites up to the mark in their religious observances. He was almost as virulent as *Obadiah against the *Edomites and exhibited the nationalism and separateness engendered by the Babylonian Exile. Yet he was also more tolerant towards worshippers of other gods, maintaining that, although these were not gods, their followers might be brought within the mercy of the true God if their prayers and offerings, however misdirected, had been sincere. Malachi's prescriptions are those of a man who is nice but muddled. He presents a picture of decay and incoherence which may be retrieved through observances of the Judaic law and the long-suffering mercy of the God of Israel. Malachi provided (chapter 3) a text for some of the most memorable passages in Handel's *Messiah*. See also Prophets.
(Malachi)

**Malchus**    A servant of the high priest, who was present when *Jesus was arrested in the garden of Gethsemane and whose right ear was cut off in the accompanying scuffle. Jesus commanded the assailant, whom *John named as *Peter, to desist and according to *Luke healed the ear. In the cathedral at Naumburg the so-called Master of Naumburg carved in C 13 the betrayal of Jesus in a scene which gives the greatest prominence to the severance of the ear.
(John 18)

**Mamre**    An *Amorite who, with his brothers Eshcol and Aner, was a friend and ally of *Abraham against the kings of the east (see under *Amraphel). Mamre was also the name of the place in Hebron where Mamre lived.
(Genesis 14, 18, 23, 35)

**Manasseh**    Elder of the two sons of **Joseph and Asenath. When presenting his sons to his father *Jacob, Joseph took Manasseh by his left hand and *Ephraim by his right, but Jacob laid his right hand on Ephraim's head and his left on Manasseh's. Joseph, displeased, tried to get Jacob to do the opposite but Jacob refused, saying that the younger would be greater than the elder. Both Joseph's sons became progenitors of separate tribes among the twelve tribes of Israel. Manasseh's tribal territory was divided, part east and part west of the Jordan. See family tree C.
(Genesis 41, 48, 50; Joshua 4, 13-17, 22)

**Manoah**    Father of *Samson. His wife was barren but an angel told him that she would bear a deliverer of Israel. Only when the angel came a second time and ascended to heaven in the flame of the burnt sacrifice did Manoah and his wife know that their visitor was a messenger from God. Rembrandt did many drawings for a picture of Manoah sacrificing, but the resulting work (Dresden, Art Gallery) has been regarded by art historians as only very partially his.

(Judges 13)

**Mark**  Evangelist and saint. His gospel stands second in the NT but is widely (if not unanimously) placed first in point of time. It is therefore the oldest written account of the ministry and passion of *Jesus. Whether Mark himself appears in the NT, otherwise than as an author, is dubious. There is a Mark in 1 Peter and a *John Mark in Acts and elsewhere, but neither can be identified with the evangelist with any confidence. There is, however, a traditional association of Mark with *Peter, and Mark was long supposed to have got much of his information from the apostle. It is, however, just as likely that he derived it from the general body of talk about Jesus prevalent between the time of the crucifixion and c. AD 70 when he wrote his gospel. Another tradition asserts that Mark was the founder of the Church in Alexandria and was martyred there. His emblem is the lion which can be seen all over Venice since, in AD 829, that city acquired his suppposed remains and placed them in the partiarchal church which bears his name.

Mark's gospel is the shortest as well as the earliest of the canonical four. It begins with a brief account of the preaching of *John the Baptist, his baptism of Jesus and the temptation of Jesus by Satan. After this preface it falls into two main parts of unequal length, concerned with Jesus' career as a teacher and, secondly, his arrest, trial, Crucifixion and Resurrection. While the second of these parts is a chronological narrative, the former is selective and purposeful rather than biographical. Mark has none of the genealogical passages of **Matthew and Luke or their interest in the infancy of Jesus. His purpose in relating Jesus' activities in Galilee and round about was to make the point that Jesus was not only no ordinary man but no ordinary prophet or teacher: that he was divine and that the Crucifixion and Resurrection in which his life culminated were unique events of unprecedented moment. That multitudes should flock to hear Jesus was one thing; but more telling than the drawing powers were the miracles which he performed and the moral prophetic lessons which, mainly in veiled parables, he addressed to the crowds and more explicitly to his chosen but often puzzled disciples. Half way through his preaching career – whose length is nowhere stated, another non-biographical trait – occurred the Transfiguration when Jesus was transformed into a personage of dazzling whiteness and, in the presence of three of his disciples, spoke with **Moses and Elijah. After this revelation Jesus outspokenly acknowledged his divinity which, up to this point, the disciples had been slow to grasp; and before his entry into Jerusalem, an almost formal procession to his Last Supper and death there, he spoke solemnly and at unusual length about the end of the world, his second coming and the Day of Judgement. Alongside these event and preparations – his contacts with crowds, his miraculous cures of humble people, his teaching in picturesque parables and his messianic revelations – was the running conflict with the serious but narrow-minded orthodox *Pharisees who dogged his movements, tried to trap him into damning remarks and finally secured his temporal downfall. Mark's simple non-literary style (more literary in most translations than in the original Greek) conceals a sense of drama which blossomed in his account of the trial and Crucifixion, of the empty tomb, Jesus' appearances to *Mary Magdalene and the disciples, and his final charge to the disciples to carry on his work. It was for this climax that Mark wrote his gospel.

Mark alone records the presence at Jesus' arrest of a young man in a white cloth who followed Jesus when all others fled but was attacked and forced to flee naked. It has been suggested that this young man was Mark himself. If so, he has inserted himself modestly in his own work like the artists or donors who appear unobtrusively in Italian Renaissance pictures or Alfred Hitchcock who does likewise in his films.

In two pictures Tintoretto painted the drama of the finding of the saint's body by Venetians (Milan, Brera) and their removal of it from Alexandria in spite of Egyptian attempts to stop them (Venice, Academy). Venice is the place to see him – preaching by Carpaccio (Academy), in mosaics outside and inside St. Mark's, and above all in a sequence of C 13 mosaics in the Cappella Zeno, the chapel where his body was first put when brought from Alexandria. According to a story in the Golden Legend Mark had a long nose, a fine fluffy beard and beautiful eyes. (The Golden Legend is a collection of stories made and published in C 13 by the Dominican archbishop, James of Voragine. An English translation was one of Caxton's first publications.) (Mark)

**Martha**  Sister of **Mary and Lazarus who lived in the house of *Simon the leper in Bethany. The sisters had contrasted characters. Martha was for ever busy and when *Jesus came to stay with them she complained that Mary was not pulling her weight. She asked Jesus to tell Mary to help her but he replied that Mary had chosen well in preferring to minister to him rather than perform general household chores. According to later legends preserved in the Golden Legend (for which see under Mark), Martha came of the royal line of Syria; went, after Jesus's ascension, to Marseilles in a boat without sails or oars; tamed a dragon from Tarascon; and worked miracles from her tomb, including the cure of King Clovis from kidney disease.
(Matthew 26; Mark 14; Luke 10; John 11 , 12)

**MARY**  The name of the mother of *Jesus; of Mary Magdalene; and of Mary of Bethany, all of whom are noted below. The Marys at the foot of the cross at the Crucifixion included, by agreement of all four evangelists, the first two of these. *John says that there were three Mary's, the third being the sister of Mary mother of Jesus and wife of Cleopas. These lists can be reconciled only by supposing that John's third Mary is identical with the third woman mentioned by the other evangelists whom, however, they identify as the mother of the sons of *Zebedee, called elsewhere not Mary but *Salome. Luke introduces yet another woman called Joanna. These discrepancies are confusing but it is nevertheless clear that these women, or some of them, repaired at the end of the Sabbath to the tomb where Jesus' body had been put by *Joseph of Arimathea. They found the sepulchre empty and were told, either by an angel or by Jesus himself, to instruct the disciples to go to Galilee where Jesus would meet them. (Matthew 27, 28; Mark 15, 16; Luke 24; John 19, 20)

**Mary**    Mother of *Jesus. She was the virgin wife of *Joseph, himself descended from the royal line of *David and from the patriarchs. Her own lineage is not recorded in the canonical Gospels although her parents are named as Joachim and Ann in the apocryphal Book of James. She learned from the archangel Gabriel that she would conceive a child of the Holy Ghost, his name to be Jesus. She went to visit her cousin *Elizabeth who was pregnant with the future *John the Baptist, and in Elizabeth's house Mary declaimed the hymn of praise and thanks to God known as the Magnificat. Joseph being obliged to go to Bethlehem for a census of tax payers, Mary went with him and there gave birth to Jesus in a manger since there was no room at the inn. From Bethlehem Joseph, warned by an angel, fled with his family to Egypt to escape the murderous design of *Herod the Great. He and his family stayed in Egypt until Herod died, when they returned to Nazareth in Galilee. Joseph died a few years later. Mary was present at the wedding at Cana in Galilee but is not again in evidence until the last phase of Jesus' life when she followed her son to Jerusalem, was at the foot of the cross at the Crucifixion, and discovered with *Mary Magdalene and other women the empty tomb at the end of the sabbath. From the cross Jesus commended Mary to the care of his beloved disciple (*sc.* *John) who took her to live with him, and she was with the apostles at Jesus' ascension. Of her death and her supposedly bodily ascension into heaven the Bible says nothing, but report has it that she died in Ephesus where John too is said to have died and where her house may still be visited.

Portrayals – mosaic, sculpted, painted – of Mary (the Madonna) with Jesus have been a central feature of Christian iconography from very early times and still are. They are to be numbered not in thousands but in tens of thousands. Hardly less popular are the principal scenes from her life: the Annunciation, the Nativity, the flight into Egypt. Occasionally Mary appears on her own, even somewhat ordinarily – for example, in Zurbaran's picture of her as a charming little girl (Leningrad, Hermitage) and Rossetti's similar conception of her (London, Tate Gallery). Devotional poetry has focussed on her no less, particularly as intercessor between mankind and a stern God: from innumerable hymns and songs, mediaeval and modern, to more sophisticated if no less emotional evocations such as Claudel's *L'annonce faite à Marie* (to which Darius Mihaud appended incidental music). Despite their dubious status Joachim and Ann appear in Christian art, e.g. Carpaccio's picture of them (Venice, Academy). The legend of their meeting after a long separation (Joachim had run away into the desert because he was taunted with his childlessness and ill used by the priests of the Temple) at Jerusalem's Golden Gate is touchingly depicted by Giotto in the cloisters of S. Maria Novella in Florence. Ruskin who, unlike other critics, had no doubts about Giotto's hand here, used this picture as a peg for one of his *Mornings in Florence*, an early guidebook in buttonholing

style. The same scene may be seen in two other Florentine churches by Taddeo Gaddi in S. Croce and by Lorenzo Monaco in S. Trinità.
(Matthew I, 2, 27, 28; Mark 15, 16; Luke 1, 2, 24; John 19; Acts I)

**Mary of Bethany**     Sister of \*\*Martha and Lazarus who lived in the house of \*Simon the leper in Bethany where \*Jesus came to lodge. While Martha busied herself with domestic chores Mary preferred to give personal attention to Jesus. Martha complained that Mary was not pulling her weight but Jesus replied that Mary had chosen well. On a later occasion in the same house a woman poured precious ointment over Jesus' head and wiped his feet with her hair. \*John identifies her as Mary, although other accounts imply that she was somebody else (see Mary Magdalene). The disciples were shocked by what seemed to them a scandalous waste since the ointment could have been sold and the money given to the poor – John says that the disciple who voiced their protest was \*Judas Iscariot – but Jesus corrected them: 'Ye have the poor always with you; but me ye have not always.'
(Matthew 26; Mark 14; Luke 10; John 11, 12)

**Mary Magdalene**     Also known as Mary of Magdala, the prototype of the reformed prostitute and a principal witness of the Resurrection. The first part of her claim to fame is very insecurely grounded. She has been identified as the unnamed woman, described by \*Luke, who found out that \*Jesus was eating in a Pharisee's house and went and washed his feet in her tears, wiped them with her hair and poured ointment on them. (A similar story is told of \*Mary of Bethany who poured ointment over Jesus' head in the house of \*Simon the leper). No good evidence has survived for calling this woman Mary Magdalene but from C 6 at the latest the equation has been widely believed.

Cured of certain evil spirits and illnesses, Mary seems to have followed Jesus and she was one of the women who witnessed the Crucifixion from the foot of the cross and afterwards went to Jesus' tomb and found it empty. Her role at the Resurrection is vividly described by *John who – assuming that he is the 'disciple whom Jesus loved' mentioned with modest anonymity in this passage of his Gospel – was observer and actor in part of the scene which he describes. Mary came alone to the tomb while it was still dark and saw that the stone in front of it had been rolled away and that the tomb was empty. She found *Peter and John, who rushed to see for themselves. After they had gone away again Mary was left there weeping and saw a man whom she took to be a gardener. She asked him if he had taken the body and, if so, where to. He was, however, no gardener but Jesus, who said to her 'Touch me not (*noli me tangere*)... but go to my brethren, and say to them, I ascend unto my Father ...' The most famous representation of this scene is Titian's (London, National Gallery) but there are very many others, e.g. by Fra Angelico (Florence, S. Marco), Correggio (Madrid, Prado) and Holbein (Palace of Hampton Court). Mary is also portrayed as the quintessential penitent: Titian again (Leningrad, Hermitage and Florence, Pitti), Donatello (Florence, Baptistery) and Jan Scorel (Amsterdam, Rijksmuseum). Tintoretto put her into a dramatic landscape (Venice, S. Rocco), Giorgione in a less dramatic one (Madrid, Prado). A drawing by Rosso Fiorentino shows her arriving with a throng of friends for a rowdy party at her house but turning aside to the next-door house where Jesus can be glimpsed through a window – supposedly the turning point in her life. Georges de la Tour gives a different version of the same fateful moment: his Magdalene is looking at herself in the mirror, with sundry symbolic objects round about (New York, Metropolitan Museum). Daumier's Magdalene is very penitent and very nude. Vaughan's poem *St Mary Magdalen* is

about the salving power of love. Christina Rossetti's *Mary Magdalene and the other Mary. A Song for all Maries* is a lullaby for Jesus. She is the Magna Peccatrix in the final scene of Goethe's Faust – which Mahler set as the second of the two movements of his eighth symphony. At the beginning of Sardou 's play and Puccini's opera, Mario Cavaradossi is discovered painting a picture of the Magdalene in the likeness of his beloved Floria Tosca. The question whether she should have an 'e' at the end of her name or not is one of the matters in dispute between the universities of Oxford and Cambridge, where the colleges dedicated to her bear the rival spellings.
(Matthew 27, 28; Mark 15, 16; Luke 8; John 19, 20)

**Mattathias**  Son of Hasmon and founder of the Maccabee dynasty; also called Hasmonean. See Maccabees and family tree E.
(Maccabees 2)

**Matthew**  One of the twelve apostles (see glossary), also called Levi son of Alphaeus. He is not named by *John. He was a tax collector in the service of the tetrarch of Galilee, Herod *Antipas, but not the *Matthew who wrote the first Gospel. Like other apostles, e.g. **Andrew, Thomas, he has been credited with far-flung and fantastic missionary activities after *Jesus' death – in his case into Persia or even Ethiopia (where he lodged with the eunuch of queen *Candace who had been baptized by the deacon Philip). The calling of Matthew by Terbruggen is in Utrecht, his martyrdom by Caravaggio in S. Luigi dei Francesi in Rome. He is traditionally depicted carrying a purse – as a publican. See also the next entry.
(Matthew 10; Mark 3; Luke 6; Acts I)

**Matthew**  Evangelist and saint. In early times the authorship of the first Gospel was ascribed to the apostle

*Matthew, but since this view has been demolished we are left with an evangelist who, distinct from the apostle, must nevertheless continue to be called Matthew since we have no other name for him. He was in all probability a Greek-speaking Jew of Syria who wrote towards the end of the decade AD 75-85. His Gospel is an edited and enlarged version of *Mark's. Nine tenths of Mark is reproduced in Matthew, abbreviated but often in the same words. (Luke, by contrast, reproduced only about half of Mark.) To this core Matthew added a beginning and an end: the genealogy and childhood of *Jesus, and a fuller account of his appearances to the apostles and others after the Resurrection. The source of these additions, some of which are common to Matthew and Luke, may have been some other document now lost or common current talk. Matthew's distinctive approach to the life and death of Jesus is the belief that Jesus was the Jewish Messiah and son of *David who had come to inaugurate the kingdom of Heaven as foretold in the OT and Jewish tradition. He is the most concerned of all the evangelists with Jesus' human antecedents and humanity, whence his emblem is a man. See also the foregoing entry.
(Matthew)

**Matthias**  One of two candidates – the successful one – to fill the place among the twelve apostles made vacant by the treason of *Judas Iscariot. He won his place by lot against *Joseph Barsabas.
(Acts I)

**Melchizedek**  Priest-king of Salem who blessed *Abraham and is said to have received in return a tithe of the spoils of Abraham's victory over his enemies. It is not certain that Melchizedek is a personal name, and the OT offers no explanation why the victorious Abraham should have given him anything; it is at least as likely that this strange king should have offered Abraham food and drink on his way back

from his battles to his home. Melchidezek is a mysterious figure who has neither father nor mother and so became a symbol of autogenerative power. His stately, elongated figure is the first to catch the eye as you begin to take in the great north porch of Chartres.
(Genesis 14; Hebrews 7)

**Mephi-bosheth**    Son of *Jonathan, son of Saul. He was five years old when his father was killed. As he was being hurried to safety he was dropped and lamed for life in both feet. *David subsequently sought him out and, for the love of his father Jonathan, endowed him with land and made him a permanent guest at his table. In later years Mephi-bosheth became implicated in *Absalom's unsuccessful rebellion against David, but David forgave him.
(2 Samuel 9, 16, 19)

**Merab**    The elder of *Saul's two daughters. She was promised by her father to *David but then given to somebody else. David got instead the younger daughter *Michal, who at first loved him but later became ashamed of his exuberant religiousness.
(1 Samuel 14, 18)

**Meshach**    One of the three friends of *Daniel who were thrown into a fiery furnace by command of *Nebuchadnezzar. He was originally called Mishael. His two friends were **Abed-nego and Shadrach.
(Daniel 2, 3)

**Methuselah**    'Man of the javelin' and synonym for longevity. He lived 969 years. *Lamech, his first son and the father of *Noah, was born when he was 187. Noah failed to reach his grandfather's age by a mere 19 years and Methuselah retained the Biblical record. There are a number of explanations for the incredible lifespans attributed to the patriarchs. None of them is convincing. Shaw's *Back to Methuselah*, described by himself as a 'metabiological Pentateuch', and as a 'legend of Creative Evolution', is a series of plays ranging over Man's past and future, as seen by Shaw. (Genesis 5)

**Micah** Prophet, a Judaean countryman who lived towards the end of the C 8 BC when **Amos and Hosea were active in neighbouring Israel. Micah was specially agitated by the poverty of the tillers of the soil, championed the poor against the rich and the countryside against the town, and joined in the general denunciation of vice, materialism and the decay of family life. He preached repentance before it was too late with the urgency of one who believes that time is running out. He is one of the most passionate voices in the OT, a revolutionary who cast his emotions and aspirations in religious form. See also Prophets and the next entry. (Micah)

**Micah** A young man who stole the silver which his mother had accumulated in order to make a graven and molten image. Micah owned up and gave the money back, whereupon his mother used a small part of her hoard for the making of the image. An itinerant *Levite came to Micah's house and Micah persuaded him to stay and live with him as his priest. But a band of *Danites, who were looking for land, carried off the Levite and also Micah's vestments and images. The Danites seized a city and there installed the Levite with his priestly gear. Micah was a victim of the

Danites' unsatisfied land hunger. See also the
previous entry.
(Judges 17, 18)

**Micaiah**    A prophet who alone among his sycophantic
fellow prophets refused to promise *Ahab victory
in his proposed campaign against Syria. Ahab had
him thrown into prison but in the ensuing battle
Ahab was killed.
(I Kings 22; 2 Chron. 18)

**Michal**    Younger daughter of *Saul who gave her as wife
to *David but subsequently took her away and
gave her to somebody else. David recovered her
after Saul's death, much to the sorrow of her
intervening husband. When David in great glee
brought the ark of the covenant to Jerusalem,
Michal looking out of a window saw him 'leaping
and dancing' before it. She despised him and later
taxed him with demeaning himself. For this lack
of understanding she was condemned never to
have a child.
(I Samuel 18-19; 2 Samuel 16; I Chron. 15)

**Midianites**    A people of mixed reputation allegedly descended
from **Abraham and his second wife *Keturah.
They were herdsmen and merchants who also
practised raiding and pillage. *Moses took refuge
among them as a young man and found a wife
among them. They lived in the sparse lands
between Egypt and Palestine.

**Milcah**    Daughter of *Haran and a central point in the
relationships of this much intermarried family,
since she married her father's brother *Nahor, by
whom she produced a grand-daughter *Rebecca

who would marry the son (*Isaac) of her other uncle *Abraham – all of which is displayed diagramatically in family tree B.
(Genesis 11, 22, 24)

**Miriam**  Sister of *Aaron and half-sister of *Moses. She was a leader in the dancing and music-making with which the Israelites celebrated their miraculous passage of the Red Sea and escape from the pursuing Egyptians. With Aaron she criticized Moses both for his leadership in the wilderness and for taking an Ethiopian wife, for which disloyalty she was afflicted with leprosy and temporarily expelled from the camp. She died in Kadesh in the desert of Sinai shortly before the Israelites' last push which ended their long years in the desert and set them on their way into the Promised Land.
(Exodus 15; Numbers 12, 20)

**Moab**  One of the two sons of *Lot whom his daughters, alarmed by advancing years and their isolation, got Lot to father on them when he was too drunk to know what he was doing. Moab was the ancestor of the *Moabites, his half-brother *Ben-ammi of the *Ammonites. The lands of the Moabites and Ammonites were east of the Dead Sea and south of the river Arnon which flows into it half way between its two ends. See family tree B.
(Genesis 19)

**Moabites**  The descendants of *Moab: see above.

**Mordecai**  A *Benjaminite in the empire of *Ahasuerus and uncle of *Esther, the queen. He was a porter outside the palace. There he overheard a plot

against the king which he revealed, so saving the king's life – and, as it turned out, his own. He refused to bow to the King's favourite *Haman and in revenge for this slight Haman planned the liquidation of all the Jews in the 127 provinces of Ahasuerus' empire. But the king, who had carelessly sanctioned Haman's designs, discovered more precisely what was afoot – which included the death of his Jewish queen. He also discovered how Mordecai had saved his life. The tables were turned, Haman was disgraced and hanged, and Mordecai was promoted to his high offices and fortunes. Mordecai is a symbol of the mutability of fortune: his Benjaminite ancestry was aristocratic, he had become a servile gate-keeper in a alien empire, he rose to power and riches through probity (allied with some skill in keeping an ear to the ground) and the better sort of patriotism. The Triumph of Mordecai by Veronese (Venice, San Sebastiano) is a puzzling picture since the painter seems more interested in two large horses than in the central character.
(Esther; The Rest of Esther)

**Moses**  Son of Amran of the tribe of *Levi. Between the arrival in Egypt of *Joseph and his brethren and the mass Exodus of their descendants several hundred years passed. In that time the children of Israel prospered and multiplied but also aroused envy and, as one Pharaoh succeeded another, lost their favoured position. Where Joseph had been an honoured immigrant and valued counsellor, his descendants were virtually slaves. From this oppression they were rescued by Moses.

***Moses and Pharaoh***  The pharaoh at the time of Moses' birth had resolved to exterminate the Israelites by having all their male children killed. A directive to midwives to do this was ineffective because, as the midwives reported, the Israelite women were sturdy enough to give birth unaided. The pharaoh then ordered that all the male children be thrown into the river; but Moses was saved by the compassion of a princess. He was put beside the river in a basket made of bulrushes where he was found by the pharaoh's daughter. She resolved to bring up the child and when she sent to find a nurse for it Moses' sister (who had been secretly watching the discovery at the water's edge) guided the servant to Moses' mother. While still a youth Moses came upon an Egyptian belabouring an Israelite. He killed the Egyptian and was forced to flee into the desert where he took refuge with nomad *Midianites and married one of them, *Zipporah (daughter of the priest *Jethro) who bore him two sons, Gershom and Eliezer. An angel appeared to Moses and spoke to him out of a burning bush that burned without being consumed. The angel told Moses that he was to save the children of Israel and lead them to a land flowing with milk and honey. Moses was reluctant to believe in this destiny and afraid that the Israelites would never believe him when he told them what he was charged to do. He pleaded his inexpertness in the art of public speaking. God showed him three miracles with which he would convince the Israelites and advised Moses to leave the talking to his brother *Aaron. So Moses set out to return to Egypt and on the way met Aaron and told him all his story. Aaron performed the miracles and persuaded the Israelites that they must follow Moses.

The next step was to persuade the pharaoh – a new one who had succeeded the one from whom Moses had fled – to 'let my people go'. But the pharaoh's first reply to this plea was to increase the burdens of the Israelites by commanding them to make their quotas of bricks without being provided with straw. When Aaron's rod turned miraculously into a serpent before the pharaoh's eyes, he ordered the Egyptian sages to try the same trick with their rods. These too turned into serpents but Aaron's serpent gobbled up their serpents. Plague upon plague – ten in all – befell the Egyptians and after each one the pharaoh decided to let the Israelites go but then changed his mind, until the tenth plague – the death in a single night of all the firstborn of the Egyptians and their animals – broke his resistance.

*Exodus* For this eventuality the children of Israel were prepared. On God's instructions each family had procured and sacrificed an unblemished lamb or kid, smeared its blood on their door posts as a sign to the angel of death to leave that house unscathed, ate their meal of roast meat and unleavened bread in readiness to depart with staff in hand and in urgent haste; and then set out, taking with them Joseph's bones and guided by a pillar of fire at night and a pillar of smoke by day. Their obvious route was northward to the Mediterranean coast, but they chose instead to go east to the Red Sea in order to throw the Egyptians off the scent. The pharaoh, having once more repented of his decision to let them go, gave chase with 600 chariots, but the Red Sea dried up to let the Israelites pass and then closed again over the Egyptians and drowned them all. Safe across, the Israelites celebrated with song and dance – and began to complain: the water was undrinkable and they had no food. Moses conjured sweet water out of a rock and God sent them manna – which was to be their food for 40 years – and quails. (Manna was probably a waxy exudation of the tamarisk tree, but to the Israelites 'who wist not what it was', it was miraculous.) But their troubles had only just begun. Enemies appeared. In the first of many engagements in his long military career *Joshua defeated the *Amalekites in a battle which was decided by the gestures of Moses watching from a hilltop: so long as he held up his arms the Israelites won and when he got tired Aaron and Hur held them up for him.

In the third month of their travels the Israelites reached the desert of Sin and Mount Sinai. There Moses encountered God. After three days of preparatory ceremonies he went up the mountain and God came down onto it amid fearsome natural phenomena and spoke to Moses in the hearing of all. The Israelites as a whole were told to keep their distance; Aaron and his two elder sons and 70 selected elders went part way, but only Moses came near to God. God gave him the Ten Commandments and 'divers laws and ordinances' and penalites to go with their breach. Moses was given two tablets of stone written on both sides 'with the finger of God' and also long and detailed instructions for the making of an ark (see glossary) to contain the tables of the Law and God's covenant with *Abraham and much sacred furniture and ornaments and garments, all of gold and gorgeous materials. Moses remained on the mountain for 40 days and 40 nights and during this extended absence disaster struck. The Israelites became impatient and asked Aaron to make them a god, which he did by turning their golden earrings and other ornaments into a golden calf, which they worshipped naked (this golden calf may have been the Egyptian bull-god Apis which the Israelites were supposed to have left behind them on the other side of the Red Sea). Moses, not for last time, found himself in a quandary, caught between a God whom he had to appease and a people whom he had to chastise. Hurrying down the mountain to the scene of the crime and outraged by what he found, he threw the tables of stone onto the ground and broke them. He ordered 3,000 *Levites to be killed. But he saved everybody else, got the two tables of stone replaced by God and secured a renewal of God's undertaking on the Promised Land.

*In the Wilderness*    The redemption of this promise took longer than the Israelites had ever imagined and the longer they wandered in the desert the more disgruntled did they become and the more testing became the challenge to Moses' leadership. The wandering sapped their morale and led them to rebel against Moses on several occasions. Their privations made them wish that they had never left Egypt; they pined for fish, cucumbers, melons, leeks, onions and garlic; their faith wilted and they complained that they were taking far too long to enter the land flowing with milk and honey. Even Moses' nearest and dearest – his brother and sister, Aaron and *Miriam – turned against him (although part of the reason was their private objection to his having taken an Ethiopian wife). God sustained Moses' authority by a series of miracles. He intervened to rally the spirits of 70 picked elders. He afflicted Miriam with leprosy. He suppressed the serious revolt of **Korah, Dathan and Abiram, whom the earth swallowed up alive with all their kin and cattle. He allowed Moses to extract water from a rock at a moment of acute drought and caused Aaron's rod to blossom and produce almonds. But God was also greatly angered by the Israelites' moaning and lack of faith after all He had done for them: 'How long shall I bear with this evil generation?' He sent plagues which killed 14,700 of them on one occasion and 24,000 on another. He decreed that none of those who had left Egypt should enter the Promised Land but that they should wander in the wilderness for 40 years until the whole of that generation had died. The only exceptions were Joshua and *Caleb who had argued for persevering against the odds notwithstanding their discovery on a hazardous spying expedition that the Promised Land was indeed flowing with milk and honey but was also powerfully defended by giants. Even Moses and Aaron were debarred from the Promised Land for some shortage of faith which the Bible does not make clear. Aaron died on Mount Hor as Moses was preparing to lead the Israelites on the last stage of their journey northward to where they would have 'one more river to cross and that the river of Jordan'.

| | |
|---|---|
| ***Towards the Promised Land*** | The Israelites were numbered for a second time. Apart from the *Levites, who were numbered separately, the able-bodied male adults – those over 20 who were able to go to war – were 601,730. Forty years earlier in Sinai they had numbered 603,550. They skirted the lands of *Edom, Moab and Ammon which, although inhospitable, Moses was instructed not to harm since their peoples were kinsmen descended from **Esau and Lot. Beyond the Arnon, which flows into the Dead Sea from the east half way up its |

length, they had to do battle with *Sihon, king of
the Amorites, and *Og, the king of Bashan – the
one east of the Dead Sea and the other east of the
Sea of Galilee. These kings were separately defeated and so *Balak, another king, resolved to
assemble a coalition against the people who 'had
come out of Egypt' and were 'covering the face of
the earth'; but Balak was thwarted by *Balaam
who, although repeatedly pressed to curse the
Israelites, ended by blessing them. Moses divided
the conquered lands east of the Jordan among the
tribes of Reuben and Gad and half the tribe of
Manasseh, who found there just what they
wanted for their flocks and herds, but he imposed
on them the condition that their fighting men
should accompany the other tribes across the
Jordan for the conquest of the Promised Land.
Besides foreshadowing the partition of their conquests these victories on the east bank of the
Jordan also gave warning of a dilemma which was
to plague the Israelites for generations to come:
their relations with the existing inhabitants. God
told them to destroy these peoples utterly, but not
all the Israelites proved immune to the attractions
of their women and, later, their gods – the
incident of the Midianitish prostitute *Cozbi was
an early example of human frailty leading to
disaster, and when in the war against the
Midianites women and children were spared
Moses was commanded to intervene and see that
all women who were not virgins and all male
children were duly killed. God and Moses repeated the warning that as soon as the Israelites
crossed the Jordan all the peoples whom they
failed to dispossess and expel would be 'pricks in
your eyes and thorns in your sides'. Moses
delivered a solemn valedictory address, rehearsing
the history of the Israelites since the Exodus from
Egypt and the ordinances – including the Ten
Commandments – proclaimed to them during
their years in the wilderness. He then went up
Mount Nebo to Pisgah where he was granted a
sight of the Promised Land and, on the day when
Joshua led the Israelites over Jordan, died. The site

**Moses'**
**great work**

of his burial was unknown.

Moses is an awesome figure. His place in the history of the Israelites is subordinate to none. He was God's instrument in conveying God's Chosen People from their serfdom in Egypt back to the lands of their patriarchs (see glossary). He was also a disappointed man who was not allowed himself to enter the Promised Land, and a lonely man who spent the last 40 years of his life sandwiched between a driving God and a driven people. In the end he is too much God's mouthpiece to be a sympathetic human figure: he lacks an individual personality. His massiveness is an invitation to sculptors rather than painters and no sculptor has realized it more powerfully than Michelangelo whose statue of Moses was meant to be part of the tomb of Pope Julius II (Rome, San Pietro in Vinculi). Freud spent hours gazing at his work and wrote a short essay on its recondite meanings and on what previous tourists had made of them. The whole of one side of the Sistine Chapel in the Vatican is devoted to scenes from the life of Moses (the other side has scenes from the life of *Jesus) by the greatest painters of the Italian Renaissance. Artists have regarded the finding of the infant Moses by the river as an event of such great moment as to require the presence of quite a crowd: thus Veronese (Madrid, Prado and Washington National Gallery), Tintoretto (Prado), Claude (Prado) and Claude's contemporary Bourdon (Washington, National Gallery). Gentileschi (Prado) includes the pharaoh's mother and daughter. For Salvator Rosa the great event has become an excuse for painting a larger landscape in the burgeoning naturalistic style of C 17 (Detroit, Institute of Art). Rosso Fiorentino purported to depict Moses with the daughters of Jethro, but Moses, hugely labouring, relegates the daughters to a distant background (Florence, Uffizi). The seventh plague — thunder and hail — is the subject of one of John Martin's doom-laden extravaganzas (Boston, Museum of Fine Art). Burne-Jones used the story of the burning bush to illustrate the Fire Tree in his Flower Book.

In the Negro Spiritual *Go Down, Moses* God tells Moses to go down into Egypt and 'tell old Pharaoh, let my people go'. William Faulkner took this title for his novel about the tabu of miscegenation; the final tragedy in the clutch of stories which make up the novel is that of the boy, 'sold into Egypt where Pharaoh got him', who becomes a murderer and is brought home in his coffin after being hanged. Handel's oratorio *Israel in Egypt* focuses on the most dramatic part of the story. On the operatic stage Moses has been appropriated by two utterly different composers: Rossini (*Moise*) and Schöenberg (*Moses and Aaron*).

Moses has been commonly depicted with horns sprouting from his head – by Michelangelo among others. This grotesque embellishment is the result of a mistranslation. The Book of Exodus describes Moses coming down from Mount Sinai with his face lit up, but the Hebrew words for beam of light and for horns are very similar and the Latin Vulgate Bible (see Introduction) got it wrong.

Among non-Biblical stories about Moses one has been depicted by Giorgione (Florence, Uffizi). This story explains why he was all his life a bad speaker. When he was three years old the pharaoh was advised to have him killed but decided first to subject the child to an ordeal by fire. He was shown a ruby and a burning coal. If he took the ruby he would be killed. He stretched out his hand for it but an angel deflected him so that he took the coal; but he burnt his tongue with it

Some 20 years after his essay on Michelangelo's statue Freud began to work out an even stranger story. He speculated that Moses was an Egyptian, a high official or general of the monotheist pharaoh Ikhnaton (c. 1391-53 BC); that he had to flee his country when Ikhnaton's religious revolution collapsed; that he took with him a personal following (who were the *Levites) and the alien Israelites; that the Israelites murdered him in the wilderness; and that his elevated, pacifist religion was there amalgamated with a different and

bellicose religion and almost obliterated by it. Although advanced with careful step-by-step logic and an alluring imagination, this rewriting of the Biblical version of events has been treated by scholars as no more that a curiosity, the intriguing wanderings of a learned mind straying beyond its own cabbage patch.
(Exodus; Leviticus; Numbers; Deuteronomy)

**Naaman** Syrian commander in-chief and a leper. His king sent him to Israel in search of a cure. Naaman was indignant: 'Are not Abana and Pharpar, rivers of Damascus, better than all the waters of Israel?' But he was persuaded to be less chauvinistic and was cured. On his way back to Damascus he was overtaken by Elisha's servant *Gehazi, who wheedled gifts of silver and garments out of him by pretending that Elisha would distribute them as alms. Elisha's insight discovered the deception and he inflicted Naaman's leprosy on Gehazi. Naaman's story has been used as a pretext for painting a lavish landscape by Claude (London, National Gallery) and by the Dutch artist Joos de Momper (Madrid, Prado).
(2 Kings 5; Luke 5)

**Nabal** A wealthy but churlish fellow, owner of thousands of sheep and goats in Carmel. His wife was the beautiful *Abigail. When *David sent ten young men to Nabal with a friendly introduction Nabal received them inhospitably. David gathered a band of 400 to teach Nabal a lesson but was met on the way and appeased by Abigail, who thus deterred him from unseemly slaughter. Nabal, however, did not escape: he was killed by God a few days later, and David married Abigail.
(I Samuel 25)

**Naboth** Owner of a vineyard which was coveted by *Ahab but which Naboth refused to give up because it was part of his family inheritance. Ahab's queen

*Jezebel got the local elders to elevate and honour Naboth and then bring false evidence of blasphemy against him. He was stoned to death. Going to the vineyard, Ahab met *Elijah whom God had sent to meet him there. 'Hast thou found me, O mine enemy?' exclaimed Ahab who was then told that dogs would drink his blood where they had drunk the blood of Naboth.
(I Kings 21; 2 Kings 9)

**Nahash**   King of the *Ammonites, was the first victim of the union of the Israelites under *Saul. When Nahash attacked Jabesh-gilead and threatened to put out the eyes of its leading citizens, Saul raised an army of 330,000 and defeated the Ammonites. After this exploit Saul was formally confirmed at Gilgal as king over all the tribes of Israel.
(I Samuel 11; I Chron. 19)

**Nahor**   One of the three sons of *Terah. The others were **Abraham and Haran. Nahor did not migrate from Ur with Terah and Abraham. He married his niece *Milcah. When Abraham wanted a wife for his son *Isaac he sent to his native land and found Nahor's grand-daughter *Rebecca. This Nahor must not be confused with another, his grandfather. See family tree B.
(Genesis 11)

**Nahum**   Prophet of the late C 7 BC. His Book is infused with a bitter hatred of *Assyria and revels in graphic description of the coming destruction of Nineveh – which occurred in 612 BC. His writing is bloodthirsty but not unpoetic. With *Zephaniah he is one of *Isaiah's principal immediate successors. See also Prophets.
(Nahum)

**Naomi**   Wife of *Elimelech and mother-in-law of *Ruth. She and her husband and two sons went from

Bethlehem to *Moab. The sons married Moabitesses and died. Elimelech died too. Naomi decided to return to Bethlehem. Her daughters-in-law started out with her but she adjured them to turn back. They both wept; the one took her advice but the other – Ruth – insisted on staying with her.
(Ruth)

**Napthali**   One of the twelve sons of *Jacob and progenitor of one of the twelve tribes of Israel. He and his brother *Dan were the sons of *Bilhah, the servant of *Rachel. His tribal territory lay between Galilee and the sea. See family tree C.
(Genesis 30, 35, 42-50; Joshua 19)

**Nathan**   Prophet and a leading figure at *David's court. In the contest for the succession to David between his sons **Adonijah and Solomon, Nathan took the side of the latter, engineered David's reaffirmation of Solomon's claim and, with *Zadok the priest, annointed Solomon king.
(I Kings I; I Chron. 17)

**Nathanael of Cana**   Twice named by *John and almost certainly the same as the apostle called by the other evangelists *Bartholomew.
(John 1, 45-50)

**Nebuchadnezzar**   King of Babylon 604-562 BC. This form of his name is a common but incorrect variant of Nebuchadrezzar. He was the most energetic ruler of the last Babylonian empire (see Assyria and Babylon) and made Babylon famous for its trade, architecture, art and astronomy. During his father's reign he was a successful general whose exploits culminated in the defeat of the Egyptians at Carchemish in 605 BC. (Among the foreigners fighting on the Babylonian side was a brother of the Greek poet Alcaeus of Lesbos.) This victory transferred Syria from Egyptian to Babylonian rule and spelt the end of Egypt's power in western Asia and – as *Jeremiah saw – the doom of the kingdom of *Judah. A few months later Nebuchadnezzar became king. His early years as king were occupied with campaigns against the cities of the **Phoenicians and Philistines and, when Judah tried to escape from his overlordship, against Jerusalem too. Jerusalem was taken in 597 BC. A new king, *Zedekiah, was installed and when he too rebelled, against *Jeremiah's advice, his capital was taken, the temple was destroyed and looted, and he was removed to Babylon with other captives (587 BC). After an abortive coup on behalf of the old royal line of Judah in which Nebuchadnezzar's governor in Jerusalem, *Gedaliah, was killed, more captives were deported to Babylon while others – including Jeremiah – fled to Egypt. Nebuchadnezzar's conquests extended into Asia Minor and north Africa and he bequeathed to his son Amel-Marduk (called in the Bible Evil-Merodach) an empire bigger than any of its Assyrian or Babylonian predecessors. But 23 years later it was gone (see Belshazzar).

Nebuchadnezzar was a great builder. His father had raised Babylon from provincial status and he himself repaired it and protected it from flood waters and embellished it with an ostentatious display of authority and pride. He built palaces, temples and halls, laid out streets and constructed canals. With an eye for landscape reminiscent of the gardeners of C 18 England he devised the famous hanging gardens which consisted of terraces and water-courses and exotic trees and were classed by the Greeks as one of the seven wonders of the world. He raised the no less famous ziggurat, a series of tiers and stairways 90 metres high. He paid for these things partly out of "voluntary" contributions and partly by the forced labour of prisoners of war. Late in life he suffered a mysterious illness which caused him to be quarantined and reduced to a vegetarian diet. This was probably some form of madness which made him imagine himself an animal and lasted long enough for his nails to grow into claws, but for pious Jews it was a punishment for flirting with the wrong gods. In religion Nebuchadnezzar was probably an eclectic, searching for the right god and hoping to find an acceptable synthesis. He was attracted to Judaism but only intermittently. Jewish writers created the familiar figure of him in the likeness of an ox eating grass on all fours and ascribed his recovery from this degradation to his reconversion to their religion. William Blake has shown him thus disfigured, naked and humiliated in a drawing in pen and water colour (London, Tate Gallery). Verdi's opera Nabucco is set in the Babylon of Nebuchadnezzar and contains Verdi's version of Psalm 137, "By the waters of Babylon", which was spontaneously sung by the crowd at his funeral 60 years after its first performance. The hanging gardens so enchanted the German Symbolist poet and recluse Stefan George that he named a series of his poems after them. Set to music by Schoenberg, they attest the vitality of the German Lieder tradition.

(2 Kings 24, 25; 2 Chron. 36 ; Ezra 1, 2; Daniel 1-4).

**Nehemiah**    He was with *Ezra the outstanding personage in the return of the Jewish exiles from their *Captivity in Babylon after the conquest of that city by the Persian King, *Cyrus the Great. He was cupbearer to one of Cyrus' successors – most probably Artaxerxes I (king 465-424 BC) – and then governor of Jerusalem for twelve years (445 – 433 BC). The returned exiles were met with hostility by Jews who had remained west of the Jordan during the Captivity as well as by non-Jews. Chief among the latter were Sanballat the Horonite, Tobiah the Ammonite and Geshem the Arabian. These enemies began by mocking Nehemiah's efforts to rebuild the city walls section by section and then angrily attacked him. But Nehemiah succeeded in creating a new Jerusalem and in building what came to be called the Second Temple. He was also a vigorous reformer who

kept the Jews' history before their eyes and ears, carried on Ezra's work of reanimating the Judaic Law, and insisted on rebuking and correcting manifold lapses and abuses – including the practice of mixed marriages, whose strict banning precipitated the secession of the *Samaritans. After Nehemiah's departure the new Judah seems to have subsided into insignificance, but it survived. Ezra and Nehemiah did not restore the kingdom of **David and Solomon but they gave the Jews a new city, a constitution and a future. Nehemiah's grief on contemplating the ruins of Jerusalem which he was to rebuild provided John Martin with precisely that mixture of architectural fancy and human emotion which inspired much of his art – in this instance, one of the series of illustrations to the Bible issued in monthly parts in mid-C 19 London.
(Nehemiah)

**Nicodemus**  A *Pharisee who came to *Jesus at night, being convinced by his miracles that he was a teacher from God. Jesus told him that in order to see the Kingdom of God he must be born again. Puzzled, Nicodemus asked how an old man could be born again or re-enter his mother's womb. Jesus distinguished birth of the flesh from birth of water and spirit (i.e. the rebirth given by baptism), but Nicodemus remained puzzled. On a later occasion, when the priests and Pharisees were debating what to do about Jesus and his subversive teaching, Nicodemus intervened to argue that Jesus must not be condemned without being heard. After the Crucifixion he helped *Joseph of Arimathea to bury Jesus' body, bringing with him a mixture of myrrh and aloes weighing about a hundred pounds. The apocryphal 'Acts of Pilate' has been ascribed to Nicodemus.
(John 3, 7, 19)

**Nimrod**  Son of *Cush and grandson of *Ham. Nimrod was a 'mighty hunter before the Lord' and ruled

vast tracts in Mesopotamia. He belonged to the Dark Age between *Noah and Abraham about which the Bible tells almost nothing. He may have been the first man to wear a crown. St Augustine and Dante (Inferno, canto 30) made him out a giant. His name has become a synonym for a huntsman. Under the pseudonym of 'Nimrod' the English Victorian author C.J. Apperley wrote *Memoirs of the Life of John Mytton* (with illustrations by Henry Alken) and other sporting works. The ninth of Elgar's *Enigma Variations* is entitled 'Nimrod' in reference to the composer's friend A.J. Jaeger (hunter in German). Nimrod's tomb was legendarily located in Damascus, where no dew ever fell on it.
(Genesis 10)

**Noah**   A righteous man who won God's favour at a time when He regretted ever having created man and had resolved to wipe him out. God divulged to Noah His plan to drown the earth and told him to build himself an ark (see glossary) 300 cubits long, 50 wide and 30 high (a Hebrew cubit was 22 inches) with a roof, a door and three decks. In the ark Noah was to take his wife, his sons **Shem, Ham and Japheth and their wives, a pair of every living creature and every kind of food. It rained for 40 days and nights, the waters covered even the highest mountains, the ark rode the waters, and every living thing not in the ark died. After 150 days God sent a wind and the water began to fall. Noah released a raven but it flew to and fro without coming back. He released a dove which, finding no foothold, came back. He released the dove a second time and she came back at evening with a fresh olive leaf in her beak. After seven days he released the dove again and it did not come back. The earth dried, the ark grounded on Mount Ararat and its entire complement emerged. Noah sacrificed to God, who promised never again to curse the earth on account of man or to kill every living creature. To confirm this promise God put a rainbow in the sky. Noah planted vines, drank himself drunk and lay naked in his tent. He was seen by Ham, who told his brothers, who covered Noah with a cloak, walking backwards in order not to see him naked. When Noah woke he cursed *Ham's son Canaan and condemned him and his descendants to be the slaves of the races of Shem and Japheth. The Biblical Ararat has most frequently been identified with the mountain of that name in eastern Turkey.

Flood stories are widespread in the Middle East and are associated by scholars with the destruction caused by the breakdown of irrigation channels in a country dependent on the supply of river water and its control. One such story appears in the Sumerian cycle of poems about Gilgamesh, king in Uruk/Erech (modern Warka) on the lower Euphrates between Ur and Babylon. This king lived c. 2700 BC. Inserted in his saga is an account of his meeting with Utanapishtim, the sole survivor of a universal deluge, about which he had been warned by a god who leaked to him a decision of the council of gods to drown the earth. The epic of Gilgamesh was rediscovered in C 19 in the debris of the royal library at Nineveh which was destroyed along with the Assyrian empire in C 7 BC. Another equivalent of Noah and Utanapishtim, Ziusudra, is also known by name.

Guido Reni painted the building of the ark (Leningrad, Hermitage). Bassano (Madrid, Prado) shows the animals being assembled for embarcation up a convenient ramp. Noah's sacrifice after the Flood and his drunkenness appear in Michelangelo's covering of the ceiling of the Sistine Chapel in the Vatican, where the same artist also devotes a panel to the fate of Noah's unhappy contemporatries about to be engulfed by the rising waters. There is a realistic version of Noah drunk by Giovanni Bellini at Besançon and another by Benozzo Gozzoli in the Campo Santo at Pisa. In a different mood Millais (Oxford, Ashmolean Museum), depicting the return of the dove, shows two of Noah's young daughters-in-law cuddling the bird. An opera begun by Halévy was completed after his death by his son-in-law, Bizet – a

filial curiosity. *Noe* by André Obey was the most successful of the plays performed by the experimental Compagnie des Quinze in Paris and London between the two World Wars. See family tree A.
(Genesis 5-10)

**Obadiah** Prophet, author of the shortest Book in the OT and the obscurest. Like *Habbakkuk's his life spanned the Babylonian conquest of *Judah, but his special feature is his venom against the Edomites. As the descendants of *Esau (also called Edom) the Edomites were closer kin to the Israelites than any of the other peoples with whom they had to share the land of Canaan after the Exodus. Since they lived east of the Jordan the Edomites were perilously exposed to the power of Babylon and forced to submit to it. For Obadiah this was treason and he described with virulent enthusiasm their coming slaughter and the seizure of their goods and lands down to the Negev. An Obadiah used to be, perhaps still is, a slang name for a Quaker. See the next entry and also Prophets.
(Obadiah)

**Obadiah** Governor of the house of *Ahab who dared to hide 100 prophets of God to save them from the persecution of *Jezebel. See also the foregoing entry.
(I Kings 18)

**Og** King of Bashan and one of the early victims of the Israelites on their way into the Promised Land. His domains lay to the east of the Sea of Galilee. After conquering *Sihon, king of the Amorites, *Moses and the Israelites attacked and defeated Og and took all his lands. These kings allowed the

Israelites to pick them off one by one, which did wonders for Israelite morale and had the opposite effect on the peoples west of the Jordan which the Israelites were about to cross. In Dryden's 'Absalom and Achitophel' Og is the poet Thomas Shadwell who was very fat: Og's gigantic iron bedstead is evidence of his own large frame.
(Numbers 32; Deuteronomy 3; 1 Kings 4; Nehemiah 9)

**Omri** King of Israel c. 876-869 BC. Omri was a general who was set on the throne by his army. The founder of the kingdom, *Jeroboam, failed to give it any dynastic stability. He was followed by four kings, of whom only one survived for as much as two years. Omri redeemed this situation. He put an end to his predecessors' predilection for making war on the sister kingdom of *Judah, which he saw to be suicidal in the light of the greater dangers from *Syria to the north and the *Philistines to the south. He also built for Israel a new capital, Samaria, on a hill which he bought for two talents of silver. But his son *Ahab undid his work.
(I Kings 16)

**Onan** Son of *Judah who defied his father's instructions to give children to his deceased brother's wife *Tamar. From his manner of evading this duty by wasting his semen comes the word onanism. God killed him for it.
(Genesis 38)

**Onesimus** A runaway slave whom *Paul met, befriended and converted to Christianity. Paul sent Onesimus back to his owner with a letter – the Epistle to *Philemon – in which he asked that Onesimus be pardoned, set free and sent back to Paul, who

seems to have marked him down as good missionary material. That is all that is known for certain about Onesimus but conjecture has led some to suppose that he made good, even that he became bishop of Ephesus and the author of the Epistle to the Ephesians.
(Philemon; Coloss. 4)

**Paul**     Previously Saul, c. AD 1-64. Tentmaker, missionary, martyr, saint. Next to *Jesus the most important figure in Christianity.

*Early life*     He was born in Tarsus, the hellenized capital of the Roman province of Cilicia, and died in Rome, probably in the Neronian persecution after the Great Fire of AD 64. Paul is famous and important for his journeys, his letters and his personal faith. He was a *Jew of the diaspora (see glossary) who began to be trained as a rabbi when he was about 14. He was proud of his cultural heritage, meticulous in the strict observances of the *Pharisees and led thereby to persecute the Christian Jews who transgressed or belittled the Judaic Law. In c. AD 32, about, two years after the Crucifixion, Paul experienced a blinding conversion on his way to Damascus. He heard Jesus calling him: 'Saul, Saul, why persecutest thou me?'. He was instantly and profoundly converted. In c. AD 34 he went to Jerusalem to meet *Peter, the first of the apostles, and *James the brother of Jesus and head of the Christian community in the chief city of the Jews. For 16 years or so after his conversion he preached in the Jordan valley, Syria and Cilicia but seems to have had little to show for it, founding no new churches or congregations. He was harried by the stricter kind of Jew, for whom the Christians were Jewish heretics, and was forced on one occasion to escape from Damascus in a basket lowered from the city's walls. His base was Antioch, the capital of Roman Syria, where there was a community of Jews, some of whom had fled from Jerusalem on account of their Christian beliefs and were already in Antioch before Paul's arrival there.

In c. AD 48, 14 years after his first visit to Jerusalem, he went there a second time to attend a meeting of Christians convoked to discuss certain stresses and strains which had been simmering for some time and were brought to head by an incident in Antioch when the more conservative Christians violently insisted – against Paul – that all Christians must be circumcised. This conflict posed the question whether Christianity must be confined to Jews so that *Gentiles attracted to Christianity must first become Jews. Paul was accompanied to Jerusalem by his friend *Titus, a half-Greek Christian who had not been circumcised. Evidently Paul was at the centre of the dispute. The upshot was to sanction Paul to go his own way in his own way, a victory for Paul but also for the large-mindedness of some of the Christian elders in Jerusalem. In return Paul recognized the centrality of Jerusalem and undertook to get other congregations to help the church in Jerusalem with money. This compromise was the prelude to the centrepiece of Paul's life – his missionary journeys which turned the church of the Christian Jews of Jerusalem into the Christian church which was to span the world. On these journeys Paul founded or fostered Christian communities and fashioned them in his own beliefs. They are astonishingly well documented: the journeys themselves in *Luke's account of them in Acts of the Apostles, and Paul's teaching in his correspondence, of which a sizeable amount survives. (But the chronology of Acts is not always correct – for example, Acts mistakenly places the first journey before the meeting in Jerusalem in AD 48.)

*Missionary journeys* From this point until his arrest in Jerusalem in AD 58 – a single decade – Paul travelled to Cyprus, to Asia Minor and into Europe as far as Corinth, visiting a number of communities more than once. His final journey, made as a prisoner after his arrest, was to Rome, where he died. His first journey was undertaken with *Barnabas and took them to Cyprus and thence to Perga, Iconium,

Lystra (where Paul was stoned) and Derbe, all of them cities in the southern part of Galatia, now central Turkey. Back in Antioch he had a serious quarrel with Peter who, conscious of the attitudes of the Jewish Christians in Jerusalem, refused to eat with non-Jews. Paul regarded this refusal as both wrong and craven because it put the Judaic Law above faith in Jesus as the touchstone of salvation. Most of Paul's comrades deserted him on this issue, including Barnabas whose refusal to go on further journeys with Paul was probably influenced by this disagreement, although the two men quarrelled over whether to take *John Mark with them: John Mark was a cousin of Barnabas and had been on their first journey, but Paul complained that he had not pulled his weight. So Paul had to find new travelling companions, among them **Silas and Titus.

On this second and most adventurous journey Paul started along the route he had already traced in Asia Minor and then went on into Europe, propelled – as he always maintained – by the Holy Spirit, which in this instance summond him by a dream: 'Come over into Macedonia and help us.' His first stop in Europe was at Philippi, a busy commercial cross-roads and military strongpoint founded by Philip of Macedon and famous as the battlefield where, in 42 BC, the future emperor Augustus had defeated Brutus and Cassius and buried the Roman republic. From there Paul went on to Thessalonica, a greater city, established in c. 4 BC by king Cassander of Macedon (whose wife was called Thessalonike) and now the capital of a Roman province. Here he had a serious brush with authority, instigated by hostile orthodox Jews, and had to be smuggled out of the city. In Beroea (modern Verria) he was again persecuted and forced onwards to Athens and ultimately Corinth. Like Thessalonica, Corinth was a Roman provincial capital and a busy place. It was a modern city, founded by Julius Caesar to replace the ancient Greek city which the Romans had sacked with ferocious frenzy in 146 BC. (The remains visible today are mostly Roman.) In

Roman times, as in Greek, it was a rich and notoriously lascivious melting-pot. The governor was L. Junius *Gallio, a brother of the Stoic philosopher and playwright Seneca, and uncle of the poet Lucan. There was a florishing community of Jews in this multi-racial town; some of them were Christians, such as Paul's hosts **Aquila and Priscilla, but most of them were unfriendly and forced Paul by rowdiness to give up his weekly appearance in their synagogue. Gallio, called upon to adjudicate between Paul and his adversaries, preferred to keep out: he 'cared for none of these things'. Paul had to teach and preach in private houses. He stayed in Corinth for a year and half, c. AD 50-51.

Next he paid a brief visit to Ephesus and a courtesy call to Jerusalem and made a longer stay in Antioch. In Jerusalem he fulfilled his promise to bring money to the mother church and also acceded to a request by James to give a personal demonstration of his Jewishness, partly no doubt to shield James from accusations of accepting money from a tainted source and partly in an attempt to abate Jewish hostility to himself. From Antioch he set out on a tour of inspection of churches in Asia Minor, in the course of which he was vigorously attacked in Ephesus by a mob incited by the silversmith *Demetrius whose trade in statuettes of the goddess Diana was being threatened by Christian denigration of her cult. Paul then journeyed on to Macedonia and Greece, his second and last visit to these places. On his return he avoided Ephesus, travelling by the islands of Mitylene, Chios, Samos, Cos and Rhodes to the mainland at Tyre and thence to Jerusalem, where the last phase of his life began. He had about six years to live and most of that time he spent under arrest.

The hostility of the Jews was unappeased and in Jerusalem Paul was accused of sacrilege and was in danger of being lynched when he was saved by the Romans, who first lodged him in gaol and then, alarmed by rumours of a plot to kill him and the consequent threat to law and order, secretly despatched him to the provincial capital Caesarea with a posse of 200 soldiers and a letter to the procurator *Felix. The procurator dithered for two years which Paul spent in prison in Caesarea (AD 58-60), but a new procurator, Porcius *Festus, took up the case and decided to send him back to Jerusalem. Convinced that he stood no chance of a fair trial in that city, Paul disclosed that he was a Roman citizen and so entitled to be sent to Rome for trial. He was at this point a victim of unlucky timing, for when king Herod *Agrippa II chanced to come to Caesarea and attended Paul's interrogation, the king told the procurator that he saw no reason why Paul should not be set free – except for the fact that he had just appealed to Rome. And so to Rome he had to go. (The king said also that Paul's eloquence had all but persuaded him to be a Christian.) Paul's last voyage was boisterous. From Caesarea the party sailed to Myra in Lycia (Asia Minor) and there trans-shipped for Italy and after touching at Crete and drifting for 14 days was wrecked on Malta. (This part of the story is suspect. Almost too dramatic to be believed, it may have been inserted in Acts for effect by the author or a later editor.) From Malta Paul proceeded to Naples and to a formal welcome in Rome where he is said to have been free to meet fellow Christians and even to preach. Here Acts ends. 'The rest of his story is silence' – so said George Moore in the last sentence of his book *The Brook Kerith*. Yet there is a strong and plausible tradition that Paul suffered martydom in Rome in the Neronian persecution of the Christians.

**His letters**  Paul was a letter-writer as well as a traveller. His surviving letters are older than Acts and are the oldest surviving Christian documents. How many letters he wrote it is now impossible to say, but their impact was such that they were in all probability collected and published c. AD 100. Until recently it was supposed that all the letters included in the NT and not expressly ascribed to somebody else (**Peter, James, John, Jude) were Paul's, but modern scholarship has destroyed this simple picture. Some are now universally, or almost universally, regarded as non-Pauline: they are Hebrews – of which Origen said in AD C3 that God alone knew who wrote it – and the three so-called Pastoral Epistles, I and 2 Timothy and *Titus. That leaves ten, which fall into three sets: first, Galatians, I and 2 Thessalonians and I and 2 2 Corinthians; second, Romans; and third, the so-called prison letters, Ephesians, Colossians, Philippians and Philemon. Thessalonians is probably the earliest of Paul's surviving letters and, like those to the Galatians and Corinthians, was written to people whom Paul knew and whose communities he had visited. His purpose in writing these letters was to keep in touch. Since he could not be everywhere at once, he could do this only by writing and sending letters by the well developed road system of the Roman empire. Frequently these were prompted by upsetting reports which he had received of squabbles in the nascent Christian communities, lapses in or queries about doctrine, or attacks on his personal authority; and there is his constant concern to insist that Christianity must not be confined to Jews, as for example when he reprimanded those among the Galatians who still held that Gentiles must become circumcised Jews before becoming Christians or remain only second-class Christians. All the letters in this group were probably written shortly after his visits to the places in question: those to Thessalonica from Athens or Corinth on his onward journey, those to Corinth in the mid-50s from Ephesus or Macedonia.

The Epistle to the Romans, which stands apart, differs from these because Paul had not yet been to Rome – although he wanted and intended to go there – and did not know personally those to whom he was writing. It was a way of introducing himself. The origins of the Christian community in the imperial city are unknown. Rome had contained many Jews since at least Pompey's campaigns in the east and there were by Paul's time about a dozen synagogues, mostly on the left bank of the Tiber. In AD 50 the emperor Claudius

expelled the Jews and presumably also the Christians, indistinguishable to the pagan eye; the
imperial biographer Suetonius wrote that
Claudius acted as he did because of the subversive
activities stirred up by 'Chrestus'. Four years later
Nero allowed them back but they remained
vulnerable to the whims of an unbalanced auto-
crat who seems to have gone out of his mind at the
time of the Great Fire of AD 64. Paul, besides
preparing his way for a visit, took the opportunity
to expand in his letter his insistence on the equal
admissability of Jews and Gentiles to Christianity.

***Prison letters
and friends***

The third set of Paul's letters are those written
from prison. Which prison is unclear. Paul was in
prison in Jerusalem and Caesarea in AD 58-60
and in Rome, if comparatively freely, from his
arrival there c. AD 61. He may also have endured
an earlier unrecorded spell in prison at Ephesus.
Of the four prison epistles one is a very short note
on a personal matter, sent to *Philemon about the
runaway slave *Onesimus. Another – Ephesians –
has come under critical scrutiny which suggests
that it was a round-robin written after Paul's
death and circulated to several churches as a
general or introductory survey of Paul's teaching
(the address specifically to the church in Ephesus
did not appear in the earliest texts and the
reference to Paul's companions which occur in the
other prison letters are absent). These letters give
glimpses of the band of brothers gathered round
Paul by his missionary activities. The closest of
them appears to be *Timothy. All the prison
letters, except Ephesians, were sent in the joint
names of Paul and Timothy – who was also the
co-author of the earlier 1 and 2 Thessalonians.
Timothy may have been a fellow prisoner with
Paul. *Aristarchus and Epaphras are explicitly so
described. Four other friends send greetings:
**John Mark, Luke, Demas, Jesus Justus. They
were clearly with Paul. Two others – *Tychichus
and Onesimus – were on their way from Paul to
Colossae or possibly to nearby Laodicea, where
another two – Philemon and *Archippus – were
to be found. Many more get passing mention in

the letters. Paul, although (one suspects) a demanding leader – Demas left him in response to the calls of 'this present life' – did not forget people. But in the end only one, Luke, possibly but not certainly the evangelist, remained with him.

## His character and impact

Paul's Christianity was formed in the instantaneous white heat of his conversion. He was already a religious man, a believing and observant Pharisee, but from the moment of revelation on the Damascus road he was totally consumed by his faith in Jesus. Whereas for the twelve apostles (see glossary) Christianity grew out of, and was a form of, Judaism, for Paul – who never met the man Jesus but had an intense communion with the risen Christ – Christianity was fundamentally different from Judaism. The Jew believed that the road to salvation was the careful observance of Judaic Law and the no less careful performance of the Temple ritual. Paul believed that what saved was faith. Jesus had changed the world: before his death and resurrection mortal men could do no more than follow the Law, but since these events the precepts of the Law were overridden by the need simply but totally to believe. The world was something which stretched finitely between its creation and its end, which was near; and God had sent Jesus into the world at this near-terminal point in order that, by his Passion, Jesus might reveal a new way to salvation. Faith now saves and nothing else does. Paul's mission was to make everybody see this. Paul was not a theologian or a systematic man of any kind. He was a missionary concerned to spread the faith, not in competition with other faiths but compulsively to show as many people as possible what had happened to the world through the coming and death of Jesus.

And by the world he meant the world, not Jewry. This is the second main feature of Paul's religion, and it was controversial. The Jews of the diaspora, to which Paul belonged, were by this time more numerous that the Jews in Judaea and they lived within the Hellenic civilization recently annexed by Rome. The first Christians were all Jews of the relatively secluded Jewish heartland who gradually realized that they had a problem over the relationship of their sect to Judaism. On this matter they were divided. Some, including *Stephen, the first Christian martyr, came into conflict with the orthodox Jewish establishment and populace, for whom the forms of worship in the Temple and the observance of the Law were – however finicky – paramount: Jews who were also Christians had either to keep a low profile or court persecution. Some of the latter fled to Antioch (where they were first called Christians) and here they came into contact with the Jews of the diaspora who were already drifting away from the spirit of heartland Judaism. For them the Temple was remote (they worshipped in synagogues – a Greek word) and the exclusivity of Jerusalem was irritating. Furthermore, the divide between Jew and Gentile, which was a fact of life in Jerusalem, was, socially at least, unreal in places like Tarsus and Antioch.

To Paul's conversion and background must be added a third cardinal factor: his temperament. If the twelve were a team, Paul came close to being a one-man band: passionate, sometimes harsh and unfair, a monomaniac thruster but also and singularly a man capable of lofty thought, not a ranter. He was too a man of courage. In spite of Rome's conquests and civil engineering, Asia Minor and Greece were not comfortable places for travellers and the crowds were largely un-policed as well as hostile to a man whom the Jews among them regarded as an apostate who had rejected the Law and its outward sign, circumci-sion – the mark, but also the condition, of God's convenant with *Abraham. Such a man as Paul raised hackles and in the first generations after his death he was more often lauded by heretics (Marcion, for example) than by what was becom-ing orthodox Christianity. But the very shape of the NT, fashioned around the end of AD C 1 shows the imprint of Paul: apart from the Gos-pels, Revelation and a handful of non-Pauline letters the NT is about or by Paul. That impact has waxed and waned but has never been less than large. It has inspired men of like temper from Augustine to Luther. On the other hand each flood tide of Pauline influence has rekindled opposition which, in its origins, amounted to a refusal to forgive Paul for upstaging the historical Jesus. In C 19 Nietzsche, not untypical of his age, attacked Paul for obliterating Jesus' ministry, gospel and passion. For a certain kind of theologian these intriguing conflicts are agonizing but also bread and butter. For the historian they exemplify the healthy complexity of the human condition. To Christianity they have done little harm.

Paul has engaged artists less than have other figures of comparable stature, but his stunning conversion is grist to the mill of the more dramatic: e.g. Michelangelo (Vatican, Capella Paolina); Caravaggio (Rome, S. Maria del Popolo) — he is lying on the ground by a large horse; Ludovico Caracci (Bologna, Pinacoteca); Peter Bruegel the Elder (Vienna, Kunsthistorisches Museum). His most massive musical monument is Mendelssohn's oratorio about him. Caravaggio's curious view of the startling event on the road to Damascus evoked Thom Gunn's poem *In Santa Maria del Popolo*.
(Acts 8-28)

**Paulus Sergius**  See Sergius.

**Peter**  Apostle, saint and the founder of the Christian church in Rome. His name was Simon but he was given the surname or nickname of Peter or Cephas, meaning rock in Greek and Hebrew respectively. He was a Galilean fisherman, brother of *Andrew, and he emerged as the first among the twelve apostles. Although *John was the 'beloved disciple', Peter was the rock on which *Jesus chose to build his church and Peter is the most prominent of the twelve in all the Gospel narratives and second only to *Paul in the account of their later doings as recorded in Acts. This prominence can be two-edged. In one of the storms on the Sea of Galilee, when Jesus walked on the water, Peter tried to do so but failed ignominiously: 'O, thou of little faith'. But none of the other apostles even tried. Peter formed with **James and John, the sons of Zebedee, an inner circle among the twelve. They were the only ones whom Jesus took with him into the house of *Jairus whose daughter Jesus restored to life; they alone witnessed the Transfiguration of Jesus; and they accompanied Jesus further than the rest into the garden of Gethsemane when he prayed there in the hours before his betrayal and arrest. Peter and John were, according to one account, the apostles whom Jesus sent ahead of him to fetch the ass and the colt for the entry into Jerusalem on the eve of their final Passover feast; they were the first of the apostles to reach the empty tomb, John the first to get there, Peter the first to go in; and after the Resurrection the same two took the lead in rallying the disciples, giving them heart in their perplexities and fears, and setting in train the fulfilment of Jesus' charge to go out and preach the coming of the kingdom of heaven. Above all, Peter stands alone at two vital moments: he was the first openly to acknowledge, in response to Jesus' questioning, that Jesus was the Christ, the Son of God; and after boasting his unique devotion to Jesus he suffered the profound humiliation of denying, out of fear and three times, that he knew Jesus. When, as foretold by Jesus, a cockcrow marked his third denial, he wept bitterly.

His activities after the Resurrection imperilled his life. When James, the son of Zebedee, was arrested and executed by order of Herod *Agrippa I, Peter was arrested too but he was rescued from prison by an angel (see Rhoda). He exercised authority in the Christian community in Jerusalem, notably and publicly at the first Pentecost; he performed miracles and undertook missionary journeys in Judaea and Syria; he gave his support to *Paul's campaign to extend the Christian fellowship to Gentiles without obliging them first to become circumcised Jews (*Cornelius, the first baptized *Gentile, was baptized by Peter). At a date no longer definable he went to Rome and was martyred there c. AD 64 in the Neronian persecution – crucified upside down, so the early Christian historian Eusebius relates. The identification of his tomb under St Peter's in Rome is accepted by some scholars as authentic and was affirmed by the Pope in 1968.

Of the two Epistles of Peter in the NT the second – a harsh polemic which bears the stamp of composition in Egypt in AD C 2 – cannot be regarded as his. The first may be his but it is well to remember that the names of leading figures were not infrequently attached to writings of this kind in order to command more attention for them. The story of an encounter outside Rome between Jesus and Peter, when Peter asked: '*Quo vadis?* ('Where are you going?'), and Jesus replied: 'To be crucified again' – occurs in the Acts of Peter, a book excluded from the canonical scriptures. Peter is the only one of the twelve apostles to have a wife mentioned in the Bible.

Peter's representation in the arts is too widespread to permit any but the most exiguous enumeration: his life in pictures by Raphael (Hampton Court); his denial of Jesus by Rembrandt (Amsterdam, Rijksmuseum) and by Duccio among that painter's gems in the Cathedral Museum at Siena; in prison by Filippino Lippi (Florence, S. Maria del Carmine); his crucifixion by Michelangelo (Vatican, Capella Paolina), Guido Reni (Rome, Vatican) and Guercino (Modena, Pinacoteca); and, more domestically, Stanley Spencer's picture of him having his feet washed by Jesus (Carlisle, Art Gallery). Peter's special association with John is celebrated in a number of scenes by Masaccio in the Brancacci chapel in S. Maria del Carmine in Florence. Sculptors and painters identify him by placing in his hands the emblematic crossed keys.

(Matthew 10, 14, 16, 17, 19, 26; Mark 3, 8, 9-11,

14; Luke 6, 8, 9, 12, 18, 22, 24; John I, 6, 13, 18, 20, 21; Acts 1-5, 8-12)

**Pharisees, Sadducees, Zealots, Essenes**

In the last two centuries BC Judaism was divided into sects of which the most prominent were the Pharisees and Sadducees. Both were relatively small elites. The Pharisees were an intellectual elite, distinguished by learning and piety, strongly attached to the letter of the Judaic Law. Their name comes from the Hebrew *perusim* meaning 'those who have been set apart'. The Sadducees were a more social elite, strongly attached to the letter of the Law as transmitted in writing. They rejected the oral Law which derived from the written Law and rejected in particular the resurrection of the dead. They were recruited mainly from the wealthy and the priestly establishment, a ruling class. They may have got their name from *Zadok, chief priest of *Solomon.

A third group, the Zealots, incidentally referred to in the Bible, consisted of the more inflexible and combative conservatives. They were organized in C 1 BC by Judas of Galilee (Acts 5) and led after him by his son Menahem and grandson Eleazar, and were almost certainly the shortlived group which retreated to Masada during the revolt against Rome in AD 66-70 and held out there until its mass suicide in AD 74. A fourth sect, the Essenes, quietists of a more retiring and contemplative disposition, finds no mention in the NT. Although Thomas De Quincey wrote two long essays proving that the Essenes never existed, these people are now widely identified with the sect which lived at Qumran and whose rich library was found in eleven caves by the Dead Sea from 1947 onward.

**Philemon**

The addressee of *Paul's letter about the runaway slave *Onesimus. Philemon held a position of authority among the Christians of Asia Minor. (Philemon)

**Philip**   One of the twelve apostles. Like most of them he is only a fleeting figure in the NT but he has a splendid series of frescoes by Filippino Lippi in the Strozzi Chapel in S Maria Novella in Florence. Legend has him martyred in Phrygia, aged 87, but not before subduing a dragon in Scythia by the force of his personality. In his martydom by Ribera (Madrid, Prado) he is about to be hoist onto the cross on which he will die. See also the next entry.
(Matthew 10; Mark 3; Luke 6; John I, 6 , 12, 14; Acts I)

**Philip**   Also called Herod Philip, tetrarch (see glossary) of Iturea BC 4-AD 34, son of *Herod the Great. He received on his father's death the northern part of his father's kingdom together with more lands further north. He was a capable ruler but he is more famous for his marriage with his niece *Salome – whose father was also called Herod Philip but was not a tetrarch. See also the foregoing entry and family tree F.
(Luke 3, 14)

**Philistines**   Where they come from has been much debated, with Asia Minor, Crete and points north as the favoured answers. They reached the south-west corner of Asia c. 13 BC and so forestalled the Israelites of the Exodus who arrived back in Asia from Egypt in this epoch. The five chief cities of the Philistine were Ashdod, Askalon, Ekron, Gath and Gaza. The Philistine confederacy existed in a state of sporadic war with the Israelites, alternatively advancing into the Judaean highlands and being pushed back again. A serious incursion in the time of *Samuel impressed upon him the need for unity among the tribes of Israel and contributed to the creation of the monarchy of *Saul and, later, *David. Although earlier leaders – for example, **Deborah and Gideon – had been able to hold their own by mobilizing some only of the twelve tribes, by C 11 BC the threat to the Israelites was more serious, partly because the Philistines were a tougher foe than the Canaanites or the Midianites had been and partly because they concerted their attacks from the west with operations against Israel by the Ammonites from east of the Jordan. *Samson's triumph over the Philistines was more spectacular than enduring. So was Saul's initial success in the person of David against *Goliath. When Saul and David quarrelled the latter found refuge with the Philistine king of Gath, but both Saul and David, in turn, warred methodically against the Philistines and lorded it over them. The Philistines held on to their independent status but eventually fell prey to *Assyria and, after the disappearance of the Assyrian empire, to Babylon, Persia, Alexander the Great and his Seleucid successors in Syria, and ultimately Rome. Their gods or *Baals included Dagon, Astarte and Beelzebub, 'the lord of the flies.' The name Palestine, a Greek derivative from Philistine, was officially affixed by the emperor Hadrian to the Roman province of Judaea after the Jewish revolt of AD 132-135. The word Philistine, denoting lack of culture, was coined in Germany in C 17 and brought into England by Matthew Arnold in his *Culture and Anarchy* (1869). In a number of his piano pieces Schumann contrasts the Philistines in this guise with the *Davidsbündler* – those leagued with David in his character as musician and civilized man.

**Phinehas**  Priest, son of *Eleazar, son of Aaron. Phinehas killed *Zimri and his Midianitish prostitute *Cozbi in order to stop the plague with which God was afflicting the Israelites in the Sinai wilderness when they took to widespread whoredom and Baal-worship. (Numbers 25). Another Phinehas was one of *Eli's two disappointing sons. (I Samuel 1, 2, 4)

**Phoenicians**  Called also in the Bible Sidonians. They were a branch of the *Canaanites. In the second millennium BC they established city states on the eastern Mediterranean coast and on off-shore islands (now part of the mainland). The most important of them were Tyre and Sidon. In the second half of that millennium they were harried by the Hittites from the north and by Egypt from the south, but the collapse of these two empires inaugurated an interlude of prosperous independence. The kings of Tyre won a general overlordship. *Hiram became the equal and ally of *Solomon with whom he partnered a commercial expedition to the far end of the Red Sea. The Phoenicians were notable seafarers, traders and colonizers. Their most famous overseas settlement was Carthage, founded in C 9 BC by Dido who fled from Tyre when her husband was killed by her brother King Pygmalion. From the same century the increasingly cruel depredations of the kings of Assyria destroyed the independence of the cities. The end of the Assyrian empire exposed them, as it exposed *Judah, to a flash-in-the-pan revival of Egyptian imperialism, followed by subjection to Babylon, Persia, Alexander the Great and his Seleucid successors in Syria, and ultimately to Rome. Each Phoenician city had its specific god – the Phoenician word for god was *Baal – but recognized also the divinity of its neighbours' gods.

**Pilate**  Pontius Pilate – procurator or governor of Judaea AD 27 -36. Pilate was the fifth governor of the province which had been carved out of the kingdom of *Herod the Great by the emperor Augustus in AD 6 when Herod's son *Archelaus proved his incapacity as a ruler. Pilate too was a poor ruler. Whether through weakness or arrogance he inflamed Jewish emotions by insisting, against precedent, on displaying the emperor's image on the banners of the legions as they moved from Caesarea on the coast to their winter quarters in Jerusalem and then compounded his mistake by caving in. After further affronts to the Jews and similar vacillations between tactlessness and unnecessary displays of force he was sacked. He had the misfortune to face and fail to cope with the dilemma into which he was put by the priestly enemies of *Jesus who had found him guilty of breaches of the Judaic Law and demanded that Pilate pronounce upon him the sentence of death applicable to these findings. Pilate seems to have sensed that he was being asked to hand over a relatively harmless prisoner to the malice of sectarian enemies and he tried to sidestep this distasteful outcome by exercising his right to release a prisoner upon popular demand. But the people – or at least a clique among them – thwarted him by asking for the release of another prisoner, *Barabbas, not Jesus.

Pilate thereupon washed his hands of an affair which presumably he expected to pass into oblivion in a month or two. Pilate's end is obscure. He is said to have committed suicide as a way of escaping the ire of the new emperor Caligula for the crime of incompetence, or – a wildly improbable surmise – the ire of Tiberius for the crime of deicide. A later tradition recounted how his body was thrown into the Tiber, regurgitated into the sea, carried to the Rhone and washed up at Vienne. The Mons Pilatus, between Vienne and Lucerne, has been supposed to get its name from him but this is probably no more than folk etymology and a mistake for *mons pileatus*, cloud-capped. A kindlier tradition, endorsed by Origen, says that Pilate became a Christian and he is commemorated in the liturgies of the Greek Orthodox and Ethiopian Coptic churches, which regard him as a martyr. The opening words of Bacon's essay on Truth: 'What is Truth said jesting Pilate, and would not stay for an answer', echo an exchange in *John's Gospel between Pilate and Jesus. Aldous Huxley picked up the phrase 'Jesting Pilate' to serve as title for one of his travel books. The trial of Jesus and the tribulations which it caused for Pilate are woven into

Mikhail Bulgakov's modern Russian parable *The Master and Margarita*. His most famous act is shown in Turner's *Pilate Washing his Hands* (London, Tate Gallery).
(Matthew 27; Mark 15; Luke 3, 23; John 18, 19)

**Pontius Pilate**    See Pilate.

**Potiphar**    A prosperous officer in the pharaoh's guard to whom *Joseph was sold by the **Midianites or Ishmaelites who pulled him out of the pit into which his brothers had thrown him. Potiphar's wife tried to get Joseph to sleep with her and when he rebuffed her accused him of trying to seduce her, for which he was thrown into prison. Unnamed in the Bible, she is called in a Persian source Zuleika. The sale of Joseph to Potiphar is depicted by Pontormo (London, National Gallery); his wife's disappointment by Tintoretto (Madrid, Prado). In Dante's Inferno Potiphar's wife suffers eternally as a bearer of false tales.
(Genesis 37, 39)

**Priscilla**    See Aquila.

**Prodigal Son**    The central character in one of *Jesus' most famous parables. He was the younger of two sons and he demanded of their father his share of their inheritance. A few days after getting it he went off to a far country and wasted it. A famine came; he took a job feeding pigs and was reduced in his distress to envying them their miserable husks; and he decided to go back home. His father, who had given him up for dead, saw him coming and ordered his servants to bring excellent clothes and shoes and ornaments and to kill the best fatted calf to make a merry feast. The elder brother was furious at this unequal treatment of the wastrel and remonstrated with his father who had never given him even a kid for a party with his friends in spite of years of obedience and hard work. The father's reply was that the elder brother would inherit all that he had but that he could not refrain from rejoicing over the return of another son whom he had believed to be dead. The Prodigal Son is the subject of Rembrandt's last great picture (Leningrad, Hermitage). The simple pathos of the old man staring out of the picture over the head of the kneeling son is one interpretation of this story which, in another view, is a celebration and triumph: e.g. Bassano and Poussin (both in Madrid, Prado). An action sequence by Murillo shows him in the ups and the downs of his career; Murillo painted two, dissimilar versions (Prado and Dublin National Gallery of Ireland). Rodin's statue orginally designed to be part of his Gates of Hell portrays the agonies of despair. André Gide and Darius Milhaud collaborated in a work for voices and small orchestra; Prokoviev used the story for a ballet, Ponchielli for an opera. (Luke 15).

**Prophets**  Prophecy means knowing and telling the future. Its sources are various: interpreting strange or natural phenomena (such as the entrails of birds), dreams and trances, a sixth sense, divine inspiration. The Hebrew prophets were inspired by God who endowed them with foresight and compelled them to proclaim what was coming. Inseparably allied with this revelation of the future was denunciation of present evils. The future which the prophets foretold was almost wholly baleful and it was baleful because the Israelites had fallen into sin by abandoning the monotheism demanded by their God. Attacking their sins was therefore a good part of the prophetic message, the sins being partly religious and partly moral and social. The prophets were the principal upholders of Israel's monotheism – in its earlier form a refusal to permit the Israelites to worship any god other than their own, in its later form a refusal to allow that any god other than theirs was a god at all. The grimmer prophets gave little hope for the future, but others proclaimed the compassion of god to the penitent.

The prophets were at the same time social critics who attacked misrule and injustice, denounced the materialism of the high and mighty, and offered consolation to the poor and downtrodden. In social terms they were conservative reformers whose nostalgia for a lost way of life found expression in violently radical abuse of the current debasement of morals. The first prophets were men with a special gift much appreciated by kings – for example, foretelling the result on the eve of a battle. They belonged to a well established class of seers so numerous that many were no better than quacks. Although few names have come down to posterity they were members of a recognized professional body and not the isolated freaks which the accidents of literary survival sometimes make them out to be. Besides advising kings they could be active in unseating one and promoting another. Such were **Samuel, Nathan, Elijah and Elisha, architects of the kingdom of Israel. By insisting on the unity of the twelve tribes and the uniqueness of Israel's God they established the essential prerequisites and chief characteristics of the Israelites' impact on the world around them. Their activities are recorded in the sequence of historical Books which comprises 1 and 2 Samuel and 1 and 2 Kings. Their later successors, beginning with *Amos, gave the religion of Israel a moral content, transcending and even deploring its purely ritualistic nature. Three of them – **Isaiah, Jeremiah, Ezekiel – came to be accounted major prophets, while another twelve were included in the OT and all fifteen constituted the prophets in the phrase 'the Law and the Prophets' which became the standard way of referring to the code of behaviour, legal and spiritual, by which Jews must live. Of the three major prophets Isaiah lived in C 8 BC, Jeremiah in C 7 BC and Ezekiel in C 6 BC. The other principal figures in the earlier phase were, with Amos, **Hosea and Micah. Deutero-Isaiah (see under Isaiah), in many ways the most inspiring of all the prophets, was a contemporary of Ezekiel. The later prophets were all profoundly affected by the Babylonian *Captivity and Exile which impelled them towards a narrow, vengeful chauvinism, apparent for example in **Haggai, Zachariah and Obadiah. Many of the surviving prophetic Books are collections of sayings from different authors and disparate periods. They achieved their permanent shape c. C 2 BC.

*Their force*    The Hebrew prophets were exceptional beings. The best of them were serious and elevated thinkers with unusual gifts of vision, courage and force of character. They had a high moral tone which transformed the religion of their people and a political impact which ensured the survival of a small race through the hazards of history. Their common feature was their insistence that the society to which they belonged and addressed themselves had become rotten. They were unsparing in their criticism of high and low alike. They had no doubt that the rottenness which they saw everywhere was the result of forsaking God, but they preached moral as well as ritual regeneration. Although there is no logical link between religion and morality and none was much in evidence in the ancient religions of the Middle East, the Hebrew prophets made this link and developed the idea of a God who was ethical as well as omnipotent: one of the major spiritual and intellectual events in the history of man. Paradoxically the least attractive and least ethical of the prophets had a hardly less powerful effect in a different way. The traumatic blow of the *Captivity, followed by the Return to Jerusalem, produced two strains of thought. In the one the Return heralded an imminent restoration of the Judaic kingdom which would quickly be widened into a world empire under the aegis of the one and only God and his chosen people. In the other the Return had a much narrower compass and the Israelites would survive only through the jealous preservation of everything that was special to them – the opposite of universalization. Although the principal prophets of this second strain exhibited an unpleasing bitterness, it is arguable that without it their people would have lost their identity and disappeared.

**Publius**   Chief man on the island of Melita (Malta), cured by *Paul when he was shipwrecked there. (Acts 28)

**Pul**   The name given in the OT to Tiglath-Pileser III, king of Assyria 747-739 BC. He was the creator in his short reign of the greatest Assyrian empire. It reached from the Persian Gulf and the Red Sea in the south to the Caspian and Black Seas in the north and included parts of Egypt, modern Turkey and Persia as well as the Tigris and Euphrates valleys and the lands of the Armenians, Canaanites, Israelites and Phoenicians. He defeated the usurper-kings Menahem and Pekah of Israel and compelled king Ahaz of Judah to pay him tribute and visit him in Damascus. His immediate successors were Shalmaneser V, Sargon and Sennacherib. See Assyria. (2 Kings 15, 16; 2 Chron. 28 )

**Quirinius**   Also Cyrenius, according to *Luke legate or governor of the Roman province of Syria. But Luke got it wrong. He was in fact P. Quintilius Varus, later and for ever famous for losing his legions in battle with Arminius in the Teutoburger Forest in AD 9 – the most disastrous episode in the reign of Augustus. (Luke 2)

**Rab-shakeh**   Leader of a delegation sent by Sennacherib king of Assyria to *Hezekiah king of Judah. Rab-shakeh's task was either to get Hezekiah to abandon his alliance with Egypt and return to being a tributary of Assyria, or alternatively to appeal over Hezekiah's head to the people of Judah to force their king back into the Assyrian sphere of influence. He failed. See **Assyria, Shebna, Hezekiah. (2 Kings 18, 19)

**Rachel**     The younger and more attractive daughter of
              *Laban and, with her sister *Leah, wife to their
              cousin *Jacob. Rachel bore two sons, **Joseph
              and Benjamin. She died giving birth to the latter
              and was buried at Bethlehem. Rossetti painted the
              two sisters together in a study based on Dante,
              (*Purgatory*, canto 27) who cast Leah as delighting
              in work, Rachel in contemplation (London, Tate
              Gallery). Her death is portrayed with roccoco
              sentimentality by Giambattista Cignaroli (Venice,
              Academy). See further under Laban and Jacob
              and, for the ramification of the family, family tree
              C.
              (Genesis 29-33, 35)

**Rahab**      A harlot in Jericho with good political sense. Two
              Israelites sent by *Joshua to spy out the land took
              lodging with her. Impressed by the Israelites'
              victories east of the Jordan, she decided to
              ingratiate herself with them. She hid the two spies
              in stalks of flax on her roof and then let them
              down by a rope out of her window which was in
              the city's wall. In return they promised that if she
              marked her house with a scarlet thread she and
              her family would be spared when the city was
              taken. And so they were.
              (Joshua 2, 7)

**Rebecca**    Wife of *Isaac. She was his cousin, fetched from
**(or Rebekah)** their ancestral country so that Isaac should have a
              wife of his own kin and not a Canaanitess. Isaac
              and Rebecca had twin sons, **Esau and Jacob.
              Esau was the elder and his father's favourite,
              Jacob his mother's favourite. She manoeuvred
              Isaac, when old and blind, into bestowing his
              blessing and his inheritance on Jacob. Claude
              painted a 'Landscape with the Marriage of Isaac
              and Rebekah' in which, as the title suggests, he is
              more interested in the natural than the human
              elements (London, National Gallery). The Rebec-
              cas were bands of Welsh farmers, dressed as
              women, who demonstrated riotously against

poverty and hardships in 1839 and 1842. See
further under Esau and family tree B.
(Genesis 24, 26-28)

**Rechab**  A servant of King *Ish-bosheth whom he killed in
expectation of reward from *David who ordered
instead that he be executed along with his fellow
ruffian *Baanah. See also the next entry.
(2 Samuel 4)

**Rechab**  A teetotaller who ordered his son Jonadab and his
son's sons never to drink wine. They persisted in
this refusal even when *Jeremiah gave them wine
and told them to drink. The Independent Order of
Rechabites, founded in 1835, takes its name from
them. See also the foregoing entry.
(Jeremiah 35)

**Rehoboam**  Son of *Solomon and Naamah, an Ammonitess;
king of Judah c. 932-915 BC. He failed to preserve
the integrity of the kingdom created by his father
and his grandfather *David, keeping only the
lands of Judah and Benjamin, the southern parts.
The other ten tribes revolted against him and
summoned *Jeroboam to rule over them. This
split, which was never healed, is ascribed in the
Bible to Solomon's backsliding in his old age when
he took among his wives and concubines a
number of women from undesirably alien races.
But God was loath to extinguish altogether the
line of David and preserved it in the lesser
kingdom of Judah. Rehoboam himself contributed to his rejection by the ten tribes. When
asked about his intentions by those who had
suffered under his father's harsh rule he consulted
first with the elders, who advised a circumspect
reply, and then with younger men, who advocated
a tough line. Although himself over 40 he preferred the advice of the younger generation and told
his prospective subjects that where his father had
chastised them with whips he would chastise them

with scorpions. So, with the cry: 'To your tents, O Israel', they disowned Rehoboam. All Judah's kings from first to last were directly descended from Rehoboam and so were of the royal line of David. Unlike Israel Judah had a record of dynastic stability, interrupted only once by the usurpation of queen *Athaliah. But Judah was a small hill state, cut off from the coast and the coastal road by the cities of the *Philistines, forced to manoeuvre precariously between more powerful neighbours and easily outraged by the more latitudinarian and cosmopolitan plainsmen of Israel. At first its enemies were Israel and *Syria; then *Assyria; finally Babylon which extinguished it. Rehoboam had 18 wives, including his cousin Maacah, a daughter of *Absalom. A drawing by Holbein shows him confronting his people in a mood likely to ensure his rejection (Basel, City Museum). A Rehoboam, like a Jeroboam, is a large measure of wine. See further under Jehoshaphat, Uzziah, Hezekiah, Josiah.
(I Kings 11-12, 14; 2 Chron. 10-13)

**Reuben**    The eldest of the twelve sons of *Jacob. His mother was *Leah. He opposed his brothers' plot to kill Joseph, but he was condemned by his father as undependable. His tribal territory was east of the Jordan. See family tree C.
(Genesis 29, 30, 35, 37, 42-50; Joshua 4, 13, 22)

**Rhoda**    An excitable girl in the house of Mary, mother of *John Mark, where a number of Christians were gathered to pray for *Peter, apprehended by Herod *Agrippa I. When Peter, having escaped from prison, knocked on the garden door she recognized his voice but was so bowled over that she ran back to the house with the news instead of letting Peter in.
(Acts 12)

**Rizpah**  A concubine of *Saul who caused bad blood between his son *Ish-bosheth and *Abner, his general. Ish-bosheth accused Abner of taking Rizpah and as a result of this incident both made their peace with *David. So Rizpah played an unwitting part in ending the seven-year war that followed the death of Saul. Tennyson's *Rizpah* is a poem of his prolific old age which justifies the cliché 'gripping'.
(2 Samuel 3, 21)

**Ruth**  A Moabitess, ancestress of the royal line of *David. She first married Mahlon, son of *Elimelech and *Naomi, who had come to Moab from Bethlehem. When Elimelech and his two sons died Naomi decided to return to Bethlehem. Both her daughters-in-law started on the journey with her but the one, Orpah, turned back when Naomi urged them not to harness their lives and fortunes to an old woman who no longer had anything to give them. Ruth, however, refused to leaver her: 'Intreat me not to leave thee .... for whither thou goest, I will go; and where thou lodgest, I will lodge: thy people shall be my people, and thy God, my God.' They arrived in Bethlehem at the beginning of the barley harvest and Ruth went to the fields to glean after the reapers for a living – and by chance in a part of the fields belonging to *Boaz, a kinsman of Elimelech. Boaz, being told who she was and how she had supported her mother-in-law, befriended her to the extent of telling his reapers to let corn fall her way. After a harvest party Ruth, at Naomi's prompting, lay down near Boaz who, upon waking during the night, was touched by this devotion in a girl who might have chosen to lie near to a younger man.

Boaz was second in degree of kinship to Naomi and Ruth. He sought out the one kinsman with closer rights and obligations in order to give him first chance to buy from Naomi and Ruth a plot of land inherited from Elimelech, but the kinsman declined to do this and formally transmitted his prior right to Boaz by the accepted ritual of taking off his shoe and handing it to Boaz. So Boaz bought the land and with it Ruth as his wife to continue the line of Elimelech, threatened with extinction by the deaths of Elimelech and his sons. Ruth bore to Boaz a son Obed, who was the father of *Jesse and the grandfather of *David. So a seed of Moab, son of *Lot, was implanted in the royal line of Israel. The author of this delightful and happy story had also a serious purpose. He was quietly making a point against the law imposed by **Ezra and Nehemiah banning mixed marriages between Jews and non-Jews.

Through Keats Ruth has provided one of the ineffaceable images of English poetry:

> '.. the sad heart of Ruth, when sick for home, She stood in tears amid the alien corn'
>
> (*Ode to a Nightingale*)

Ruth seems to appeal to organists. The prodigious English organist and composer Samuel Wesley, son of the almost equally prodigious Charles, wrote an oratorio on Ruth. (He did so at the age of eight and soon afterwards fell into a hole in the ground and put himself out of action for ten years). The Belgian organist and composer César Franck began his career as an orchestral and choral writer with a work on the same subject. (Ruth)

| | |
|---|---|
| **Sadducees** | See under Pharisees etc. |
| **Salome** | One of the most famous women of the NT, although not named in it. Her father was a disinherited son of *Herod the Great, and her mother was *Herodias. Salome married her half-uncle Herod *Philip the tetrarch (see glossary) and then her remoter cousin Aristobulus, king of Lesser Armenia, but her unique fame comes from the story of her lascivious dancing which so pleased her stepfather Herod *Antipas that he promised to give her anything she might demand up to half his kingdom. At her mother's promp- |

ting she demanded the head of *John the Baptist who had enraged and humiliated Herodias by denouncing her unlawful marriage to Antipas

Nothing more is known about Salome except that she had children by her second marriage. A late legend relates how she met her death by falling into a freezing river where her head was caught between pieces of ice and severed from her body – too apt to be true. A mosaic in St Mark's in Venice shows Herod's banquet and Salome dancing at it. Lippo Lippi, among many others, painted her at this high point of her life but with the decorum demanded by his picture's place in the cathedral at Prato; Gustave Moreau likewise with eerie melodrama (Cambridge, Mass., Fogg Art Museum). Benozzo Gozzoli catches her heartlessness by showing her bemusing Antipas while the Baptist's head is being cut off in a small vignette behind her back (Washington, National Gallery). Titian shows her as a resplendent female holding the head aloft on a platter like a tennis champion displaying her trophy to the crowd (Madrid, Prado). Flaubert's story *Hérodias* ends with three men taking the Baptist's head away but finding it so heavy that they have to take turns carrying it. Massenet's opera *Hérodiade*, based on this story, was not allowed to be performed in London until its frightful happenings had been move from the Holy Land to Ethiopia. Oscar Wilde's play *Salomé* (1893), written in French, translated into English by Lord Alfred Douglas and published with illustrations by Aubrey Beardsley, was not deemed fit for public performance in England until 1931. It furnished the libretto for Richard Strauss's opera of the same name. Wilde changed the Bible story. To the vengeance of Herodias he added the sensual Salome's passion for the hairy preacher. Salome's obvious appeal to the choreographer caught the imagination of the French composer Florent Schmitt whose *La tragédie de Salome* is a balletic counterpart to Strauss's contemporary opera. Vaughan's poem, *The Daughter of Herodias*, describes her as the 'young sorceress' and hints at her icy death. See also the

next entry.
(Matthew 14; Mark 6)

**Salome**  Mother of the apostles \*\*James and John, sons of
\*Zebedee. She was one of the women at the foot
of the cross at the Crucifixion and, according to
\*Mark, also one of those who took spices to
anoint his body as soon as the Sabbath ended,
finding the tomb empty. They were instructed,
either by an angel or by Jesus himself, to tell the
disciples to go to Galilee and meet him there. She
may have been a sister of Jesus' mother Mary. See
also Mary and the foregoing entry.
(Matthew 27; Mark 15, 16; Luke 23, 24; John 19,
20)

**Samaritans**  Inhabitants of Samaria; also the name of a sect.
The city of Samaria was built by \*Omri king of
Israel as his capital. Its capture by Sargon of
\*Assyria in 722 BC marked the extinction of the
kingdom of \*Israel. It was repeopled by the
Assyrians, captured by Alexander the Great,
absorbed into the empire of his Seleucid successors, captured by Pompey, and restored to fortune
by \*Herod the Great who made it a capital once
more with the name of Sebaste.

The Samaritans, who believed themselves to
be the residue of the ten tribes of Israel lost after
the debacle of 722 BC, constituted a separate sect
which spilt from the main Judaic stem when the
Jewish exiles returned from Babylon to Jerusalem
in C 5 BC (see Ezra, Nehemiah). One consequence
of the Return was antagonism between those who
returned and those who had never been carried
away either to Nineveh or to Babylon. The latter
thought the former too self-righteous and exclusive and objected in particular to the rigorous ban
on mixed marriages upon which Ezra and Nehemiah insisted. The Samaritans accepted only the
first five books of the OT. Their differences with
orthodox Jews were accentuated and embittered
in the period of the \*Maccabees. A small Samar-

itan community has survived into C 20 at Nablus (ancient Shechem).

**The good Samaritan**
A man on a journey from Jerusalem to Jericho was attacked by thieves and left half dead by the side of the road. A priest came along but passed by on the other side. So did a Levite. A Samaritan, however, took pity on the victim, gave him first aid, carried him to an inn and gave the inn-keeper money to look after him with a promise of more money if needed. Jesus told this story to show that a man should be judged by what he does and not by what he is. In the Middle Ages it was used by propagandists who cast the uncaring priest and Levite as Jews and the Samaritan as Jesus. The C 27 artist Domenico Fetti shows the Good Samaritan hauling the victim onto his donkey against a background of wispily exotic trees (New York, Metropolitain Museum).
(Luke 10)

**The Woman of Samaria**
Sitting alone by *Jacob's Well, *Jesus asked a woman of Samaria to give him a drink. She was amazed since Jews did not have dealings with Samaritans. Jesus told her that if she knew who he was she would have asked him for water since water from him stilled thirst for ever, whereas water from the well merely slaked it for a time. The woman asked for the water of which Jesus spoke. After further conversation she realized that she was speaking with a prophet and when they went on to talk of the coming of the Messiah Jesus told her that he was the Messiah. Rembrandt fashioned the scene at the well about a dozen times (e.g. Birmingham, Barber Institute): Kenneth Clark pointed out that the prominence given to the well shows that Rembrandt knew that it was a symbol of purity. A more stilted version of the conversation between Jesus and the woman of Samaria was made by Allori for S. Maria Novella in Florence. She makes a brief appearance in the closing scene of Goethe's *Faust* and in Mahler's eighth symphony, whose second movement is a setting of that scene.
(John 4)

**Samson** A Judge of Israel and son of *Manoah. Samson is proverbial for his great strength and for demonstrating man's vulnerabilty to woman. His life was enmeshed in the conflict between Israel and the *Philistines. Samson saw and desired a woman of the *Philistine city of Timnath. On his way to it he ran into a young lion and killed it with his bare hands. On a second journey with his parents he saw the lion's carcase and in it a swarm of bees and honey. He ate some of the honey and gave some to his parents. At his pre-marriage feast Samson posed a riddle. To anybody who could guess the answer within seven days he would give 30 sheets and 30 changes of garments, but if nobody could guess right they would give him the same. The riddle was: 'Out of the eater came the forth meat, and out of the strong came forth sweetness.' The baffled guests got Samson's intended wife to wheedle the answer out of him. Samson had to pay up but he did so by first going to Ashdod and there killing 30 Philistines and taking their garments off them. (Lions were still common in western Asia in Biblical times: Tiglath-Pileser I of *Assyria killed over 700. The idea that bees might be created out of putrifying flesh was familiar to Greeks and Romans as well as Jews.)

Meanwhile Samson's prospective father-in-law had given his daughter to another man, upon which Samson caught 300 foxes, tied them tail-to-tail in couples, fixed burning brands between the knotted tails and loosed them in the Philistines' cornfields. The furious Philistines seized and burned the prospective father-in-law and his daughter. Samson retaliated by smiting the Philistines 'hip and thigh', but his own people were so scared by these commotions that they seized Samson, bound him and handed him over to the Philistines in order to appease them. But Samson broke his cords and killed a thousand Philistines with the jawbone of an ass. He proceeded to the Philistine city of Gaza where, in the course of a visit to a prostitute, he was surrounded but escaped and when beset by enemies at the city gates burst through them taking the gates and posts with him.

He fell in love with *Delilah and the Philistines pestered her to discover the secret of his phenomenal strength. At first he put her off with false answers but in the end he revealed that no razor had ever cut his hair and that if it did he would be no stronger than the next man. They came and shaved his locks while he was asleep and put out his eyes and put him in prison in Gaza to grind corn. But his hair began to grow again and when the Philistines sent for him to make mock of him at a party he got a boy to guide his hands to the pillars of the house where they were and pulled it down, so killing another 3,000 Philistines and himself. The fateful cutting of the hair of the strong man sleeping with his head on his woman's knee is shown with opulence by Sebastiano del Piombo and by Rubens (both London, National Gallery). The act of putting out his eyes is painted with terrible realism by Rembrandt (Frankfurt, Art Gallery) who handled the story of Samson several times, including his riddling at his wedding feast (Dresden, Art Gallery). Milton's *Samson Agonistes* begins when the tragic hero is already 'eyeless in Gaza at the mill with slaves' and ends with the report of his fearful vengeance and death. The text of Handel's oratorio, his most operatic in the vulgar use of that word, is a compressed version of Milton's epic and contains the famous aria: 'Let the bright Seraphim . . . ' Saint Säens' most successful opera, *Sanson et Dalila*, was first performed in Germany by Liszt because the French found it too modern for their taste. The strangest depiction of Samson is by Guido Reni who shows him triumphant, curiously elegant, almost balletic, with a carpet of corpses at his feet (Bologna, Academy).
(Judges 13-16)

**Samuel**  The last of the *Judges of Israel. Samuel inaugurated its first two kings *Saul and *David. His parents were Elkanah and *Hannah and although

Elkanah had children by another wife he had none by Hannah. From this unhappy lot Hannah was rescued by the priest *Eli and when she bore Samuel she gave the child to Eli as a servant. One night God spoke to Samuel but Samuel thought the voice was Eli's. When the call was repeated Eli realized that Samuel was being called by God and he got Samuel to tell him what God was saying to him. So he learned that Samuel would take his place when his house was destroyed as a result of his sons' transgressions – a calamity which occured when the Philistines captured the ark of the covenant (see Eli). Under Samuel's leadership Israel turned the tables on the Philistines and recovered the cities of the coast. The people, however, wanted a king (for an earlier attempt see Abimelech) and persisted even when Samuel painted a grim picture of how a king and his captains would treat them. God said to Samuel: 'Make them a king'. That king was Saul. But Saul fell short notably in his lenient treatment of *Agag and the Amalekites, and Samuel was obliged to step in, himself hew Agag in pieces and tell Saul that God repented of choosing him to be king and rejected him. Samuel's mission after this meeting was to find and designate a successor to Saul – in fact David. Samuel made a spectral appearance after his death when summoned by the witch of *En-dor at the behest of Saul, whose coming defeat and death he foretold. Reynolds' picture of the infant Samuel once hung, in reproduction in sepia, in countless middle-class night nurseries. Samuel's anointing of David has been another attractive subject for painters and sculptors, for instance on the facade of Orvieto cathedral where the multiple imagery is in itself something of a Who's Who in the Bible. Holbein drew Samuel's most hazardous undertaking, when he was forced to convey God's anger to king Saul (Basel, City Museum).
(I Samuel 1-4, 7-13, 15, 16, 25, 28)

**Sanabassar**   See Sheshbazzar

**Sapphira**   See Ananias

**Sarah**   Originally Sarai, wife of *Abraham. She was married to Abraham before he set out from Ur on his long trek to the land of Canaan. She remained childless into old age and when she overheard three men – angels in disguise – tell Abraham that she would have a child, she laughed. But she did and he was *Isaac. See family tree B, the next entry and, for the less pleasant side of her character, *Hagar.
(Genesis 11, 12, 16-25)

**Sarah**   Daughter and sole surviving kin of Raguel. She married Tobias, son of *Tobit, after seven previous marriages had been wrecked by the evil spirit Asmodeus, See also the foregoing entry.
(Torbit 3, 7, 8, 10-12)

**Saul**   Son of Kish of the tribe of *Benjamin. His story begins with him roaming the country in search of his father's lost asses and ends with his suicide. In between he was chosen by God and anointed by *Samuel as first king over all the tribes of Israel but was rejected by God after failing to kill enough *Amalekites. The latter part of his life was consumed by wars with the *Philistines and by conflict with *David whom he alternately loved and tried to kill. This conflict was made all the more bitter by the love of his own son *Jonathan for David. He lived in C 11 BC.

Saul was a 'choice young man, and goodly . . . from his shoulders and upward he was higher than any of the people'. Samuel, forewarned by God of Saul's approach and destiny, received him with honours above his years and station, told him where to find the lost asses and anointed him 'captain' over (God's) inheritance'. He then summoned all the tribes and presented Saul to them and 'all the people shouted, and said, God save the king'. Thus was the kingdom insituted by God and the people. It was renewed and Saul made king at Gilgal after the first test of his leadership – the defeat of *Nahash, king of the *Ammonities, who had been harassing Israel from the east in collusion with the Philistines in the west. Saul and Jonathan then turned against the Philistines and Amalekites in the west and south-west. Saul's acid test, which he failed, came with the war against the Amalekites. Saul was commanded by God to destroy the Amalekites utterly, but after defeating them he spared their king *Agag and, in deference to his people, spared also the best of the Amalekites' flocks and herds. God, incensed by these half measures, sent Samuel to seize Agag (whom he 'hewed in pieces before the Lord in Gilgal') and to tell Saul that God had rejected him. This was the last meeting between Saul and Samuel alive.

Saul became depressed and hoped to find relief by finding a 'cunning man with a harp'. This man turned out to be David who so pleased Saul that he made David his armour-bearer and one of his captains. But Saul became jealous of David and suspicious, particularly after David's success against *Goliath and consequent popularity. Saul gave David his younger daughter *Michal as wife 'to be a snare to him' and demanded in return 100 foreskins of the Philistines. He thought in this way to get David killed but David killed 200 Philistines – and got Michal, who loved him and saved his life. For the rest of his reign Saul oscillated between trying to get David killed and relenting (see David). Pursued by failure Saul, in disguise and in despair, consulted the witch of *En-dor, who raised for him the dead Samuel who reminded him of his transgression over Agag and foretold his final defeat by the Philistines and death. His three sons – Jonathan, Ishui and Melchi-shua – were killed in battle with the Philistines and he himself committed suicide by falling on his sword after his armour-bearer refused to kill him. 'Saul and Jonathan,' lamented David, 'were lovely and pleasant in their lives, and in their death they were not divided . . .' Saul's head was cut off and his body fixed to a wall in

Beth-shan but his body, and his sons' bodies, were recovered by men of Jabesh-gilead where they were cremated and the bones buried under a tree. Many years later David reinterred them in the sepulchre of Saul's father Kish.

Saul's high promise turned to failure and psychological collapse. He is a human, tragic figure whom it is easier to weep for than condemn. Rembrandt conveys the fullness of the looming calamity of the brooding monarch trying to find solace in music (The Hague, Mauritshuis). *The Suicide of Saul* by Peter Brueghel the Elder (Vienna, Kunsthistorisches Museum) is a fantastic panorama with Saul dying in a corner of the picture as his army takes to flight. The Romantics loved Saul. Byron's *Song of Saul before his Last Battle* gives him a retrieved dignity at the end. Alfieri wrote his most accomplished tragedy about Saul. Robert Browning, in his *Saul*, is at pains to tell that although David cannot heal Saul's tortured soul *Jesus will; but what remains in the mind after reading that poem is something more human than theological – the young David, wearied by his all-night harping and abashed by the feeling that he has failed, stumbling home very sad. Handel took a less complicated view. In his oratorio *Saul* he is unreservedly on Saul's side and wrote a famous and fitting funeral march for this moody man.
(I Samuel 9-31; I Chron. 10)

**Semites**  A major branch of the human race; legendarily the descendants of *Shem, the eldest of *Noah's sons. In scholarly terms the word semutic denotes the large group of languages prevalent in the Middle East and northern and north-eastern Africa. They include *Hebrew and modern Arabic. Almost the entire cast of the OT is semitic. See also family tree A.

**Sergius Paulus**  A hesitant convert who took the plunge when the sorcerer *Bar-jesus, who was obstructing the missionary efforts of **Paul and Barnabas, was struck with blindness.

**Seth**    Son of **Adam and Eve, ancestor of
**Methuselah and Noah. In a legend not in the
Bible Seth got from the archangel Michael a
branch of the forbidden tree of Eden with which
to heal the dying Adam but arrived back to find
Adam already dead. He planted the branch on
Adam's grave, where it grew into a tree which
eventually provided wood for the cross on which
*Jesus was crucified. This legend is depicted by
Agnolo Gaddi in the church of S. Croce in Florence.
See family tree A.
(Genesis 4, 5)

**Shadrach**    One of the three friends of *Daniel who were
thrown into the fiery furnace by comman of
*Nebuchadnezzar. He was originally call Hana-
niah. His two friends were **Aled-nego and
Meshach.
(Daniel 2, 3)

**Sheba**    Queen of, unnamed in the Bible but called
elsewhere Balkis or Bilkis and by other names. For
so famous a personage the Queen of Sheba
occupies a surprisingly small space in the Bible –
11 verses in 1 Kings, repeated in 2 Chronicles. They
testify to *Solomon's fame and riches. These were
such that the queen could not believe what she heard
without seeing for herself. So she travelled to
Jerusalem, found Solomon even wiser and richer
than she had supposed and gave him great gifts of
gold and spices. He gave her 'all her desire' – as to
which posterity has speculated with prurient
surmise. With more scholarly surmise posterity
has also debated where she came from. Some
place her in Arabia in what is now Yemen; others
on the other side of the Red Sea in what is now
Ethiopia. Saba (Sheba) in south-west Arabia was
rich enough to qualify as the realm of the great
queen – but not until several centuries after
Solomon's time. Contrariwise the queen, in a
tradition which goes back to Josephus and was
commonly accepted in Europe in the Middle Ages,
was an African; and Ethiopians have had no

doubts about claiming her as the ancestress of their royal line, fathered on her by Solomon. At Chartres, and in many other images, she is shown with an African servant. A persistent legend gives her a malformed foot, which, in western Europe, is usually webbed – hence *La Reine Pédauque* (*pied d'oie*, goosefoot). At Chartres her foot is hidden by her dress but on other French churches it is not. There is a glorious pair of C 12 statues from Corbeil, now in the Louvre: majesty portrayed as dignity. Solomon is said to have been intrigued by stories about her feet and to have laid down a floor of crystal which caused her to lift her dress because she mistook if for water – an ungallant trick. Tintoretto's portrait of her makes her every inch a queen (Madrid, Prado). Her reception by Solomon by Piero della Francesca is in the church of St Francis at Arezzo; Veronese's picture of the same scene is characteristically luscious (Turin, Galleria Sabauda); Handel's musical version is a tripping evocation which is a favourite way of beginning a concert, and Goldmark's bubbly *Queen of Sheba* is on the borderline between opera and operetta. In his poem *Solomon and Balkis* Robert Browning is in no doubt that the queen wanted from the king something saucier than wisdom; Yeats lovely poem *Solomon to Sheba* makes them definitely lovers.
(I Kings 10; Chron. 9)

**Sheba** A Benjaminite who raised a revolt against *David after the collapse of *Absalom's revolt. David sent **Joab and Abishai against him and they besieged him in Abel of Beth-maachah. To save their city the inhabitants cut off Sheba's head and threw it over the wall to Joab.
(2 Samuel 20)

**Shebna** Leader of a trio chosen by king *Hezekiah of Judah to parley with *Rab-shakeh, emissary of king *Sennacherib of Assyria. Hezekiah had switched from paying tribute to Assyria to alliance with Egypt in the desperate hope of getting rid of

the Assyrian yoke. Rab-shakeh's mission was to scare Hezekiah back into the Assyrian sphere of influence. The parley took place outside the walls of Jerusalem in the hearing of people on the walls. In response to Rab-shakeh's threatening overtures, which were aimed partly at the Jerusalemites on the walls, Shebna and his colleagues asked the Assyrians to speak in Syrian, which they said they could understand, but Rab-shakeh refused. Hezekiah and his advisers were distraught by the outcome of the exchanges and sought the advice of *Isaiah. The prophet tried to calm their fears and promised them that God would defend Jerusalem. This promise was redeemed when Sennacherib's army was destroyed in the night by the angel of death. Shortly afterwards Sennacherib himself was murdered in his capital of Nineveh by his sons. See also Assyria.
(2 Kings 18, 19; Isaiah 22)

**Shechem**    Son of Hamor, a princely neighbour of *Jacob. Shechem raped Jacob's daughter *Dinah. Shechem and Hamor asked for Dinah as Shechem's wife but her brothers **Simeon and Levi preferred to slaughter Shechem and his compatriots. See Dinah.
(Genesis 33, 34)

**Shechemites**    People of Shechem, a city which supported *Abimelech's attempt to make himself a king and then deserted him. His mother was a Shechemite. See also the preceding entry.

**Shem**    Eldest son of *Noah and eponymous progenitor of the semitic races. With his brother *Japheth he managed to cover Noah's nakedness without seeing it. *Abraham was descended from him. See family tree A.
(Genesis 5-11)

**Sheshbazzar**    A prince of *Judah who was made governor of Jerusalem by the Persian king *Cyrus and was

entrusted with the return to the Temple of the immense quantities of precious vessels which had been looted from it by *Nebuchadnezzar. In the apocryphal Book of Esdras he is called Sanabassar.
(Ezra 1, 5; 1 Esdras 2)

**Shilonites**   People of Shiloh, the holiest place of the *Israelites until *David captured Jerusalem and made it his capital. See further under **Joshua, Eli, Ahijah, Benjaminites.

**Shimei**   A partisan of the house of *Saul who cursed *David and threw stones and dung at him when he seemed on the point of being overthrown by the rebellion of his son *Absalom. When David triumphed Shimei grovelled and was forgiven but from his deathbed David advised his successor *Solomon to have Shimei put away. At first Solomon tolerated Shimei and allowed him to remain unharmed in Jerusalem for three years on the condition that he did not try to leave the city. But when two of Shimei's servants ran away Shimei followed them to get them back. On his return Solomon had him killed.
(2 Samuel 16, 19; I Kings I, 2)

**Shishak (or Sheshonk)**   Founder of the XXII Egyptian dynasty. He restored Egyptian power after one of its periods of decline, sacked Jerusalem c. 925 BC soon after the death of *Solomon, and re-established – albeit temporarily – Egyptian hegemony over the Promised Land.
(I Kings 11; 2 Chron. 12)

**Shulamite**   A purely literary creation the Shulamite is a young girl of bewitching beauty and the ultimate symbol of an eroticism which is wholly unvulgar. She appears in a number of love lyrics which suggests that she ends where she began in the arms of a rustic swain to whom she has remained faithful in spite of exciting opportunities for a richer life. The Song of Solomon, or Song of Songs, which is a sequence of love lyrics addressed to the Shulamite,

has baffled and embarassed commentators mainly because of its presence in a collection of religious writings. It belongs in that large literary category of allegories in which serious ideas are clothed in the language of love – the attractions obvious, the ultimate meaning not so clear. It was composed many centuries after *Solomon's time and has no historical value beyond its testimony to the magic of Solomon's name.
(Song of Solomon)

**Shunammites**  Two Shunammite women won a place in Biblical history. The one, *Abishag, was chosen to comfort *David in his old age and keep him warm. The other, unnamed, provided *Elisha with bed and bread and was rewarded with a child even though her husband was old. The child died but Elisha revived it by lying on it, mouth to mouth, eyes to eyes, hands upon hands.
(1 Kings 1; 2 Kings 4)

**Sihon**  King of the *Amorites whose capital was at Heshbon. His domains lay to the east of the Dead Sea. He refused peaceful passage to *Moses and the Israelites who therefore attacked and defeated him and took all his lands. Sihon was caught at an unlucky moment. He had recently expanded his kingdom in war against the *Moabites but had not had time to establish sure control.
(Numbers 32; Deuteronomy 2; I Kings 4; Nehemiah 9)

**Silas**  One of *Paul's main missionary companions. He was sent with *Judas Barsabas by the Christians of Jerusalem to Antioch with Paul and *Barnabas and attached himself to Paul when Judas returned to Jerusalem. Paul chose him to take the place of *John Mark as a travelling companion after he had become dissatisfied with John Mark on their first trip together.
(Acts 15)

**Simeon**  The second of the twelve sons of *Jacob. His mother was *Leah. With his brother *Levi he

wreaked cruel and deceitful vengeance on
*Shechem and the Shechemites in retaliation for
the rape of their sister *Dinah. On his deathbed
Jacob cursed Simeon and Levi and condemned
them to be scattered in Israel. See also the next
entry.
(Genesis 29, 34, 35, 42-50; Joshua 19)

Simeon    A good and devout man of Jerusalem to whom it
was revealed that the infant *Jesus was the
Messiah. He took the child into his arms and
praised and thanked God in the words since
known as the *Nunc Dimittis:* 'Lord, now lettest
thou thy servant depart in peace . . .' T.S. Eliot's
'A Song for Simeon' repeats the Biblical theme,
working in several phrases from the Bible.

*SIMON*    A common name in the NT, akin to *Simeon
which is found in both OT and NT. Eight Simons
are noted below. They are Simon Maccabaeus;
Simon Peter, commonly called Peter; Simon the
Zealot, one of the twelve apostles; Simon the
leper, with whom *Jesus lodged in Bethany;
Simon of Cyrene, who carried the cross to
Calvary; a supposed brother of Jesus; and two
Simons, the one a magus and the other a tanner
whom Peter encountered on his travels after the
Resurrection.

Simon    Brother of *Judas Maccabaeus. He ruled the
Maccabee principality from 142 to 134 BC with
the title (from 140 BC) of high priest. See
Maccabees and family tree E.
(I Maccabees 5, 9, 12, 14-16 ; Maccabees 8)

Simon Peter    See Peter

Simon the Zealot    Also the Canaanite, one of the twelve apostles. He
is not named by John. It is uncertain whether he

met his death by crucifixion or by being sawn in two. His emblem is a saw. For the Zealots see under Pharisees etc.
(Matthew 10; Mark 3; Luke 6; Acts I)

**Simon**
A leper in whose house in Bethany *Jesus rested on his way to Jerusalem. This was where *Mary, sister of *Martha, poured some precious ointment over Jesus' head out of an alabaster box.
(Matthew 26; Mark 14; Luke 10; John 11, 12)

**Simon of Cyrene**
A passer-by who was impressed to carry the cross on the road to the Crucifixion.
(Mark 15; Luke 23)

**Simon**
One of the supposed brothers of *Jesus. See under *James the Less.

**Simon**
A magus or sorcerer of Samaria who was converted and baptized by the deacon Philip (see under Stephen). Simon tried to buy from the apostles a share in their power to heal by laying on hands but was told by *Peter that the power could not be had for money.
(Acts 8)

**Simon the tanner**
Host to *Peter in Joppa.
(Acts 9)

**Sisera**
Captain of the armies of *Jabin, king of Canaan, whose forces were routed by Barak and *Deborah and who was killed by *Jael who drove a tent-nail through his head.
(Judges 4, 5)

**Sodomites**
The people of Sodom, a city on the west shore of the Dead Sea, closely linked with Gomorrah.

When *Lot parted from his uncle *Abraham because their combined flocks and herds had become too large to be managed as a single entity, Lot chose to make his home in these rich 'cities of the plain'. Five of these cities formed a league to defend themselves against an aggressive alliance of eastern cities, but they lost and were destroyed (see *Amraphel). Their fate was ascribed to the wrath of God incurred by their unnatural sexual tastes. These proclivities were not explicitly referred to in the OT but may be deduced without difficulty from the episode in which Lot felt obliged to offer his daughters to some rowdy Sodomites in order to protect a passing male guest from their importunities.

**Solomon**  Son of *David and king of Israel c. 968-928 BC, a byword for wisdom and opulence. His succession to the throne was contested but after dispersing the opposition he enjoyed a long and exceptionally prosperous reign, amassing wealth in preference to making war. Supported by the dying David, he triumphed over his elder brother *Adonijah who made a bid for the throne with the support of some of David's most powerful counsellors. These were wiped out by Solomon. Early in his reign God spoke to him and asked him to name a gift. Solomon asked for wisdom and God was so pleased with this answer that he gave Solomon not only wisdom but long life and riches too. Solomon quickly displayed his wisdom. He was confronted by two harlots, each of whom had had a child and was claiming to be the mother of the only one to survive. He solved the dilemma by ordering that the child be cut in two and that each woman be given a half: by abandoning her claim the real mother identified herself.

*His magnificence*  Solomon inherited from David and put into effect plans for building a temple; it was to be 60 by 20 cubits and 30 cubits high (a Hebrew cubit = 22 inches), covered with gold and replete with sumptuous ornaments. The building took seven years. Solomon also built splendid palaces for himself and his first wife, the daughter of the Egyptian pharaoh. He raised armies of workers whom he sent to neighbouring Lebanon to work there for one month in three. In all his public works Solomon was assisted by *Hiram, king of the Phoenician city of Tyre (whose realm included Lebanon), who supplied cedars and firs in exchange for food and oil and sent skilled labourers to work on the buildings. He was rewarded with 20 cities in Galilee – but he did not like them. After the solemn dedication of the Temple, God again spoke to Solomon and promised him a perpetual kingship for himself and his descendants, provided they continued to serve Him faithfully and rightly.

Solomon built a navy, again with Hiram's help, and together the two kings despatched a joint expedition to Ophir at the far end of the Red Sea to fetch gold and timber and precious stones. The Queen of *Sheba, dazzled by reports of Solomon's magnificence, visited him and was even more dazzled by the reality. Yet there was a fly in all this ointment. Solomon was as lavish in his affections as in everything else, and among his 700 wives and 300 concubines were many strange women of foreign race and false religion by whom Solomon was induced to forget the rules of racial purity and exclusive worship. God, angered by these lapses, decreed that Solomon should lose his kingdom but He was moved to postpone this penalty until after Solomon's death and to modify it to the extent of allowing Solomon's progeny to inherit a piece of it. In Solomon's closing years God revived the threat to Israel from *Edom – in the person of *Hadad who had been lurking in Egypt since being defeated by David and *Joab. Other old enemies raised their heads, and within Israel itself – where Solomon's appetite for luxury made for harsh rule – *Jeroboam was encouraged to challenge Solomon's son. Jeroboam took refuge in Egypt to await Solomon's death and the chance to seize a kingdom where Solomon's line had become unpopular.

*His reputed works*  Solomon has been credited, but no longer cred-

ibly, with the composition of thousands of sayings and hundreds of songs, including the Book of Proverbs; Ecclesiastes ('Vanity of vanities, saith the Preacher . . . the son of David'); the Song of Solomon or Song of Songs (see Shulamite); and the apocryphal Wisdom of Solomon (a composition of C 3 BC, Greek in style and thought, which includes the marvellously comforting passage beginning: 'The souls of the righteous are in the hand of God, and there shall no torment touch them'). Solomon has not lacked for artists to proclaim his glory or his wisdom. Besides countless mediaeval carvings and glass windows he has been treated by the most eminent Renaissance painters e.g. the appropriately magnificent *Judgement of Solomon* at Kingston Lacy, once ascribed to Giorgione but now, in part or wholly, to Sebastiano del Piombo; Raphael's design (executed by his pupils) in the Vatican; and Rubens' dramatic version (Madrid, Prado) in which the child is being held by a foot upside down. Duncan Grant painted Solomon with the Queen of Sheba, the king – whose keenly semitic face is modelled on Lytton Strachey's – pensively assessing the queen (London, Tate Gallery). Handel found in Solomon a peculiarly apposite theme – the theme of wordly success with which to please the Hanoverian court in London. Solomon's renown, comparable with Alexander the Great's, has carried his name to strange places, as witness Rider Haggard's *King Solomon's Mines* and various mountain tops called Takht-i-Suleiman (throne of Solomon).
(I Kings I-11; I Chron. 22, 23, 28, 29; 2 Chron. 1-9)

**Sosthenes**  The head of the synagogue in Corinth. During *Paul's visit to that city most of the Jews were hostile to him and demonstrated violently against him in the hope of getting the Roman governor *Gallio to imprison or evict him. But Gallio could not be bothered with such things, even when Sosthenes was seized and beaten in his presence. Presumably Sosthenes belonged to the minority of

Jews who welcomed Paul or at least wanted him to have a fair hearing. He was later co-author of Paul's first letter to the Corinthians after he had left them.
(Acts 18; I Cor. I)

**Stephen** First Christian martyr. He was one of seven deacons chosen to help the twelve apostles in their work of preaching the divinity and resurrection of *Jesus. The others were Philip, Prochorus, Nicanor, Timon, Parmenas, and Nicolas of Antioch. For his missionary activities he was driven out of Jerusalem and stoned to death. Rembrandt shows his end (Lyon, Art Gallery) and so does Burne-Jones – on glass (Morton, Lincolnshire, St Paul's). According to the Golden Legend – for which see under Mark – Stephen's body was rescued by *Gamaliel, re-discovered in C 5 and ended partly in Rome and partly – an arm – in Capua.
(Acts 6, 7)

**Susanna** The alluring wife of the prosperous Joakim, owner of a large house and fine garden which were used for meetings of the better sort of citizen, including two elders who longed to seduce Susanna. Contriving to be the last to leave a certain meeting, they parted from one another but each then secretly doubled back and so ran into the other. They confessed their several but similar designs and together surprised Susanna in the garden where she had gone to bathe. She was alone, having sent her servants to fetch something from the house. The elders demanded sex upon pain of proclaiming that they had caught her with a young man. She shouted for help and they put their threat into effect. She was reviled, tried and condemned to death, but *Daniel stood up for her and insisted on questioning the two elders separately. Upon being asked under which tree they had found Susanna with the young man, they gave different answers and so discredited themselves. The peeping elders waiting to pounce on the radiant Susanna have provided painters with an irresistible theme and Susanna herself has been depicted in a gamut of reactions: by Titian (Vienna, Kunsthistorisches Museum) admiring herself in a mirror; by Veronese (Prado) and Bassano (Nîmes, Musée des Beaux Arts) surprised and recoiling; by Domenichino (Munich, Alte Pinakothek) surprised and grabbed; by Tintoretto (Prado) grabbed and fondled. Guido Reni's elders (Florence, Uffizi) get the closest look, while Guercino's (Madrid, Prado) are stealing up on her from behind, still unseen. Her trial for adultery is a showpiece in the grand manner by Antoine Coypel (Prado). Daniel's defence of Susanna is echoed in the trial scene in Shakespeare's *The Merchant of Venice* where Shylock and Gratiano, each in turn when he thinks he is winning, hails Portia as a new Daniel come to judgment. Such is the artistry of this Bible story that it came to be regarded as true. The great scholar Origen thought so, until he was put right by one of his correspondents.

(The History of Susanna)

**Syria**  The northern part of the lands between Egypt and Asia Minor (modern Turkey) with, in the south, the Promised Land disputed between the Israelites and their Canaanitish and other enemies. On the coast to the west were the cities of the *Phoenicians, while eastward Syria reached into the desert and to the Euphrates. The Aramaean kingdom of Syria, whose capital was Damascus, was formed at about the same time (c. 1200 BC) as the Exodus of the Israelites from Egypt. Both peoples flourished and warred with one another in a period when the great powers of the Tigris/Euphrates and Nile valleys were in occlusion. A strong Israel meant trouble for Syria and *vice versa*. In C 10 BC *David took Damascus; in C 9 BC Kings **Omri and Ahab of Israel (c. 876-851 BC) hammered Syria. The spread of Assyrian power from the east forced these traditional enemies to patch up their quarrels and at the battle of Karkar in 853 BC they checked the Assyrian advance. But they reverted to fighting one another and in C 8 BC Israel, in alliance with Judah, briefly occupied Damascus. When the expansion of Assyria was resumed by the usurper Tiglath-Pileser III – called in the Bible *Pul – Syria was extinguished in 732 BC and Israel ten years later. The ultimate decline of Assyria over the next hundred years did not save Syria, which passed into the hands of Babylonians, Persians, Macedonians and Romans. By the beginning of the Christian era its chief city was no longer Damascus but Antioch, where *Luke practiced as a doctor and *Paul had his headquarters for a number of years. See also Ben-hadad and Hazael.

**Tabitha**  (In Greek) Dorcas. A woman of Joppa, full of good works, who was restored to life by *Peter after he was shown all the coats and other garments which she had made for others. Whence a Dorcas is a sewing bee. Peter raising her from the dead is among Masaccio's scenes from the apostle's life in the Brannacci chapel in S. Maria del Carmine, Florence.
(Acts 9)

**Tamar**  A Canaanitess married to *Judah's eldest son Er. He died without issue. Judah required his second son, *Onan, to give her children, but Onan resorted to the unfruitful practice since named after him. For so wasting his seed God killed him. Judah had a third son, Shelah, but he was too young. Desparing of her prospects, Tamar enticed Judah himself into lying with her by pretending to be a harlot and after first exacting from him his seal and other tokens. When her pregnancy became obvious Judah condemned her to death for extra-familial sex, but she produced the tokens and was reprieved. She had twins called Perez (or Pharez) and Zerah. The former was the ancestor of *David who had therefore Canaanitish blood –

as well as that of the Moabitess, *Ruth. See also the next entry and family tree C.
(Genesis 38; Ruth 4)

Tamar    Daughter of *David. She was passionately desired by her half-brother *Amnon who, following a plan devised by his friend and cousin *Jonadab, pretended to be ill and asked for Tamar to look after him. He raped her but immediately came to hate her and had his servant throw her out. She was avenged by her full brother *Absalom who contrived the murder of Amnon two years later. In a picture by Le Sueur (once thought to depict Tarquin and Lucretia) Amnon threatens Tamar with a knife (New York, Metropolitan Museum). See also the foregoing entry.
(2 Samuel 13)

Terah    Father of **Abraham, Nahor and Haran. He was descended from Shem, with seven generations intervening between the two of them. Terah led the migration from Ur, in which he was accompanied by Abraham. Of his other sons Haran was already dead and Nahor stayed behind. Terah settled in Haran and died there. See family tree A.
(Genesis 11)

Tertullus    An orator hired by the high priest *Ananias to lay accusations against Paul.
(Acts 24)

Thaddeus    Also Lebbaeus Thaddeus, one of the twelve apostles named by **Matthew and Mark. In Luke's Gospel and in Acts he is called Judaeus, son of James. *John does not name him.
(Matthew 10; Mark 3; Luke 6; Acts I)

Theophilus    Friend of *Luke whose Gospel was addressed to him, as also Acts. From the way he is addressed in both works he must have been a most superior person, perhaps a Roman senator or governor. (Luke I, Acts I)

**Thomas**  Called Didymus or Twin, one of the twelve apostles. According to *John, Thomas was not with his fellow apostles when *Jesus appeared to them after the Resurrection and showed them his wounds. They told Thomas what they had seen, but Thomas refused to believe them without seeing for himself. Although they were in a locked room Jesus appeared and showed his wounds and Thomas saw and put his hand in Jesus' side and believed. Thomas acquired the reputation of having carried the gospel as far as southern India. If he did so, which is unlikely, he must have returned, since his remains were venerated from an early date at Edessa in Syria. Guercino's *Incredulity of St Thomas* (London, National Gallery) shows Thomas in the act of putting his finger on Jesus. There is another version of the scene by Gerrit van Honthorst (Madrid, Prado), and a grand picture, by Cima of Conegliano, of the resolution of his doubts has recently returned to the National Gallery in London after more than a decade in the skilful and patient hands of the restorers.
(Matthew 10; Mark 3; Luke 6; John II, 14, 20, 21; Acts I)

**Tiglath-Pileser III**  King of Assyria. See Pul.

**Timothy**  Sometimes Timotheus, son of a Greek father and a Jewish mother, one of Paul's closest companions and co-author or amanuensis of a number of his letters; also the addressee of 1 and 2 Timothy; clearly an invaluable helper and faithful friend about whom nothing except that can confidently be said. (Acts 16-18; Romans 16; I Cor. 14, 16; 2 Cor. I; I Thess. I, 3; 2 Thess. I; Coloss. I; Phlipp. 2; Philemon; 1 and 2 Timothy)

**Titus**    A Gentile of Antioch, taken by *Paul to the conference in Jerusalem in c. AD 48 at which the admissibility of uncircumcised non-Jews to the Christian community was debated. Paul refused to circumcise Titus who became a symbol of Paul's determination to extend the Christian faith to Gentile as well as Jew. Titus accompanied Paul on his second long journey and became an important member of his staff.
(2 Cor. 2, 8, 12; Gal. 2; 2 Timothy 4)

**Tobias**    Son of *Tobit

**Tobit**    A Jewish captive in the Assyrian capital Nineveh who devoted himself to giving illicit help to his fellow captives. He was found out, lost his job and was made destitute, but his lot improved with a change of regime: the new king Esarhaddon (see Assyria) thought well of him. One day Tobit sent his son Tobias to find a poor man to share their Pentecostal meal. Tobias came back with the news that a Jew had been strangled and his body abandoned in the marketplace. In defiance of regulations Tobit went to collect the body to give it burial. Being ritually polluted by these charitable acts, he lay down to sleep outside his house and while he was asleep he was blinded by the droppings of sparrows onto his eyes. He was blind for eight years.

In time past Tobit had deposited ten talents with a man of Rages in Media (modern Rhey on the outskirts of Teheran) and he sent Tobias to find this man and get the money back. Since Tobias did not know the way, he took, at one drachma a day, a guide who was the archangel Raphael in disguise. They took also a dog with them. On reaching the Tigris they came upon a big fish which attacked Tobias. At the angel's command Tobias tackled and caught the fish, cut it up and ate it, keeping back its heart, liver and gall. Arrived at the Median capital Ecbatana, Raphael took his companion to lodge with *Raguel who was a cousin of Tobit. Raguel had an only daughter *Sarah and thoughts of marriage entered everybody's head. But Sarah had a peculiar history. She had been seven times married and on each occasion the consummation of the marriage had been prevented by an evil spirit, Asmodeus, who killed the bridegroom on the nuptial night. Tobit was reluctant to become the eighth victim but he was persuaded by Raphael to take the risk and instructed to burn the fish's heart and liver in the bridal chamber. When he did so Asmodeus fled to uppermost Egypt and to everybody's surprise (except Raphael's) the pair emerged next morning alive and happy. Meanwhile Raphael journeyed on to Rages where he collected the ten talents. Returning to Nineveh, Raphael restored Tobit's sight with the fish's gall. Tobit ended his days in Ecbatana where he lived long enough to rejoice over the destruction of Nineveh. This engaging, if rambling, tale has everything: nice people; an angel, a devil and a whiff of magic; an animal; and a happy ending. Such stories – Ruth and Susanna are others, but without the magic – humanized the OT and kept it close to generation after generation of ordinary people. In c. 1200, for example, one Matthew of Vendôme retold the story of 'Tobias senior and junior' in Latin verses which, although dedicated to the bishop and dean of Tours, were clearly meant to be read beyond the cathedral close – a mediaeval counterpart of the more modern popularization achieved by Negro spirituals.

Tobias and angel, with dog, are shown as happy travelling companions by Filippino Lippi (Washington, National Gallery), Pollaiuolo (Turin, Galleria Sabauda) and Titian (Venice, San Marziale). In Savoldo's painting the fish is a friendly creature poking its nose out of the water with incautious curiosity (Rome, Villa Borghese). Botticelli unwarrantably gives Tobias three angels (Turin, Galleria Sabauda). Rembrandt loved the story well enough to paint it several times: for example, the angel flying away in a blaze of yellows as Tobias watches open-mouthed from a

corner of the picture (Paris, Louvre); or blind Tobit and his wife in tender companionship (Amsterdam, Rijksmuseum). Guardi too took time off from painting Venetian palaces and canals to portray Tobit and his wife (Venice, San Raffaelle).
(Tobit)

**Tubal-cain**   Son of *Lamech by his second wife, Zillah. He was a smith, a worker in brass and iron, the patron of those who turn swords into plough-shares. See family tree A.
(Genesis 4)

**Tychichus**   Companion of *Paul on his last visit to Jerusalem and when Paul was in prison.
(Acts 20; Coloss. 4; Ephesians 6; 2 Timothy 4, 21; Titus 3)

**Uriah**   The Hittite, husband of *Bathsheba and victim of *David's concupiscence. As soon as David caught sight of Bathsheba from his roof-top he deter-mined to have her, and having seduced her he sent Uriah, cuckolded and unsuspecting, to his general *Joab with a letter instructing Joab to put Uriah in the front line of the fighting, where he was killed. The treatment of Uriah is the biggest stain on David's record. Uriah was a Hittite only in a secondary sense. By his time the Hittites and their empire had disappeared from the scene – the last Hittite empire was extinguished c. 1200 BC (see introduction) – but their name continued to be applied to those who lived in what had been its southernmost extension. Uriah with David was painted by Rembrandt (Leningrad, Hermitage). An example of a Uriah in modern literature is provided by Kipling's Jack Barrett in his poem 'Uriah'
(2 Samuel 11)

**Uzziah**  Also called Azariah, King of Judah c. 786-758 BC. He was a leper, smitten with the disease for his presumption in usurping the functions of the priests in the Temple. In his earlier days he was a great conqueror who, by reasserting Judah's dominance over *Edom, the cities of the *Philistines and the nomads of the Negeb, made Judah's southern borders secure as far as the frontiers of Egypt. But a greater conqueror was coming: *Assyria. Judah's problem was to know whether to join or evade alliance with **Israel and Syria against the growing menace of Assyria. Uzziah did not, perhaps could not, resolve this dilemma, which he left to his successors. His grandson Ahaz, king c. 735-715 BC, reaped the whirlwind: he refused to join an anti-Assyrian coalition but when his refusal brought upon him an invasion from Israel and Syria, he turned to Assyria for protection and ended up an Assyrian satellite. See further under Hezekiah, Josiah.
(I Kings 15-17; 2 Chron. 26; Isaiah I; Amos I, 6; Zechariah 14)

**Vashti**  Wife of *Ahasuerus king of Persia. She disobeyed his command, delivered by his seven chamberlains, to appear before him and disclose her beauty to the people. She was put away as a bad example to other wives.
(Esther 1-2)

**Zacchaeus**  A rich publican of Jericho who was unusually short. He climbed a sycamore to be able to get a better view of Jesus who called to him to come down because he wanted to lodge with him. The bystanders muttered that Zacchaeus was a sinner and no fit host, but Jesus made the point that he had come to save the lost. Zacchaeus gave half his property to the poor and made fourfold restitution to those whom he had wronged with false accusations. Francis Quarles' poem 'On Zacchaeus', as delightful as it is short, ends: 'Down came Zacchaeus, ravished from the tree; Bird that

was shot ne'er dropped so quick as he.'
(Luke 19)

**Zacharias**  A priest with a wife *Elizabeth, both of them
beyond the child-bearing limit. Officiating one
day in the Temple, Zacharias saw the archangel
Gabriel standing to the right of the altar. The
angel told him that he and Elizabeth would have a
son, a new *Elijah. Zacharias asked for a sign to
substantiate this unlikely event and the angel,
chiding him for his lack of faith, condemned him to
be dumb until the child's birth. The child was
named *John – to be the Baptist – and Zacharias
recovered his speech. There is a picture of him
looking very surprised in smart Flemish Renaissance costume, by Jan Prevost (Madrid, Prado),
and Stanley Spencer painted him and Elizabeth,
seen through a window near the Thames and
engaged in a variety of homely outdoor activities.
(Matthew 24; Luke 1, 11).

**Zadok**  Priest. With *Nathan the prophet he played a
decisive part in securing the throne for *Solomon
upon the death of *David when the great men of
David's entourage were split between Solomon
and his brother *Adonijah. Zadok was rewarded
with the office of chief priest which his family held
until the time of the *Maccabees. The Sadducees
(see Pharisees, Sadducees) may have got their
name from him. 'Zadok the Priest and Nathan the
prophet anointed Solomon King . . .': so begins
the anthem which Handel composed for the
coronation of George II in Westminster Abbey in
1727.
(I Kings 1-2; I Chron. 15, 16, 18)

**Zealots**  See under Pharisees etc. and Simon the Zealot.

**Zebedee**  Father of the two apostles, **James and John. His
wife *Salome tried to get special positions for her

sons in heaven but was rebuked. She was one of the women at the foot of the cross at the Crucifixion.
(Matthew 4, 10, 20, 28, Mark I, 3, 15, 16; Luke 5, 6; John 21)

**Zebulon**  One of the twelve sons of *Jacob and ancestor of one of the twelve tribes of Israel. His tribe and that of his nearest brother *Issachar were located west of the Sea of Galilee in the northern part of the Promised Land. See family tree C.
(Genesis 30, 35, 42-50; Joshua 19)

**Zechariah**  Prophet of the late C 6 BC who, like *Haggai, put his energies into support for ** Zerubbabel and Jeshua in their Return to Jerusalem from the Babylonian *Captivity, the rebuilding of the Temple and the restoration of its observances. He had visions of the unrolling of a new world order and of a nameless Messiah who would bring universal peace. The Book of Zechariah contains fragments which, no earlier than C 5 BC and possibly much later, constitute a most unattractive diatribe full of hate against the surrounding peoples in the vein of the laager mentality. These chapters (which include a reference to the price of 30 pieces of silver echoed in the NT) show how the role of a prophet degenerated through the ages from religious and moral exhortation to a narrow and vengeful chauvinism. See also Prophets.
(Zechariah; Ezra 5)

**Zelophehad**  Zelophehad having no sons, his land devolved on his daughters. A question arose – and was put to *Moses – about the land of any daughter who might marry outside her tribe and so take away part of the tribe's land. Moses decreed that a daughter with tribal land was free to marry any man within the tribe but not outside it.
(Numbers 36; Joshua 17)

**Zephaniah**  Prophet and probably great-grandson of King *Hezekiah. He was a man of educated background and uncompromising directness who concentrated his attack on the ruling class of Judah in the later C 7 BC, with a vigorous accompaniment of attacks on the *Philistines and the (now declining) *Assyrians. His is a voice of vengeance and pessimism telling of the wrath to come but, like *Amos, he glimpsed the salvation of a remnant destined to keep the house of *David alive. See also Prophets.
(Zephaniah)

**Zerubbabel**  A scion of the royal line of *David and the leader, with the priest Jeshua, of the first expedition of Jewish exiles from Babylon to rebuild Jerusalem. The history of the Return is not easy to reconstruct because the principal sources – notably the Books of **Ezra and Nehemiah – are hopelessly muddled and in many respects evidently wrong. It is, however, clear that the Persian king *Cyrus, who took Babylon in 538 BC, encouraged the Jews to go back to Jerusalem with the gold and silver vessels which *Nebuchadnezzar had carried off from the Temple, and with expectations of religious tolerance and political autonomy. Zerubbabel's expedition consisted of **Levites, Benjaminites and Judahites and was not well received by the other tribes which had remained west of the Jordan, particularly after Zerubbabel rebuffed their offers to help with the rebuilding of the city and the Temple. They reported to the king in Babylon that Zerubbabel intended to restore an independent kingdom in Judah, but after research in the official archives the king ruled that Zerubbabel's work had been duly authorized and should go on. With the support of the prophets **Haggai and Zechariah, Zerubbabel and Jeshua pushed ahead, but by the end of the century their venture seems to have run into the ground. It was later renewed by **Ezra and Nehemiah.
(Ezra 2-4; Nehemiah 12; I Esdras 3-6)

**Zilpah**  Servant of *Jacob's wife *Leah and mother of his sons **Gad and Asher. See also Bilhah and family tree C.
(Genesis 29-30, 37)

**Zimri**  An Israelite of the tribe of Simeon who introduced a Midianite called *Cozbi into the camp of the Israelites in the wilderness of Sinai. She was a prostitute and *Phinehas the priest killed both of them – but not before 24,000 Israelites had died of the plague with which God afflicted them because of the spread among them of whoredom and Baal-worship. This Zimri is not to be confused with Zimri king of Israel, for whom see under *Jeroboam.
(Numbers 25)

**Zipporah**  Daughter of *Jethro the Midianite and wife of *Moses.
(Exodus 2, 4)

**Zophar**  The Naamathite, one of *Job's comforters.
(Job 2, 11, 20, 42)

# Genealogical Appendix

A. From Adam to the sons of Noah
B. Abraham's extended family
C. The children of Israel
D. Ruth and the line of Jesse
E. The Maccabees
F. The Herods

## A. From Adam to the sons of Noah

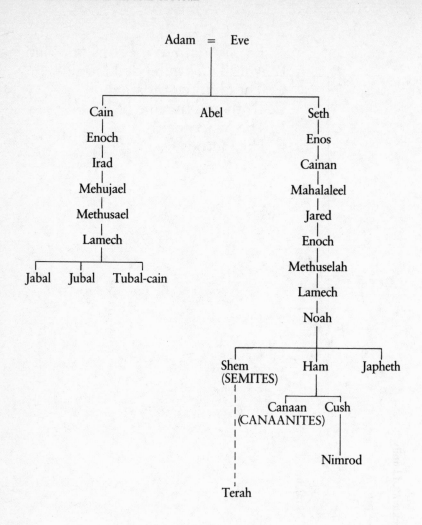

## B. Abraham's extended family

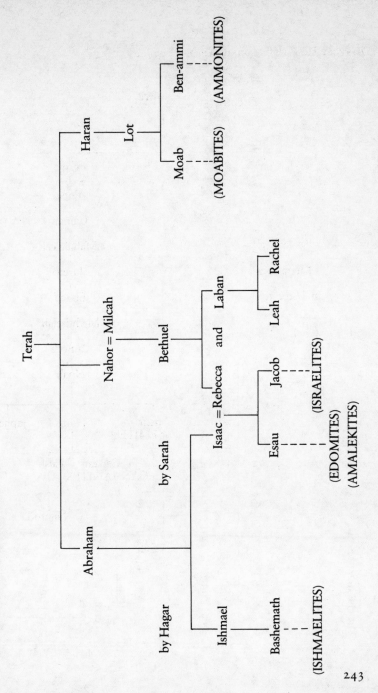

## C. The children of Israel

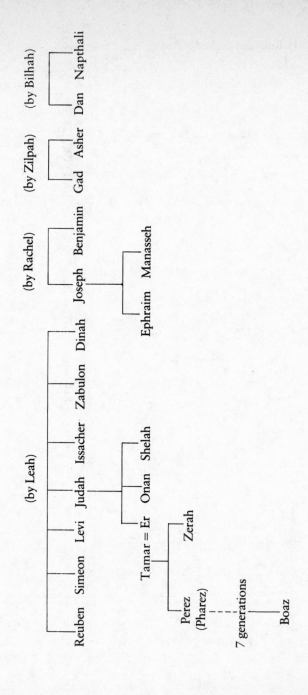

## D. Ruth and the line of Jesse

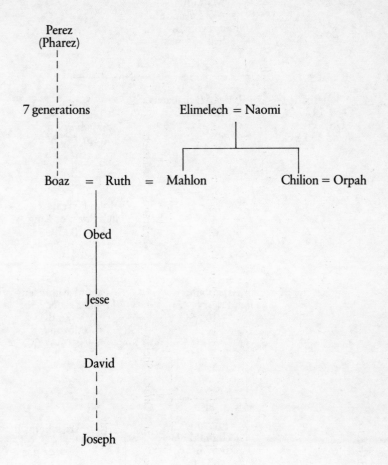

Perez
(Pharez)

7 generations

Elimelech = Naomi

Boaz = Ruth = Mahlon        Chilion = Orpah

Obed

Jesse

David

Joseph

## E. The Maccabees

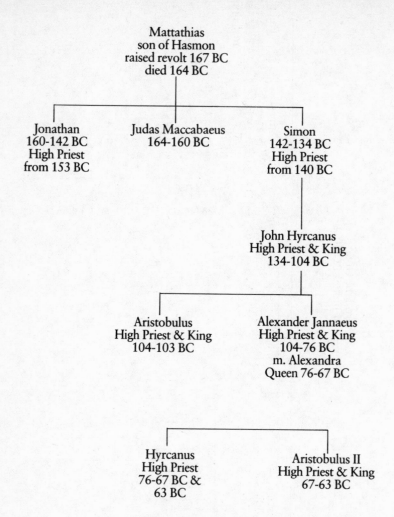

Mattathias
son of Hasmon
raised revolt 167 BC
died 164 BC

Jonathan
160-142 BC
High Priest
from 153 BC

Judas Maccabaeus
164-160 BC

Simon
142-134 BC
High Priest
from 140 BC

John Hyrcanus
High Priest & King
134-104 BC

Aristobulus
High Priest & King
104-103 BC

Alexander Jannaeus
High Priest & King
104-76 BC
m. Alexandra
Queen 76-67 BC

Hyrcanus
High Priest
76-67 BC &
63 BC

Aristobulus II
High Priest & King
67-63 BC

**F. The Herods**

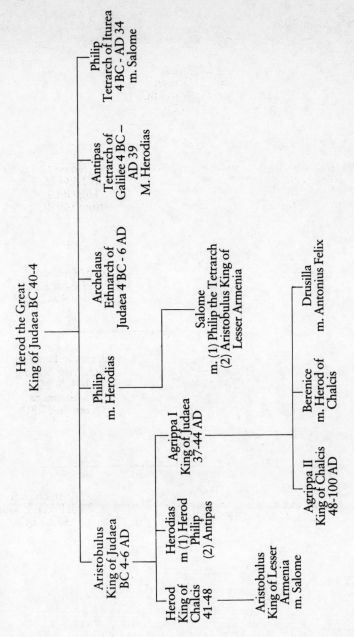

Herod the Great
King of Judaea BC 40-4

Aristobulus
King of Judaea
BC 4-6 AD

Philip
m. Herodias

Archelaus
Ethnarch of
Judaea 4 BC - 6 AD

Antipas
Tetrarch of
Galilee 4 BC –
AD 39
M. Herodias

Philip
Tetrarch of Iturea
4 BC - AD 34
m. Salome

Herod
King of
Chalcis
41-48

Herodias
m (1) Herod
Philip
(2) Antipas

Agrippa I
King of Judaea
37-44 AD

Salome
m. (1) Philip the Tetrarch
(2) Aristobulus King of
Lesser Armenia

Aristobulus
King of Lesser
Armenia
m. Salome

Agrippa II
King of Chalcis
48-100 AD

Berenice
m. Herod of
Chalcis

Drusilla
m. Antonius Felix

# INDEX

A page number in bold type
indicates the specific reference for
the subject in the alphabetical
sequence.

# Y

*Compiled by Valerie Lewis*
*Chandler, BA, ALAA*